BRYNMAWR

A STUDY OF A DISTRESSED AREA

BASED ON THE RESULTS OF THE SOCIAL SURVEY
CARRIED OUT BY THE BRYNMAWR COMMUNITY
STUDY COUNCIL

BY

HILDA JENNINGS, M.A.

ALLENSON & CO., LTD.
7, RACQUET COURT, FLEET STREET
LONDON, E.C.4

First Published 1934

EDGAR G. DUNSTAN AND CO., DRAYTON HOUSE,
GORDON STREET, LONDON, W.C.

FOREWORD

The story of Brynmawr, as a typical small community in the Distressed Area of the South Wales Coalfield, which is told in the following pages, is based on facts obtained by the citizens of Brynmawr in the course of a social survey undertaken during the three years from September, 1929, to August, 1932, in the hope of finding a basis for reconstruction. All sections of the community have taken part in the Survey, which has been planned as a community self-study in which the experience of employed and unemployed and the point of view of men of every shade of opinion should have its due weight. The enquiry work was divided between a number of Groups of voluntary survey workers, and while it is impossible to give the names of the 150 workers who took some share in it, the names of the officers of the Community Study Council and of some of those who gave most time and energy to the Survey are mentioned below :—

OFFICERS OF BRYNMAWR COMMUNITY STUDY COUNCIL

Chairman .	.	ALDERMAN EDGAR JONES (Miner)
Vice-Chairman	.	D. H. HERBERT (Shop-keeper)
Hon. Secretaries {		T. EVANS (Post Master)
		TUDOR MORRIS (Steel Worker)
Treasurer .	.	J. M. BOWEN (Bank Manager)
Former Hon. Sec.		THE REV. H. S. WILLIS

The following are among the officers and members of the Survey Groups who took most part in organising and carrying out the work of enquiry.

v

COMMERCE GROUP

Chairman . . R. C. GRIFFITHS (Shop-keeper)
A. BREST (Shop-keeper)
O. HOLFORD (Shop-keeper)
G. F. SPACKMAN (Shop-keeper)

EDUCATION GROUP

Chairman . . T. W. PRICE (Head Master, County School)
Group Leader . LEWIS LEWIS (Head Master, Church School)
Hon. Secretary . MISS K. PERROTT (Head Mistress, Council Infants' School)

Recreation Section F. WILLIAMS (Miner)

FINANCE GROUP

Chairman . . J. M. BOWEN (Bank Manager)
Hon. Secretaries { W. MORRIS JONES (Head Master)
*CHARLES WILKINSON (Bank Clerk)

HEALTH AND HOUSING GROUP

Chairman . . *J. K. WATKINS (Teacher)
Group Leader . MRS. JENKINS
Hon. Secretary . F. SIMS (Miner)
NURSE KING (School Nurse and Health Visitor)
J. J. QUIRK (Surveyor and Sanitary Inspector)

INDUSTRIAL GROUP

Group Leaders . *J. JOHN (Colliery Manager)
H. O. LLOYD (Assistant Manager, Employment Exchange)
Hon. Secretary . I. RICHARDS (Miner)

MUNICIPAL SERVICES

COUNCILLOR J. ELWYN JONES (Teacher)
ALDERMAN EDGAR JONES (Miner)
ALDERMAN ENOCH GRIFFITHS (Miner)
S. SHORT (Clerk to Urban District Council)

POPULATION GROUP

Hon. Secretary . D. H. HERBERT (Shop-keeper)
*TUDOR MORRIS (Steel-worker)
Group Leaders . REV. H. J. PHILLIPS
REV. W. F. SCOTT

TRANSPORT GROUP

Chairman . . *E. J. WATKINS (Station Master)
Hon. Secretary . W. H. RICHARDS (Miner)
*W. DOWDING (Bus Company Official)

* Denotes members who wrote part of the Survey Reports on which this book is based. Mr. Tudor Morris was responsible for the final analysis of the figures obtained from the Population Group's returns and the tables reproduced from their returns.

LLANELLY PARISH AND GOVILON SURVEY COMMITTEE

Chairman . .	THE REV. W. G. DAVIES (Rector)
District Hon. Secretaries and Group Leaders . .	COUNTY COUNCILLOR EDGAR MCINTOSH (Insurance Agent)
	J. B. DAVIES (Miner)
	COUNTY COUNCILLOR MATHEWS (Miner)
	E. L. RICHARDS (Head Teacher)
	E. R. MORGAN (Sanitary Inspector)
	S. PEARCE (Head Teacher)
	I. G. TOSSELL (Head Teacher)
	REV. E. J. SAMUEL (Minister)
	ALDERMAN W. POWELL (Farmer)
	W. POWELL (Farmer) (Secretary Farmers' Union)

Mr. Alexander Farquharson, of Le Play House, gave much advice and guidance especially in the initial stages of the Survey, and was at all times ready to assist with suggestions and helpful criticisms arising out of his long experience of Survey work. The Agricultural Economics Department of University College, Aberystwyth, also advised, and Mr. Llefylys Davies, and Mr. D. Hopkinson spent some time in the district. Mr. Hopkinson prepared the Agricultural section of the Survey. Mr. Clifford Davies, B.A., and Mr. Rees Davies, Tredegar, while not members of Survey Groups, helped considerably. Dr. Jordon, Tuberculosis Officer for Breconshire, and other officials of the various Local Authorities gave help and information. Miss Marion Richards prepared most of the original diagrams and charts, Miss Mariel Russell and Miss E. W. Spear also helped with them, and Major Rybot advised on the work and himself re-drew many of them. Mr. Alfonso Lewis, Mr. Phillips, Mr. I. Richards, Mr. Burrows and Mr. Sims (unemployed miners), also gave a great deal of time to work in the Survey Office. The material for the general sketch of the industrial position in South Wales, included in the introductory chapter has been largely drawn from the Industrial Survey of South Wales made for the Board of Trade by the University College of South Wales and Monmouthshire.

CONTENTS

CHAPTER   PAGE

FOREWORD V
Describing Organisation of Survey of Brynmawr.

I. INTRODUCTORY 1
South Wales as a Distressed Area.

II. THE GROWTH OF THE COMMUNITY OF BRYNMAWR 16

III. THE DEVELOPMENT OF NATURAL RESOURCES . 26
Iron and Coal.

IV. ORIGIN AND NATIONALITIES 41
English and Welsh Immigrants. Movements of Population.

V. INDUSTRIAL RELATIONSHIPS AND COMMUNITY LIFE 62
The Development of Trade Unionism and present Industrial Organisation.

VI. LOCAL ADMINISTRATION AND THE POLITICAL MOVEMENT 72
Early Work of Board of Health. Formation of Urban District Council. Political Influences in Local Administration.

VII. HOUSING 84
Growth of Town. Present Housing Conditions and Effects on Health.

VIII. TRANSPORT, COMMUNICATIONS AND TRADE . . 98
Roads and Railways, Brynmawr as a Distributive Centre. Analysis of Businesses in Town.

IX. RELIGIOUS AND CULTURAL INFLUENCES . . 117
Peasant Culture. Craftsmanship. Religious Influences on Culture and Education. Recreation. The Development of Educational Facilities. Present Position as Regards Education.

X. EXTENT AND EFFECTS OF UNEMPLOYMENT . . 135
Duration and Length of Unemployment. Effects on Groupings and Loyalties. Boys, Youths and Adults.

CONTENTS

CHAPTER   PAGE

XI. PRIVATE AND PUBLIC FINANCE 152

Incomes; Savings; Dependence on Public Funds; Public
Finance. Public Assistance. Means Test. Rates.

XII. THE REGION TO THE NORTH OF BRYNMAWR . 177

Llanelly Parish and the Crickhowell Rural District.
Occupations and Former Industries. Use of the Land.
Possible Developments.

XIII. AN EXPERIMENT IN RECONSTRUCTION . . . 198

Distress and Help from Outside the Area. The Survey.
The Work and Aims of the Community Study Council.
Town Development. Brynmawr and Clydach Valley
Industries Ltd.

XIV. SUMMARY AND ANALYSIS OF PRESENT POSITION . 220

Possible Lines of Future Development.

XV. THE IDEAL AS MOTIVE 234

MAPS AND CHARTS

		PAGE
1.	VARIATIONS IN UNEMPLOYMENT SINCE 1921	13
2.	BRYNMAWR: POPULATION	15
3.	BRYNMAWR: ROADS	17
4.	GEOLOGICAL MAP . . . . . . *to face page*	26
5.	OLD LEVELS AND WORKINGS IN NEIGHBOURHOOD OF BRYN- MAWR	37
6.	WORKPLACES OF BRYNMAWR MEN	40
7.	POPULATIONS OF LLANELLY AND LLANGATTOCK (1801–61) AND BRYNMAWR (1861–1931)	47
8.	BRYNMAWR: POPULATION 1911–31	48
9.	INWARD AND OUTWARD MIGRATION	53
10.	OCCUPATIONS OF NON-NATIVES	55
11.	NATIVES AND NON-NATIVES EMPLOYED AND UNEMPLOYED	61
12.	TRAMROADS FORMERLY RADIATING FROM BRYNMAWR	85
13.	GROWTH OF TOWN, 1800–1930 . . . *to face page*	86
14.	BRYNMAWR: TYPES OF HOUSES	89
15.	PROPERTY OWNED BY NATIVES AND OUTSIDERS *to face page*	96
16.	PROPERTY OWNERS AND TENANT OCCUPIERS, 1930 *to face page*	96
17.	BRYNMAWR AS KEY POINT FOR DISTRIBUTION TO SOUTH WALES COAL FIELD	115
18.	IMPORTATION OF FOOD SUPPLIES, 1930	116
19.	DISTRIBUTION OF SCHOOL POPULATION	134
20.	WORK PLACES OF BRYNMAWR MEN, 1921 and 1929	136
21.	AGE GROUPS OF EMPLOYED AND UNEMPLOYED MINERS	146
22.	AVERAGE WEEKLY INCOMES FOR YEAR ENDING 31ST MARCH, 1929	162
23.	AGRICULTURAL POSSIBILITIES	194
24.	LLANELLY PARISH: HOUSE OWNERSHIP	195
25.	CLYDACH VALLEY: FORMER INDUSTRIES	196
26.	CLYDACH VALLEY: CULTIVATION AND WOODLANDS	197
27.	SITE OF BRYNMAWR OPEN AIR SWIMMING BATH *to face page*	207
28.	SWIMMING BATH AND GARDENS MADE BY VOLUNTARY LABOUR . . . . . . *to face page*	207

BRYNMAWR

A STUDY OF A DISTRESSED AREA

BRYNMAWR

CHAPTER I

INTRODUCTORY: SOUTH WALES AS A DISTRESSED AREA

EVERYWHERE to-day we hear doubts of the stability of the economic and social structure. The very foundations on which it has been built up are questioned. In one place, the private ownership of capital or the system of international credit is repudiated; in another, men speak of representative government and democracy, in which every individual has his responsibility and part to play, as impossible ideals; yet elsewhere, the family as the spiritual and economic unit and Christianity and belief in personality as an expression of more than material forces are cast aside. In the universal confusion, the people wander bewildered, as sheep without a shepherd, a company of the blind led by blind leaders, trying one expedient after another, and finding no firm ground on which to stand. Many point to the signs of decay and destruction; few pause to ask whether there are any absolute values on which humanity may build a new and more stable world.

In distressed areas such as South Wales we see the process of disintegration at an advanced stage. The signs of economic failure are obvious; to those who live among its people the spiritual distress is no less plain. It has become a truism to say that the aggregation of the unemployed in the area is due to excessive dependence on the industries of coal-mining and iron and steel working to the exclusion of the lighter

industries, which spread the risks of unemployment in more
prosperous districts such as the West Midlands.

There is little attempt to ascertain how and why a people
once pre-eminent in rural crafts,[1] happy in the possession of
a common culture of hand and imagination and in a simple
village life amidst supremely beautiful scenery, have acqui-
esced in the mechanisation of industry and society and in the
crowding together of population in valleys disfigured by coal-
tips and undermined in such a way that their congested,
smoke-blackened homes are as insecure as their means of
livelihood.

Men of different schools of thought point to the greed
of employers in exploiting natural resources, to the intran-
sigeance of the workers, whose first aim is said to be to secure
the largest possible share of the proceeds of industry with
the maximum of inconvenience and loss to the owners, to the
folly of governments, or to the world-wide diminution of
demand. These, or any combination of these, they say,
provide sufficient explanation why South Wales is becoming
an economic parasite. If more reasons are required, one
has but to turn to the contemplation of political folly and
dishonesty, and to the extravagant finance of individuals
and local government authorities.

The capacity and daring of early employers, the self-sacrifice
and idealism of pioneer Trade Unionists, the thrift by which
workers acquired their own houses, the passion for individual
liberty and responsibility which inspired the struggle for
democratic government, are forgotten or thrust aside as of no
historical significance.

Yet the important questions from the point of view of the
future are surely what human qualities and traditional attitudes to society and life have drawn strength from permanent
and absolute values, and why men have been tempted from
the firm rocks to the treacherous shifting sands of materialism
and mutual antagonism.

The intensive study of a small community set against the
wider background of its contacts with the outer world offers

---

[1] See Chapter IX: "Religious and Cultural Influences."

an opportunity of understanding the dynamic forces at work in society. It is for this reason that the Survey of Brynmawr, a town on the edge of the South Wales Coalfield and in many ways typical of it, has been undertaken.

The situation in South Wales as a whole has been revealed to some extent by the Industrial Survey published in 1932, from which some facts should be noted as a prelude to the more intimate study of a small part of the region which is the main theme of this book.

Unemployment on a large scale has now persisted in South Wales for a period of over ten years,[1] and since June, 1927, has been consistently heavier in proportion to the total number of insured workers in the main basic industries than in Great Britain. In 1931, over one-third of all the insured workers in South Wales were unemployed.

The predominance of the heavy basic industries and the lack of alternative openings for employment have been potent causes for the widespread nature of the distress throughout the region since 1921. In 1923, the coal-mining industry and the manufacture of iron, steel and tin-plate accounted for nearly two-thirds of the insured population and in spite of migration and the growth of the distributive trades, still remained of paramount importance in 1930.[2]

Coal-mining in particular is the most important avenue for employment and since the South Wales area normally exports on an average 50 per cent of its own output and accounts for more than 40 per cent of the total coal exports of the United Kingdom, the causes which have brought about the general decline in the British coal industry have affected it even more severely than other coalfields. The slower rate of increase in the world demand for coal since the end of the War together with the development of coalfields abroad have hampered the

---

[1] See graph at end of Chapter (Appendix I).
[2] See *Industrial Survey of South Wales* which shows the following percentages:

	Percentage in Coal-mining	Iron, steel and tin-plate.	Distributive Trades.
1923:	51·8	10·0	6·6
1930:	44·8	11·5	10·2

B

export trade, while the development of substitutes for coal has diminished demand both abroad and at home. South Wales has thus lost many of its principal markets. The effects of decreased demand for South Wales coal have been felt to different degrees in different parts of the region, the production of anthracite being better maintained between 1923 and 1930 than that of steam and bituminous coal, and the northern edge of the coal area, where the coal measures are nearest to the surface and were first worked, feeling the depression most intensely and continuously. Migration within the coalfield has been a natural result of the localisation of the acutest distress, but in spite of this and of emigration out of South Wales the surplus of workers in the coal-mining industry of the area in 1932 is still probably not less than 30,000.[1]

In the metal industries, the position is different in that while "the demand for coal has contracted, the effectual demand for iron and steel products has expanded, and the existence of a considerable potential demand for them is unquestionable."[2] Yet there has been a substantial amount of unemployment among metal workers for some years. Some of the unemployment figures denote temporary stoppages only, but even the wholly unemployed percentages in June and December of 1930 were as high as 14·4 and 26·3. The industry, expanded by war-time demand, is still in process of adjustment and the effects of the general depression in it since 1927, shown by the steady decline in exports due to the failure of South Wales steel producers to compete in the world markets on favourable terms, have been felt, as has the coal-mining depression, in very different degrees in different parts of South Wales.

In particular, the shifting of the steel works from the hills to the sea, together with contraction in demand for some of the products of the industry and the rapid technical advances, which have greatly increased the output obtainable from a given labour force, have produced in the eastern districts a

---

[1] See *Industrial Survey of South Wales.* Between 1921 and 1931, 70,000 persons migrated from the four counties of Monmouthshire, Glamorganshire, Brecknockshire and Carmarthenshire.

[2] Ibid.

surplus of workers which does not exist in the west where the production of tin-plate can absorb the bulk of the output of steel.[1] Hence, since it is unlikely that Newport and Cardiff will be able to absorb any considerable number of steel-workers from outside their own areas even if considerably increased activity should take place after a revival in trade, it is probable that in the Merthyr, Tredegar and Ebbw Vale and neighbouring districts the number of iron and steel-workers who are permanently surplus to the requirements of the industry and for whom employment should be found in other industries is about four thousand.

It appears, indeed, that, although there may be a revival of prosperity in the iron and steel industries, and there is potentially a much greater home market available for the tinplate industry in particular, these industries cannot be expected to provide employment even for all those normally attached to them, and certainly will not make good the loss of employment capacity in the coal-mining industry and hence of effective demand for goods and services by the bulk of the population.

The inter-dependence of industry, transport and commerce and the effects of what is practically a monopoly of industrial activity by the coal, iron and steel industries are such that when the latter are continuously distressed, all other productive and trading concerns must suffer. This fact is brought out in the following paragraph quoted from the *Industrial Survey Report* :—

"So large a proportion of the population do the coal and iron and steel industries employ directly and so great a part of the remaining commercial activity of the region consists in importing and exporting their raw materials and their products that when they become depressed every other industry and service must languish too; except possibly tin-plate manufacture, which may profit from a fall in the price of their products and exports the greater part of its own output. The distributive trades in South Wales, as in Great Britain, have employed a larger proportion of the population in recent years. The printing trades and the amusement trades and the road transport industry may have experienced a comparative prosperity. But railway transport and the

[1] See *Industrial Survey Report*, Chapter III, "Metal Industries."

docks, and the business of exporting, ship-repairing, and building have
suffered. The business of shop-keepers, printers, amusement caterers,
bus-proprietors, and even the salaries and fees of local government
officials, teachers and professional men, depend ultimately in such a
region, upon the spending power of miners and steel-workers and the
profitability of mining and steel-making to the owners of these enterprises."

The indirect effects of the decreased spending power of those
normally engaged in the basic industries have been felt to
different degrees by the various derivative and dependent
branches of trade, industry or service in South Wales. The
port returns show a decrease in employment of seamen between
1923 and 1929 due to the shrinkage of coal-exports; for the
same reason the employment position is worse in the South
Wales ship-yards than in those of the United Kingdom as a
whole. On the railways the unemployment percentage increased more in the Wales Division than it has in Great
Britain as a whole. Brewing, bottling and malting firms have
experienced a steady decline in trade co-incident with the
worst phases of the depression in the Coalfield. The Survey
Report states that in the hotel and restaurant and amusement
trades

"Fluctuations in employment have followed very closely the fluctuations of the fortunes of the basic industries of the area and though
they have tended to expand while the latter have contracted there
is no reason to suppose that, in the absence of a decided improvement
in employment in coal-mining they are likely to be able to employ
many more persons unless seaside resorts in the region so increase their
attractiveness as to draw visitors from outside the Industrial Region,
or to persuade inhabitants of the region who now go elsewhere for their
holidays to visit them. So far as we are able to judge from the rather
scanty information available, it would seem that the local resorts depend
almost entirely upon the earnings of workers in the larger industries,
and have suffered depression while those industries have been depressed."

In the building trade the decline in house-building during
the years of industrial depression has been so great that
there is now a surplus of about 3,000 builders, although many
of the builders' labourers have sought other occupations.
The brick-making industry is of course affected by the decline

of the building and contracting trades, and several firms have closed down.

Even in road transport, where there has been a rapid expansion in Wales as elsewhere in recent years, the percentage unemployed, which was lower in Wales than in Great Britain in 1923, was higher in 1930. Moreover, not only has the employment capacity of industrial and commercial undertakings outside the coal, iron and steel industries declined with the depression which they are experiencing, but in the nine years, 1921 to 1929, the total number of factories and workshops declined by more than 20 per cent in South Wales as compared with 8 per cent in Great Britain, and this disproportionate decline was mainly indicative of a cessation of activity due to industrial depression, although amalgamation of businesses played some part in it.

As has been seen, the distributive trades now employ a greater proportion of the population of South Wales than in 1921, but it is probable that some of the development is parasitic and not a legitimate growth in response to new demand. Too often, the decrease in the capital resources and turnover of the tradesmen leads to the substitution for adult workers of girls and boys who are still dependent upon the earnings of their parents in organised trades, and who are dismissed, without having received any training to fit them for other occupations when they become old enough to demand a higher wage.

Two possible remedies for the economic situation have both been tried in greater or less degree. The first and by far the most extensively tried is transfer of the unemployed surplus to districts outside the distressed areas. The results of the adoption of schemes of Public Contracts in relief of unemployment are far better as regards subsequent employment *outside* South Wales than within it. This is natural, as in more prosperous areas there are some openings for other employment when the contract comes to an end. Yet about 40 per cent of the persons transferred through the agency of the Ministry of Labour's schemes return to the distressed areas after a period of temporary employment elsewhere. Again, the sample investigations undertaken by the Ministry of Labour indicate that owing to continuous unemployment over a long period, family ties, attachment to their own country and lack of the youth, energy and self-confidence which would enable them to uproot themselves from familiar surroundings and settle among strangers, house-ownership and physical defects, 42 per cent even of the men between 18 and 45 years of age were unable, unwilling or unfit for transfer. Men who by reason of age were unlikely to be suitable for transfer were not included in the scope of the investigation. Since so great a volume of transfer has already taken place the proportion of those among the surplus workers who cannot be transferred for the various reasons outlined is likely to increase. Moreover, the continuance of transfer at the rapid rate at which it was proceeding up to the end of 1931 would involve a further contraction among the trades and industries which cater for the needs of those formerly engaged in basic production. Some of the equipment of the region in docks and railways, warehouses, shops and hotels, and houses would thus become definitely redundant or be wasted because of partial utilisation, while in other parts of the country the community will be expending its labour power upon new docks, new roads, new drainage and building, new ships and new amenities generally.

It appears, therefore, that a deliberate effort to secure the introduction of new industries into the region is "not only desirable on sentimental or compassionate grounds, but is justifiable as a sound measure of public economy." Experiments in the establishment of such new industries have so far only been tried by small groups of volunteers and not on a large scale as a result of official action. One such experiment at Brynmawr, on the northern border of the South Wales Coalfield is described in detail later on. It is interesting to note from the Industrial Survey Report that a number of the smaller industries in South Wales have maintained their existence throughout the depression in spite of declining demand and migration of population. Examples of such industries are furnishing, stone-quarrying, printing (although unemployment among printers during recent years has been more severe in the Industrial Region of South Wales than in Great Britain as a whole) and fishing and tobacco manufacture. In the Swansea district in particular, where there is the greatest diversity of manufacturing industry in South Wales, the greater stability afforded by the presence of a variety of even small industries is apparent. In this area the number of insured workers actually increased by 10·9 per cent during the period 1923–1930, and the number "in employment" (counting "temporarily stopped" workers as employed) was only 7 per cent less in December, 1930, than in December, 1923.

While conditions with regard to industry, employment and trade are not uniform throughout South Wales, the main features remain the same in kind, although varying in degree. This holds good also with regard to the psychological effects of unemployment and to certain social factors affecting the industrial communities of the Coalfield. Industrial and social movements are intimately related and both are largely determined by the quality of human life and the direction of human desires. No study of South Wales which does not include enquiry into the origins of the people, their racial make-up, inherited and acquired social relationships, and attitudes of mind can form a sufficient basis for a plan for the future. Certain distinctive features, which are common to the South Wales Coalfield, are worthy of special consideration. These include the traditions of the Welsh peasantry and their cultural and social aptitudes prior to the Industrial Revolution, the extent to which successive incursions of workers from without Wales have modified racial characteristics and influenced the mode of living together, in fact all the diverse effects of cosmopolitanism, the manner in which class bias and that antagonism between employers and wage-earners, which is commonly attributed to the South Wales Coalfield even more than to other industrial areas, have grown up; and those special ties to locality and country which react unfavourably on schemes of transfer to districts outside Wales.

The student of life in South Wales will seek to learn also what have been the ideals which have inspired individual and common effort, and how far they now unite or disintegrate the people, what is the attitude to private and public finance, and what are the forces which make for the stability and endurance of distressed communities. It may be that in family attachments and the cohesion of the community, there will be found the basis of a plan for reconstruction. At all events, it is only by the study of the smaller units of society that we can learn those intimate facts with regard to the imaginations and desires of men which are the real factors which guide their destinies. In the self-help of small communities there may even be a firm economic foundation on which to build.

It was in the belief that self-knowledge was essential for reconstruction that the citizens of Brynmawr undertook the task of making a Social Survey of their town. The story of Brynmawr which follows is based on the facts ascertained in this way, and it is hoped that it in its turn may throw light on problems which affect the wider area of South Wales. Nowhere in the Coalfield has unemployment been more prolonged, or the accompanying economic, social and spiritual distress been more acute. In this small town with a population of less than 8,000 situated on the northern outcrop of the Coalfield, the exploitation of mineral resources commenced at an early date in the last century and the local coal resources are almost exhausted, yet coal-mining is still the main occupation and tends to bound men's hopes for themselves and their children. The metal industries do not play so large a part in the life of the town as in some areas in South Wales, but proximity to Ebbw Vale means that a small section of the population shares in the fluctuating fortunes of the iron and steel industry. As elsewhere in South Wales the distributive trades are increasingly important from the point of view of the percentages of the population which they employ, while transport has a considerable employment capacity but has suffered owing to the mining depression. The figures quoted in Appendix II with regard to the

numbers employed in the various occupations in 1921
and 1929 show the same general trends as those already
described as affecting the whole region, while the mobility
of labour within the coal-mining area is illustrated by the
fact that as the adjacent mines closed down the miners
of Brynmawr sought work at collieries in the Ebbw Vale
district, the Tredegar Valley and the Eastern and Western
Valleys.[1]

Unemployment has followed the universal trend of the
South Wales Coalfield but has been aggravated by the fact
that the town is now largely a dormitory one, so that Brynmawr
is officially regarded as a "Black spot" even in the Distressed
Areas. Migration from it outside the Coalfield has been
heavy, and this rather than a decrease in the rate of natural
increase has caused the steep decline in population since
1925.[2] Industrial distress has reacted on the trading fortunes
of the town, and the impoverished resources of the individual
have affected public finance, so that debts have been accumulated and rates have gone up.

Yet despite the cosmopolitan nature of the people and its
long history of industrial and political revolt, throughout its
changing fortunes Brynmawr has maintained its cohesion as
a community. To-day it presents in miniature a picture of
those industrial, social and psychological factors which make
up the problem of the Distressed Coal-mining Areas. Just
as South Wales shows the culmination of processes at work
elsewhere in western civilisation, so Brynmawr may be looked
on as indicative of what the tide of industrial and social change
is likely to bring to other communities at present less far from
the centre of mining activity. If then a way can be found
by which this area can once more make itself self-supporting
and self-respecting, there is hope that with due regard to
varieties of local history and circumstances, and with the

[1] The Brynmawr Survey enquiries showed that in 1929 the following
numbers of men living in Brynmawr worked in the various mining districts:—
Western Valley (Monmouthshire), 180. Ebbw Vale, 150 miners and 72 metal
workers. Eastern Valley (Monmouthshire), 98. Tredegar Valley, 90. Lower
Western Valley, 45.

[2] See Appendix III.

necessary measure of co-operation within the whole region, the present drift to disintegration may be arrested in other communities also. Knowledge of facts and conviction of what are the real values of human life alone can give the incentive to the determined and united effort which will be necessary for the attainment of this end.

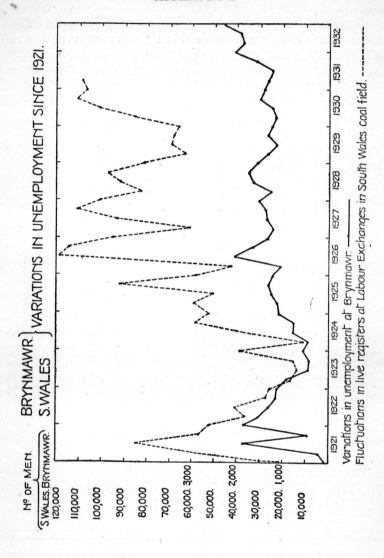

APPENDIX II

NUMBERS ATTACHED TO VARIOUS OCCUPATIONS IN 1921 AND 1929 RESPECTIVELY (BRYNMAWR)

Occupation	No. in 1921	No. in 1929	Increase or Decrease
Mining and Quarrying .	1640	1414	— 226
Commerce and Finance .	398	390	— 8
Professional Occupations	129	117	— 12
Metal Workers . .	147	114	— 33
[1]Transport Workers . .	132	114	— 18
Personal Service . .	248	94	— 154
Makers of Textile Goods and Articles of Dress (including Bootmakers) .	97	38	— 59
Builders, Bricklayers, etc. .	75	25	— 50
Clerks, Draughtsmen, Typists, etc. . .	54	55	+ 1
Stationary Engine Drivers, etc.	38	10	— 28
Workers in Wood . .	35	14	— 21
All Other Occupations .	236	131	— 105
TOTALS . . .	3229	2516	— 713

[1] The decrease in the number of transport workers reflects the tragic change in the industrial position of Brynmawr. It is the more significant when the growth of road traffic within the period is remembered. Although the Bus Company alone employs 50 Brynmawr residents, the combined rail and road employment capacity has decreased, mainly owing to the drop in goods and passenger traffic which is directly due to the depression in the mining industry.

APPENDIX III

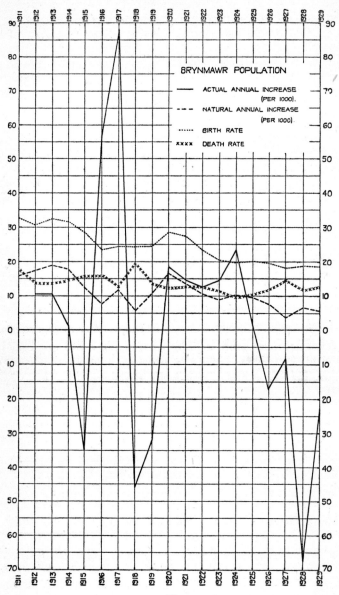

BRYNMAWR POPULATION

——— ACTUAL ANNUAL INCREASE
(PER 1000).

– – – NATURAL ANNUAL INCREASE
(PER 1000).

.... BIRTH RATE

xxxx DEATH RATE

CHAPTER II

THE GROWTH OF THE COMMUNITY OF BRYNMAWR

"OUR fathers called Brynmawr the City of the Hills, but to me it is the City of the World." Words such as these, spoken by an old man almost at the end of a long life lived in Brynmawr, are a sign that the town has achieved individuality. In the minds of its citizens and of its neighbours it is recognised as a community unique in its life and influence and not to be confused or interchanged with those around it.

Many strands in the make-up of the people and their common history have been woven into a common emotional tone and a body of common ideas and associations of ideas. As a result of this process of interweaving into the texture of life, reactions to circumstances tend to take certain lines and are based on assumptions drawn from the previous history of Brynmawr and on certain accepted standards of values.

The place itself has played its part in the growth of the community. Brynmawr stands at the extreme northern edge of the South Wales Coalfield on the border of Brecknockshire and Monmouthshire. A few miles to the north lies the fertile valley of the Usk, while in the more immediate vicinity coal and iron outcrop on the mountain side. Up to 1800 it was practically uninhabited. The great hill fringed on one side by the long line of willows, which gave it its early name of Waun-y-Helegyn, or the field of the willows, remained for centuries untenanted except by the inhabitants of two or three farm-houses and shepherds' cottages. The turnpike road running from Abergavenny to Merthyr passed through the little village of Clydach two miles away through the turnpike gate,

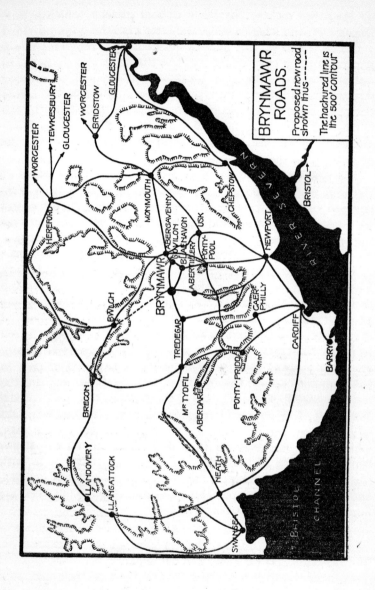

BRYNMAWR ROADS.

Proposed new road shown thus – – –

The hachured line is the 500 contour

17

up the steep rock to the bleak upland plateau, which is now Brynmawr, and where a stage and later a coaching-inn provided a change of horses. The plateau reached out to rough mountain grazing land on the one side, and to the north and south fell to narrow wooded valleys, musical with the sound of running streams and rushing waterfalls. Narrow mule-tracks cut across the open space, bringing iron-ore from the hill slopes to the north and limestone from the quarries of the Llangattock mountain to the iron works of Nantyglo and Beaufort, a mile or so away to the south and west.

The new settlement, in which lived some of the workers at the iron works and the men, women and children who were engaged in the extraction of iron-ore, was thus ringed round by a mile or two of uninhabited ground which divided it from the earlier settlements of Clydach, Beaufort and Nantyglo. At first the focus of social interests was in these settlements. A newcomer to Brynmawr in 1820 might have found work locally in the iron-ore gathering grounds, or have walked daily to one of the Iron Works. For his Chapel, for his shopping at the Company Shop and even for his children's school, if they were privileged to attend one, he would have been forced to go to Nantyglo. There he would have learnt local history and gossip about local personalities and have taken part in the building up of the workers' organisations and in the religious meetings and services of the Independents or Baptists. Insensibly, too, he would acquire the prevalent attitude, half admiring and half satirical, to the employers and their doings, expressed in the doggerel English song set to an old Welsh tune which told of the doings of Crawshay Bailey, who with his brother had purchased the Nantyglo Iron Works in 1813, and whose organising power and engineering exploits became famous throughout South Wales:—

> "Crawshay Bailey had an engine
> It's a-puffing and a-steaming,
> And according to its power
> It can go four miles an hour.
> Did you ever see, did you ever see
> Such a funny thing before?"

Yet the mere fact that the worker had his home and family at Brynmawr would have introduced him to a new set of interests. As the congested streets in the older part of the town sprang up, the neighbourhood would play an ever increasing part in his thoughts and conversation and those of his family. The children playing together in the narrow roads or on the mountain-sides, the women meeting at the wells from which they daily drew their water, he himself talking with his fellows in the public-house, would evolve new human interests as they grew to know each other in daily intercourse. Births, deaths and marriages would be made known, friendships and antagonisms would spring up, and in a very short time the fabric of thought and conversation would be tinged by the common knowledge and assumptions of the growing settlement.

Into the little community came a constant flow of newcomers from Wales and England, each the subject of speculation, and each adding some new ingredient to the common life. Difficulties in providing houses and house-furnishings, added hardships owing to the severity of climate and the poorness of roads would be common to all; all, too, would have a tale of past history and their reasons for and difficulties in migrating to this isolated spot, which would provide the material of romance and adventure to be imagined and talked over in the home and public-house. Gradually the cleavage between the English and Welsh was overcome as the English language gained ground and the habit of living together as pioneers in a strange place affected the customs of immigrants whatever their place of origin.

Owing to the geographical position of the town at the head of the mining valleys, it was the natural meeting-place of bands of workers, who were combining in the attempt to extort better wages and freedom from the Truck system. Since, whatever their place of work, almost all the inhabitants of Brynmawr were in some way dependent on the iron industry, these meetings and processions would be deemed of great importance and would help to relate the common interests of Brynmawr to those of the place of occupation. The workers living in the town soon found the need for a permanent local

c

meeting-place, and the Brynmawr public-houses became the centres of local lodges and branches of the Secret Union Clubs.

In other ways also the centre of social interests and activities shifted from Nantyglo. The march of men, women and children bearing the chapel furniture from the Mother Church at Nantyglo to a separate chapel at Brynmawr in 1828 was symbolic of the inevitable transfer of interests to the home town and of the process of building up a body for the life of the new community. Buildings and organisations as well as social groupings were bound to spring up to provide a mode of expression for the common life. Thus chapel after chapel was built; little schools were held in chapels and cottages; the few shops in private houses were added to by a line of shops in what was to be the main street in the centre of the town. Even the Company Shop established a Branch in Brynmawr itself.

Moreover, common needs which could not be provided for individually began to make themselves felt. Cholera visited the town, and could not be stayed either by the precautions of individual families or the ministrations of the churches, to which new converts rushed in terror; the water-supplies were polluted and insufficient; the chapel burial grounds became overcrowded. Thus in 1851, a Board of Health was elected, and discussion of its doings, of the services which it instituted and the rates it imposed became a standing feature of the life of Brynmawr. To the social and industrial organisations was added the machinery of government, and thus on all sides the common life, which at first had been fluid and shapeless, acquired fixed methods of expression; groupings and activities were no longer altogether shifting and spasmodic but were stabilised in social institutions.

The grandchild of the immigrant of 1820 grew up to be a man shaped not only by his native temperament and physique, but by an ever-growing body of community influences. Unconsciously he accepted innumerable assumptions and traditions and acquired without deliberate effort or teaching a miscellaneous assortment of knowledge which influenced both his personal life and his reactions to society. His attitude to authority, his conception of the obligations of neighbourliness, his ideas with regard to the place of women and the part which they should play in life, the kind of knowledge and skill which he desired, the demands which he made of his environment, and his standards of public and private honesty and disinterestedness, were all largely determined by the effects of community life on his parents and himself. Without being told, he knew that the two opposing worlds of the chapel and the public-house were open to him, and that for the one he must give up the excitement of fairs, brawls and travelling theatres, and possibly also the sterner movement of industrial revolt. When topics such as temperance, Sunday closing, the Company Shop, or strikes were under discussion he expected a certain attitude of mind and emotional excitement to show themselves. He anticipated criticism of the doings of the local Board but instinctively assumed that his civic pride in Brynmawr, its market, its central position and its coaching inn, justified him in feeling superior to the inhabitants of neighbouring towns. Whether he was by nature a leader or follower, he belonged to Brynmawr and was largely what he was owing to its influences.

The many-sided expressions of community life touched the individual at so many points, that even when one bond was snapped there were other close ties which bound him to the place. Thus, in the period when depression in the iron industry had not yet been counterbalanced by the growth of coal-production for export, the community of Brynmawr showed a surprising stability, and civic pride and optimism even gave rise to new developments and experiments. Some workers left the town, but many were kept there by the fact that they had built or bought their houses, by family ties, attachment to a chapel, and by the more intangible attachments to place and people which played so large a part in their lives. To see the Milfraen Mountain and judge the weather signs by it, to walk down the Clydach Valley on a Sunday afternoon, to join in the intensely social and gregarious life of streets and courts, to share the swift onrush of emotion in the presence of human drama in the lives of those around them, the ecstasy of "Revivals" or Singing Festivals, the keen theological argument, the recurring excitement of controversy and dispute, had become, almost without their knowledge, necessities without which they could not live. So, when work was slack, many of them clung to the place, falling back on their savings, getting some credit from the family tradesmen, who were themselves indirectly dependent on the two main industries of iron and coal, and eking out their scanty resources by making the most of their position on the edge of the agricultural as well as of the industrial districts. A cow or a few sheep and a pig could be kept on the mountain grazing land behind the houses on the outskirts of the town. All around collier-farmers and their families combined agriculture and industry as a source of income and in this and other times of depression the men turned more of their attention to the land.

Contact with farmers bringing their produce to the weekly market might lead to some temporary employment; a friend in the chapel or public-house might find them work. At the worst they must have recourse to the Poor Law despite the hurt to their pride which this involved. Thus they managed to remain rooted in the community until the coming of "Coal as King" justified their optimism and Brynmawr once more entered on a period of prosperity.

In this period from 1880 onwards the common life became yet more varied as a few subsidiary industries, such as the boot factory, which was opened on a very small scale by a tradesman in 1850, grew, and schools, musical societies, lectures and dramatic performances opened out new cultural vistas and led to new groupings and institutions. The coming of the railways and improvements in the roads had led to the beginning of that process by which the town became the natural shopping and amusement centre of surrounding towns and villages. The demand for coal-miners brought in yet new immigrant workers. All was activity, and excitement. Now an explosion or accident in the mine brought home the universal fact of death, stunning the imagination by its suddenness and the horror of the manner of its coming, yet bringing the people together in little knots and clusters or in solemn procession on the funeral day. Now the annual Sunday Schools' Walking brought the people out into the streets, as young and old, marshalled chapel by chapel, marched through the town with linked arms, moving rhythmically as they sang. Or again, when the public-houses turned out their customers at closing-time a sudden quarrel would cause the more sober to form a ring, equally ready to stand by and see fair play whether two of themselves were the protagonists or whether the struggle was between some drunken brawler and a policeman.

Generation after generation found the community consciousness modified and enlarged by the alien traditions of newcomers, by the penetration of the common life by some ideal, by the memory of further individual and common efforts and experiments. Certain traits such as warmth of hospitality, a family pride which sacrificed even elementary needs to the maintenance of the accepted standards of appearance on the ceremonial occasions of life, such as a funeral or a Schools' Walking, family cohesion in times of distress, warmth of colour in human relationships, a fiery loyalty to Chapel, Trade Union or other chosen organisation, came to be taken as a matter of course.

Taken equally for granted was the perpetuation of certain feuds and antagonisms between individuals and groups. A slight to the dignity of family or group might well prevent the participation of either in some common effort or interest long after the original cause of trouble was forgotten by the wider circle of friends and acquaintances. Hence within the community have come sectional groupings, the members of which share the common influences but are not easily able to join together for a common purpose.

The quality of life within the various social institutions is of course as much affected as is the life of the individual by the nature of the community life. Just as each individual reads varying degrees of intensity and significance into simple universally known stories such as those in the New Testament according to his own temperament and experience, so a church in Brynmawr with precisely the same theology as that of one in

England has a different quality of life. Because of the kind of home life, social relationships and natural surroundings, the various subsidiary groups and organisations have their distinctive emotional tone, and the relative health or disease of the community to a great extent determines their unconscious standards and their effectiveness for their own purpose.

Closely related to the quality of social life and the generally accepted standards of family and neighbourhood relationships was the growing up of a conception of leadership. First the old Ironmasters assumed supreme power over the lives of their workers. Then leaders sprang up from diverse sections, exerting an influence sometimes over the lives of one or other of the various groups of citizens only, but in some cases guiding the aspirations of the community and influencing its fortunes at many points. From the workers sprang leaders in revolt, nameless leaders of the terrorist body known as " Scotch Cattle " and "King Crispin," the Chartist shoe-maker; later Mr. Hicks, shopkeeper from Bristol and founder of the Boot Factory, known as the King of Brynmawr, and Chairman of its Board of Health, held sway for many years, while for nearly half a century John Thomas, the "stern, unbending Calvinist" and capable Town Clerk, combined leadership in religious and social movements with enthusiastic membership of the Abergavenny Cymreigyddion, the pioneer of the modern Welsh Renaissance. Towards the end of the nineteenth century workers, who not only influenced their fellow wage-earners but took their share in guiding the fortunes of the town, came to the front. Such was William Davies (Bricks) who worked in the mines from the age of eight, and could neither read nor write, yet by force of character came to serve as a member of the local Council and even of a deputation to the House of Lords, which urged the extension of the railway from Nantyglo to Brynmawr. Qualities of enthusiasm, persistence and vision appear to have outweighed nationality or education, and through all the gathering momentum of industrial and political revolt, the conception of leadership as "kingship," the recurrent desire for a "king" to unite warring individuals and groups seems to have persisted.

Old-standing religious ideals remain a force in some sections of the community and decline in others; new political ideas such as Communism are preached unremittingly by a few enthusiasts. Coal is slowly being dethroned in men's minds as the ten years' mining depression in South Wales is recognised to be due to more than temporary causes; persistent unemployment since 1921 has altered standards of living and caused a heavier migration from the district than ever before. Yet the life of Brynmawr is still shaped by the dynamic forces of nature, race, common traditions and common history. It remains a community and still exerts its power over individuals through community attachments. Probably no force which has influenced its past and present can safely be ignored in the consideration of its future. Through self-study its citizens can learn to recognise their assets and deficiencies, and may to some small extent at least determine which of the many strands in the texture of the past shall be re-woven into the future. Whether he wills it or not each citizen of to-day has his immortality in the lives of those who follow him, and the generations to come will be in some way different according to the part which he plays in the community of his own day. We cannot "pluck out the heart of the mystery" of Brynmawr, but it is well that we should study its history if we wish to plan a future for it instead of drifting down the stream of declining prosperity and disillusionment.

CHAPTER III

THE DEVELOPMENT OF NATURAL RESOURCES

ENGLISH Ironmasters and English capital first developed the natural resources of the district surrounding Brynmawr. The first iron works were founded two miles away down the Clydach Valley as early as 1615, when a relative of the Hanburys, a Northamptonshire family which had already erected furnaces at Pontypool, built a small forge at Clydach. The interests of the small population—only 86 in 1673—remained predominantly rural, however, until 1793 when Edward Kendall, a native of Derbyshire, who had obtained a lease of the mines and minerals in the parishes of Llangattock and Llanelly, sub-leased those in Llanelly Parish to Messrs. Frere, Cooke and Company, under whose management a swiftly expanding industry was built up, until as many as a thousand men found employment there. Even before this Mr. Kendall himself started the Beaufort Iron Works, on the other side of the hill. Similar works had been opened at Nantyglo in 1789, and, after a period of difficulties between the proprietors and a stoppage of the works for seven years, during which plant and buildings deteriorated and many workmen moved away, became one of the greatest centres of industry in the district.

A geological map of the South Wales Coalfield shows Brynmawr at the edge of the carboniferous rocks containing coal measures, millstone grit and limestone.[1] The coal measures outcrop in an escarpment to the north of the town running from Waenavon to Beaufort, and are inter-stratified with

---

[1] See Map opposite.

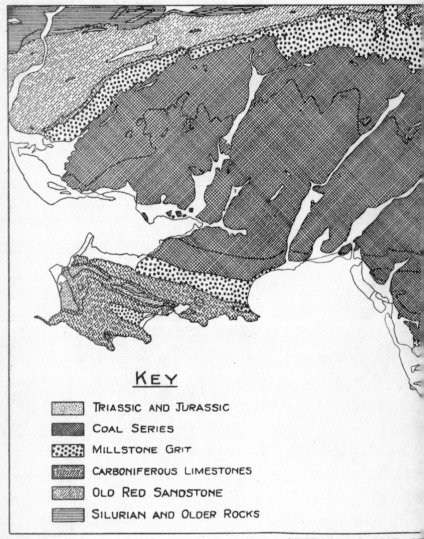

KEY

	Triassic and Jurassic
	Coal Series
	Millstone Grit
	Carboniferous Limestones
	Old Red Sandstone
	Silurian and Older Rocks

GEOLOGICAL MAP O[

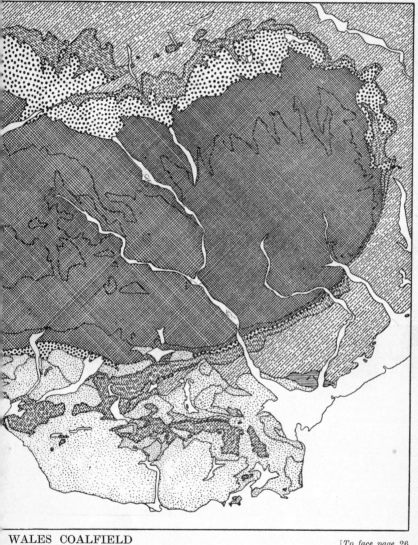

WALES COALFIELD

iron-ore and fireclay.   Immediately beyond them to the north
is a limestone belt, and beyond that again a region where red
sandstone predominates and the valley of the Usk and its
surrounding hillsides offer rich and fertile ground for agriculture.

Iron-ore was the first mineral, the value of which was
recognised in the district, and the Clydach Valley leading up
to Brynmawr is still made beautiful by the thick line of beech
trees planted to serve as charcoal for the Iron Works. With
the discovery of the use of coal for smelting and its general
adoption towards the end of the eighteenth century came the
opening out of small coal levels by the ironmasters.   The coal
produced was both used in the iron works and taken on the
backs of mules and later by canal for sale as house-coal in
Brecon and Abergavenny.

Many workers at the Clydach, Nantyglo and Beaufort Iron
Works made their homes at Brynmawr, but the industry
of the town itself was the gathering of the raw materials,
iron-ore, blackband and coal.   Clydach Dingle on the
northern outskirts of the town was the first scene of
this industry. Here the earth was "patched," or its
surface removed, in order to reach the ironstone strata.
Iron-ore and blackband were collected and stacked in great
heaps which were burned to remove the grossest impurities
before the minerals were sent to the furnaces.   Streams were
plentiful and sometimes the ironstone was scoured by rushing
water.

At the same time levels were driven into the hillside and
the hill gradually became honeycombed with subterranean
passages. The map of the old levels and workings in
Appendix I indicates something of the activity which must
have gone on in the early days of the development of the
region.

At first most of the work was above ground, and the little
community of workers must have been well inured to the hardships of climate, torrential rains, piercing winds and falls
of snow, as well as to the heavy manual labour.   From Clydach
and Llangattock would come the sound of blasting of limestone,

while at night not only the fires of the burning stacks of mineral along the outcrop, but the greater glow from the furnaces would light up the sky. When in 1822, the solid rock in the Clydach Valley was blasted to make a way for the tramroad down which the manufactured iron was taken from Nantyglo to the new Canal, the contest between rugged nature and the organising ability and strength of will of man as seen in the Ironmasters, must have impressed itself on the minds of the workers and made the more imaginative of them conscious of taking part in an epic struggle.

The differences in the geology of the districts to the north and south of Brynmawr entirely altered the mode of life of the communities in the two directions. Below Clydach, at Gilwern, around Llanelly Church and at Crickhowell were the conservative, slow-moving agricultural villages and little towns; a little farther away was the larger town of Abergavenny with its ambitions as a genteel health resort, where fashionable invalids drank goats' milk and inhaled the soft warm air, and its miscellaneous industries, such as shoe-making and cloth-making, its agricultural market, and its civic pride and literary interests. In the other direction, from Clydach southwards, the mineral resources first brought together great numbers of people of different origins and few mutual interests save their common means of livelihood, and then impressed upon them common characteristics by the call for endurance, initiative and skill in their extraction.

The pioneer workers in the little levels had to contend with great difficulties in evolving methods of working the coal, dealing with water and ventilating the mines. Hence skill and craftsmanship were valued among the colliers almost as much as in the iron works.

Scarcity of timber for supporting the roofs of the mines meant that the coal had to be left solid on one or both sides of the roadways, though connections were made at intervals with parallel roads for ventilation.

The mines were so shallow that there was no great danger of explosive gas, but the air became foul with carbon-dioxide, which could not be properly dealt with by the means of ventilation available—a ventilating furnace at the bottom of the up-cast shaft, or, if the difference in height between the intake and outlet was sufficient, dependence on the natural air current only. The workers suffered much discomfort under such conditions, and the death-rate from lung disease among miners was comparatively high in the early days of the mines. Methods of testing for gas were very primitive, often indeed consisting of the use of a candle over which clay had been placed.

The irregular surface with widely differing altitudes lent itself to a system of natural drainage by means of adits, the watercourses adapting themselves to the gradients in the seams, and sometimes serving the double purpose of drainage and haulage of coal. The stone arches, built where the strata were broken and great stresses were expected, are evidences of the skill and good workmanship of their builders. Where natural drainage was impossible the water was collected at special pits and pumped to the surface by beam pattern pumps. From time to time tragedies occurred owing to the flooding of the pits and the trapping of miners at their work, and the element of constant risk and exposure to sudden death was ever present; thus a certain recklessness and hardihood were knit into the temper of the community.

In the early days of the mining communities, the owners, although foreign to the locality, were in close touch with their workmen, some of whom had followed them from the mining districts of England. Mr. Frere, and later Mr. Powell at Clydach and the Baileys at Nantyglo lived as well as worked among their employees; they were not only equipped with organising ability, but also capable of judging personally of the skill and character of individual workmen, and were prepared to take an active part in their personal affairs. Thus Mr. George Frere after his retirement from the management of the Clydach Works was able to recall his old workmen one by one: "John Williams, the smith, of whom I was justly proud; John Herbert, a puddler, who turned over a new leaf for the better before I left; George Griffiths, the smith, who had the habit of spending his money faster than he earned it, tho' he was a good hand at earning it too." There is an intimate note in these reminiscences which might well have come from a village squire attached by the tradition of many generations to the people of his estate. The same "Mr. George" is said to have been swift to criticise and reprove his workmen for their conduct; he would confiscate and destroy ruthlessly the "fetchings" of beer, which the men clubbed together to obtain from the inn, if he met one of them bringing the supply to the works. Even his riding whip was "an object of dread" to his workmen if he returned from "the chase" to the works and found anything wrong there. He was himself a hard worker and an attentive manager; "his ears ever open to the sound of the old forge hammer," and if the machinery was out of gear, he could be seen in the works "even in the depth of night with little more than his night clothes on among his night workmen."

Even more outstanding than the personality of Mr. Frere, was that of Crawshay Bailey. It was owing to his organising ability and that of his brother Joseph that, during the period when the iron industry boomed throughout South Wales, the works at Nantyglo and Beaufort took so large a share of the trade, and at the height of their prosperity were able to employ over three thousand men.

Five hundred and thirty houses stood on the five thousand acres of surface property belonging to the firm. There were twelve blast furnaces, seven at Nantyglo, five at Beaufort, with a full equipment of forges, rolling mills and refineries. The minerals cropped out at the surface and could in places be "dug out as potatoes from a garden." All could be reached by means of shallow levels varying from 40 to 200 yards in depth. Twelve seams of coal were worked, having a combined depth of 40 feet of mineral and under the property was an estimated quantity of 150 million tons of coal, two veins being of the finest steam coal, while the ironstone was unlimited in quantity. 1,100 tons of coal were raised in a day, and 68,000 tons of iron manufactured in one year.

Two private railways connected the works with the Great Western and the London and North Western Railway systems, while a third, eight miles in length, brought limestone from the quarries of Llangattock. Above and underground were three hundred miles of tramroads. There were shipping wharves at Newport connected to the works by a private railway since replaced by the London and North Western Railway Company.[1]

Like the Freres, Crawshay Bailey lived near his workmen, and the "Big House" which he inhabited represented an almost feudal power over the neighbourhood. Nor was it altogether the magnitude of the works, nor the many points at which as an employer he touched his workmen's lives which accounted for the awe in which he was held. It may even be that the personal force of character which enabled him and the other Ironmasters to shape the life of the district has permanently influenced the tradition of leadership and the prevalent conception of power.

First the place, then the people. As usual in a rapidly expanding mining district the younger men[2] came in greatest numbers; hence the tendency to impulsive action and the desire for excitement of whatever nature were greater than in well-established communities, where older and more experienced men formed a greater proportion of the population. Many of the newcomers were single men or had left their wives and families behind until they should have an assured living and a settled home to offer them. Males were thus in excess of females[3] and this again influenced the social habits of the

---

[1] See *History of Breconshire*, by Theophilus Jones (Glanusk Edition).

[2] A study of the Census statistics for 1822 for Brecknockshire and for the Crickhowell district, in which Llanelly and Llangattock parishes are included, shows a higher proportion of men between the ages of twenty and forty in the partly industrialised area of Crickhowell than in the County generally. It seems probable, therefore, that the early industrial immigrants were largely men under forty years of age.

[3] In 1811, males predominated in Llanelly and Aberystruth, which were already chiefly industrial, while in Llangattock, which was then largely agricultural, females were slightly in excess of males. By 1822, when Llangattock also had become industrialised, males predominated there also, while the excess of males over females had increased markedly in Llanelly and Aberystruth. (See Census Volumes for Breconshire 1811 and 1822.)

community and their reactions to the outward circumstances of their lives.

The women, whether married or single, took their share in the work of gathering the iron-ore and in the coal levels. Often they took their babies to work with them and from an early age the children were employed in the less skilled operations, such as turning over the rubbish and picking out the nodules of ironstone. Even to-day a local coal-level is known as "Peggy's Pit," the name being derived from that of a woman driver of outstanding personality who was employed as a haulier in the mine.

Early life in Brynmawr must have been both simple and lacking in comfort and security, and the iron-workers of the district seem to have experienced considerable difficulty in obtaining even the bare means of livelihood. Thus in 1800 two hundred men, women and children congregated along the Beaufort road, stopped the horses and mules which were being led to the Dowlais Company Shop, drove them into the Beaufort Works and declared that the barley meal and bran which they carried should not be taken out of the county.

While the Ironmasters and Colliery Owners were transforming the once quiet hills and valleys and communities were being evolved by the joint influences of nature and man, the development of steamship and rail transport was bringing rival raw materials within the scope of the South Wales Iron Works. By the middle of the nineteenth century it was found that iron-ore of superior quality could be brought in from England or even imported profitably from Spain. The local blackband contained only 37·8 per cent of metallic iron as compared with 55 and 60·3 per cent in the various iron-ores in Spain.[1] In addition the working of the mines by the patchwork process was prohibitively expensive in view of the thinness of the veins and the thickness of the burden to be removed before they were reached. Already by 1865 imports were one third of local products; by 1878 they were four times and in 1890 a hundred times the local product. Nor does it

[1] See Appendix II.

seem that there can be any revival of the iron-ore industry in the district until the cheap ores now so easily obtained elsewhere are exhausted.

Difficulties with regard to the quality and cost of extraction of local ores, together with the gradual superseding of iron by steel, led to a decline in the iron trade which culminated in the closing down of the Clydach and Beaufort Iron Works in 1861, and in the sale of the Nantyglo Works by the Baileys in 1870, followed by the end of their activities shortly afterwards. The neighbouring works at Ebbw Vale and Blaenavon were converted into steel works.

The communities which had grown up around the Iron Works were by this time not entirely dependent on them, but the demand for coal also was diminished temporarily by the closing of the works, and for the twenty years between 1860 and 1880 there was great distress in Brynmawr and the surrounding towns and villages. Once again the younger men proved to be the first to move, as they had been the pioneers of immigration into Brynmawr. Thus, while in 1821 males between the ages of twenty and forty constituted ·3 of the total male population of the Crickhowell district, after the twenty years' depression due to the closing of the Iron Works in 1861, only ·13 of the male population of Brynmawr Urban Sanitary District were in this age-group. On the other hand, by 1891, when the coal mines were beginning to call for more men, the proportion had already risen to ·16.

Throughout the period of depression and declining population, the excess of males over females was maintained in the Brynmawr Urban Sanitary District, although immigration from Breconshire resulted in reversing the ratio of the sexes in the county as a whole. Legislation with regard to the employment of women and children in the mines and lack of alternate openings for women entirely altered their position in the life of the community. Instead of being important contributors to the family income they became dependent on the earnings of the men, and this economic dependence, together with the excess of males, was no doubt one reason

why the women have tended to marry early and the proportion of married to single women is high.[1]

With the period of production of coal for export and the
development of the collieries associated with the Ebbw Vale
Steel Works from 1880 onwards, coal-mining began to take
the place which iron had formerly held in men's thoughts.
A small contingent of skilled and semi-skilled steel-workers
travelled daily from Brynmawr to Ebbw Vale, but the bulk
of the population, including the fresh settlers who came in
from both England and Wales, found work in the coal mines
at Blaina and elsewhere.[2] The workers became proud of
the superior quality of South Wales coal and belief that
demand must inevitably continue and that a high price
could justly be asked for it, played some part in determining
their attitude to wage-questions, and in building up the
optimistic tradition which has been a feature in the life
of the community.

During the War period the demand for coal and for munitions
brought unprecedented prosperity to the district, but since
1921 the long-maintained faith in coal as the common means
of livelihood has been severely tried. The depression which
set in after the 1921 strike has been broken only by a temporary
revival, due to the occupation of the Ruhr and the cessation
of coal-mining there; in 1923 and 1924 and from 1926 onward
the population of Brynmawr declined at an unprecedented
rate. The fact that the Coalfield generally was suffering from
depression, while the western anthracite area tended to super-
sede the eastern bituminous region and industry in the latter
receded further from the outcrop area to the south and west,
meant that the Brynmawr miners, living far from the newer
and more profitable collieries, had little chance of employment.
Even the steel industry shows signs of moving permanently
to the ports, where raw materials can be transferred directly

---

[1] The 1921 Census showed that in the Brynmawr Urban District only
16·8 per cent of all women over 12 years of age as compared with 32·3 per
cent for the whole of England and Wales were occupied.

Appendix III gives the comparative percentages of women of variou sages
married and of the marital condition of males and females of all ages.

[2] See Appendix IV.

from the ship's bunkers to the furnaces, while the "finished" products can be distributed more easily and economically. Consequently steel-workers formerly employed at Tredegar, Ebbw Vale, Dowlais and Blaenavon are out of work, and since the steel works normally consumed large quantities of local coal the employment of miners also has been further contracted by the failure of their demand.

The natural mineral resources of Brynmawr and the immediate neighbourhood seem unlikely to provide the means of livelihood for the present population. There are not sufficient reserves of coal to make coal-mining possible on a large scale, although work may yet be found for a few men —perhaps a hundred—for some years to come, in the various levels and slants in shallow seams. The deeper measures to the south of Brynmawr are almost certainly waterlogged, and no venture to exploit them can be successful without a cheap supply of electrical power for pumping. This may be forth-coming in due course, but while there are vast supplies of good coal in virgin areas in other districts, it is unlikely that an area which has been robbed of its best will be extensively worked. The amount of coal still available in the barren and disturbed area around Nantyglo is difficult to estimate, but probably even if it proved possible to work it economi-cally at some later date it would not afford employment for more than a few hundred men for a period of perhaps ten years.

Is there any future for Brynmawr, or must it be content to live only in the lives of its former citizens?

The once thriving industrial centre of Clydach is now once more a green common lying silent between the little houses on the hills on either side, which once looked on to the busy works with their glowing furnaces and noisy forges. The valley from Brynmawr to Clydach is quiet except for the sound of waters and the occasional thunder from the limestone quarries which have lost most of their market with the closing of the steel works.

Brynmawr, in other times of depression, has shown a tenacity of life which seems to prove that the community is

D

well-rooted. Coal, though for long enthroned as "King" in men's minds, may yet prove less important than the spiritual life of the community which has sprung up with the use of natural resources. In the long run, perhaps the continued existence of the community may depend less on the kindness of nature than on the will to live.

APPENDIX I

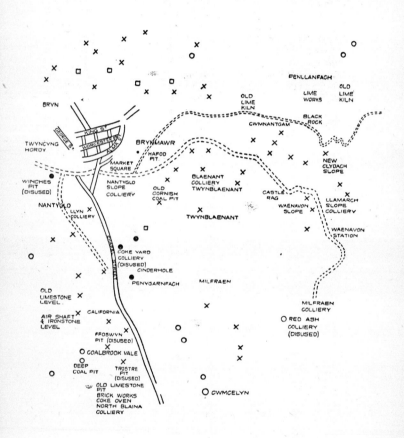

OLD LEVELS AND WORKINGS IN THE NEIGHBOURHOOD OF BRYNMAWR.

☐ = OLD WORKINGS COAL AND IRONSTONE
✕ = OLD COAL LEVELS.
○ = QUARRIES
● = OLD COAL PITS
-- = RAILWAYS

APPENDIX II

PERCENTAGES OF METALLIC IRON IN LOCAL AND OTHER ORES

District	Ore	Metallic Iron
Breconshire	Blackband	37·8
	Iron Ore	31·0
Yorkshire	Iron Ore	32·0
	Clayband	37·0
	Blackband	38·0
Northamptonshire	Iron Ore	35·0
Staffordshire	Iron Ore	35·0
Shropshire	Iron Ore	37·0
Leicestershire	Iron Ore	35·8
Oxfordshire	Iron Ore	33·6
Whitehaven	Iron Ore	58·5
	Siderite	44·0
Spanish	Rubio	55·0
	Haematite	60·3

PERCENTAGES OF WOMEN OF VARIOUS AGES MARRIED 1921
(*Excluding Widowed and Divorced Persons*)

	15 and under 20	20 and under 25	25 and under 45
Brynmawr Urban District .	3·7	39·3	80·6
Crickhowell Rural District .	3·5	31·3	73·3
Compare :			
Brecknockshire . . .	2·5	28·4	70·1
Monmouthshire . . .	3·0	40·6	80·0
Whole of England and Wales	1·8	27·0	68·5

MARITAL CONDITION OF MALES AND FEMALES OF ALL AGES 1921

	MALES			FEMALES		
	Percentage Single	Percentage Married	Percentage Widowed including divorced	Percentage Single	Percentage Married	Percentage Widowed including divorced
Brynmawr Urban District .	58·8	37·7	3·5	54·2	39·4	6·4
Crickhowell Rural District .	59·8	35·6	4·6	54·7	37·7	7·6
Compare:						
Brecknockshire .	60·0	35·7	4·3	55·6	36·7	7·7
Monmouthshire .	59·1	37·7	3·2	54·3	39·9	5·8
Whole of England and Wales . . .	55·0	41·4	3·6	53·5	38·3	8·2

N.B—These proportions are of course considerably affected by the age distribution.

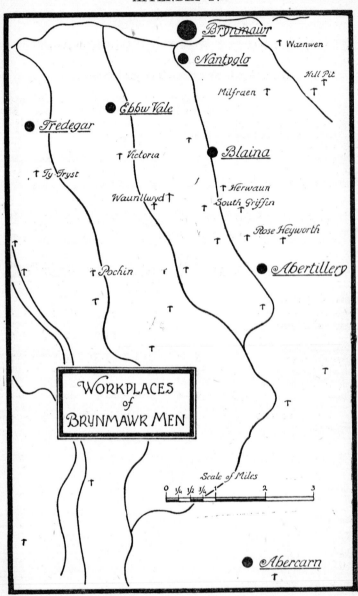

Picks represent collieries

CHAPTER IV

ORIGIN AND NATIONALITIES

IT is not generally realised in England how great has been the admixture of peoples in the South Wales Coalfield, nor how cosmopolitan is the present population. The ports of Cardiff, Swansea and Newport are understood to contain foreign seamen and other immigrants; Pembrokeshire is known to include the curious phenomenon of "Little England," but the Coalfield generally is assumed to be almost entirely populated by persons of Welsh stock. No assumption could be more mistaken. In the early-developed districts on the northern borders of South Wales the mixture of peoples has persisted for over a century and a quarter. The extent to which persons of various origins and nationalities have immigrated into these districts can be judged from the example of Brynmawr.

Surrounded on three sides as the place was by swiftly developing iron works and itself possessing supplies of iron-ore on its northern slopes, it was almost inevitable that it should be used both as the home of some of the workers who were crowding into the works in the narrow valleys near by, and as the gathering ground of the raw material.

The first workers at the Iron Works were drawn from the surrounding agricultural districts and were of Welsh nationality. The distress which was present among agricultural labourers in Breconshire and Monmouthshire between 1795 and 1801 made them glad to exchange their average weekly wage of 6s. to 9s. a week for the 2s. 6d. or 3s. a day which they could earn at mining collieries or in lime kilns. These workers from the adjacent moorlands were of the Iberian type which is still marked among the colliers of South Wales, short and dark, and, as described by Professor Lloyd in his History of Wales, "impulsive and wayward, but susceptible to the influences of music and religion."

Something of their mode of life, interests and characteristics is revealed in the accounts of Monmouthshire and Breconshire written by Archdeacon Coxe and Theophilus Jones in the early years of the nineteenth century. A simple diet, to a great extent produced by their own exertions, pride in the appearance of house and garden, a love of poetry, story and music, and a cheerful sociability are portrayed by both writers.

Theophilus Jones tells us how even the "Middling" farmers were content to kill one beast in November or December and to salt and roof a pig about Christmas. "This was the principal stock and capital for the ensuing year, a piece of this out of the pot formed one day's dinner, the broth in which it was boiled, with a dessert of bread and cheese washed down by water or whey, followed for the two or three succeeding days, and flummery and milk and vegetables, as potatoes, turnips, etc., with brown bread and skim cheese filled up the week."[1] Archdeacon Coxe gives a similar picture of Monmouthshire, and adds that almost every cottager had a garden, and "the greater part were even enabled to keep a cow, which ranged the commons for subsistence."[2]

Fuel, whether coal or wood, was plentiful, and the abundance of lime made it customary for the houses to be whitewashed inside and out annually, so that they presented a "neat and cheerful" appearance.

The Welsh language was predominant, and Archdeacon Coxe says that when he visited Blaina, two miles from the site of Brynmawr, the English language was so little known

---

[1] Notes from the *History of the County of Brecknock* by Theophilus Jones (1809) Glanusk Edition.

[2] Notes from Archdeacon Coxe's *Historical Tour through Monmouthshire* (1802).

that without assistance the Parish Clerk could scarcely understand or answer his questions intelligibly.

Farmers and peasants had their own culture and found a natural zest in life. "The songs and traditions of the peasantry," were repeated and the poetry of David ab Gwyllim was read by the firelight. Harpists visited the farms, and the young people met frequently in parties to dance country dances, some of which had four and twenty variations, all of which were to be danced through, as well as "variations in the figure of the dance to correspond to those of the tune."

The growth of nonconformity revealed a second strand in the make-up of the native people, a capacity for religious fervour and the power to adopt habits of life to the demands of an intellectual conception. Owing to its influence many social customs were changed during the second half of the eighteenth century and dancing, in particular, fell into disrepute. The more athletic amusements such as hunting and ball playing, "to which drinking frequently if not always succeeds," survived. In the course of these "Carousals" Theophilus Jones noted that "What they call singing" was introduced "with great satisfaction to themselves and apparently to the great delight of all parties," though the "Ballads" and "Cadences" with long drawn out last notes seem not to have appealed to his taste. Possibly, already the suppression of the natural love of song, dance and story by nonconformity was leading to an artificial divorce of recreation from the finer qualities of the mind and spirit, and to a cleavage in the community life. This cleavage, symbolised by the distinction between the life centring round the public-house and chapel, has been one of the constant factors in the history of Brynmawr.

While certain cultural activities were suppressed at least among the Nonconformist congregations, the country itself with its wooded dingles, swift streams and waterfalls, and its vast and lonely mountain spaces was ever present to stir the imagination as well as to brace to physical endurance. Legend and superstition died hard, and a minister of a congregation of Independents, who published an account of the Parish of Aberystruth[1] (in which Blaina, Nantyglo, and afterwards part of Brynmawr were included) in 1779, laid stress on the prevalent belief in fairies and "other spirits of hell" which were said to frequent the Parish "as much or more than any Parish in Wales."[2]

In these "superstitions" and beliefs of the original Welsh stock may be found the key to lasting tendencies which to-day puzzle students of Welsh psychology. What, for instance, is the origin of the "deep seated" respect for death which has caused trouble time after time in South Wales owing to the refusal of colliers to continue work after a fatal accident in the mines? Perhaps the clue to this obstinate refusal is contained not in the recent history of industrial controversy, but in that old Welsh folk-song which tells of the inescapable presence of Death and of his dignity. Certainly a deep pre-occupation with the natural and universal facts of human life still prevails.

As early as 1801 there were as many as 937 people living in Llanelly Parish and 1,000 in Llangattock Parish.[3] During the next thirty years the growth of the settlement of Brynmawr accounted for part of the increase in population in the two parishes in which it was included. This increase averaged 1,000 for each decade in Llanelly and over 500 in each decade in Llangattock, and was largely due to immigration. The immigrants came not only from Breconshire and Monmouthshire, but from more distant Welsh Counties such as Carmarthenshire and Cardiganshire, and both worked in the Iron Works and crossed the mountains for purposes of trade. In this way, the preponderance of the Welsh workers was maintained, and their racial characteristics can be seen in the history of the early chapels of Brynmawr. The devotion of

[1] See *A geographical, historical and religious account of the Parish of Aberystruth in the County of Monmouth* by Edmund Jones.

[2] See also *Historical Memoranda*, by John Lloyd, for account of a prosecution at the Brecon Quarter Sessions, in 1789, of a man who undertook to track down a witch, who had bewitched a cow's milk, in return for a payment of five shillings.

[3] Separate statistics for Brynmawr are not available for the period prior to 1861, up to which date they are included in the Census Volumes in those for the two parishes of Llanelly and Llangattock.

the ministers shown in their long and lonely journeys over the mountains with utter disregard of wintry weather, scanty clothing and poor food, was equalled by the self-sacrifice of the scattered congregations which at first met in cottages but whose zeal soon found the means to build little chapels. Perhaps the very repression of the natural lighter interests and the degradation of enjoyment of a secular nature, intensified the force of emotion in its narrowed channel; at any rate, religious fervour rose periodically to a high pitch of intensity. A typical Welsh "Revival" took place immediately after the building of the first Brynmawr chapel in 1827, when "an indefinable wave of feeling swept over the place and scenes of hysterical ecstasy were witnessed." By 1832 the membership of the chapel, which was entirely Welsh, had risen to 250, and, with industrial prosperity, religion also seemed to prosper, new members constantly flowing in at the rate of 20 or 30 a month.[1]

Even before 1830, some English workers had entered the district, and at Clydach a purely English Wesleyan Sunday School was opened in 1807 in what had been a roadside inn called the "Trap," and a chapel was built for the joint use of English and Welsh Wesleyans in 1822. In Brynmawr itself, an English Baptist Church was built in 1836. There are no records available to show the places of origin of the early English immigrants into the Brynmawr district, but references to workers from Staffordshire and other industrial areas in neighbouring iron works, such as those at Merthyr, seem to indicate that the English pioneer immigrants into South Wales were not drawn direct from the land as in the case of the Welsh immigrants to the iron-ore districts. In any event, they must have brought with them very different traditions and habits of life, influenced not only by their different racial characteristics but by the different nature of the country from which they came. The wild and rugged mountain scenery, great, lonely spaces, and poor roads may well have affected the imaginations and courage of all but the

[1] See *History of Rehoboth Congregational Church of Brynmawr* by Rev. Crwys Williams.

more hardy newcomers. Again, the difference in language must have been a bar to speedy assimilation, and to the growth of understanding and unity between the two racially divided sections of the population of Brynmawr.

During the first sixty years of the century the population of the County of Brecknockshire, although largely agricultural except along its southern borders where minerals outcropped, nearly doubled, rising from 32,325 in 1801 to 61,627 in 1861. Monmouthshire, the character of which changed almost wholly from that of an agricultural county to that of an industrial one, quadrupled its population within the same period. The population of Llangattock increased fivefold to 5,700 and that of Llanelly increased tenfold to 9,600.

From 1841 to 1851 the rate of increase was accelerated in both parishes, no doubt as a result of the increased activity of Clydach, Nantyglo and Beaufort Iron Works owing to the opening out of new markets by the development of railways in England and other countries. After this, came a decade of declining population followed by the closing of Clydach and Beaufort Iron Works in 1861, and a period of industrial depression lasting for the next twenty years. The graph on the following page shows the early variations in the Parishes of Llanelly and Llangattock, the subsequent increase of population in Brynmawr during the great coal exporting period from 1881 onwards, and the close correspondence of fluctuations in population and industrial prosperity.

Side by side with influxes of English workers, the recruitment of Welsh workers from Breconshire, Radnorshire, Monmouthshire, Cardiganshire, Carmarthenshire and other Welsh Counties went on. That the inflow of these workers was very considerable is shown by the constant admission of new members to the Welsh Church of Rehoboth, and the phenomenal number of converts of that Church in the revivals of 1839, 1849 and 1859.[1] Welsh Baptist and Calvinistic

---

[1] Rehoboth admitted more converts on each occasion than any other Church in South Wales: 400–500 in 1839, 500–600 in 1849. See *History of Rehoboth Congregational Church of Brynmawr* by Rev. Crwys Williams.

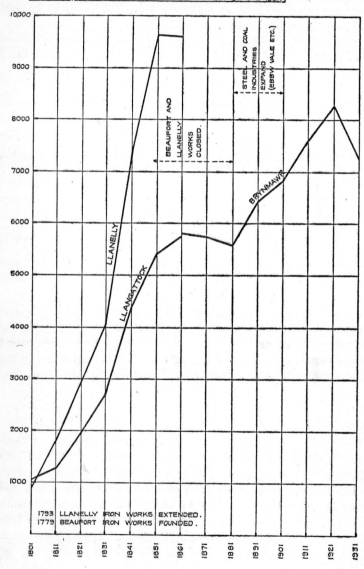

POPULATIONS OF LLANELLY AND LLANGATTOCK (1801-61) AND OF BRYNMAWR (1861-1931). FIGURES FROM CENSUS REPORTS (BRYNMAWR NOT SHOWN SEPARATELY BEFORE 1861).

47

Chapels were also built in 1837 and 1845 and a second Welsh Congregational Church, which was built in 1850, used both languages, a fact which seems to show that the English speech was gaining ground even among the native Welsh inhabitants.

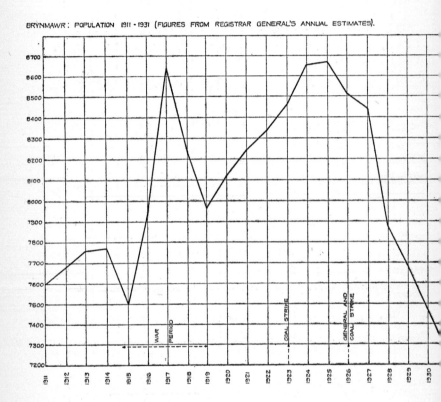

BRYNMAWR: POPULATION 1911-1931 (FIGURES FROM REGISTRAR GENERAL'S ANNUAL ESTIMATES).

An English Congregational Church was built in 1848 and an English Wesleyan Church followed.

In their evidence before the Commission of Enquiry into the state of Education in Wales in 1847, the Curates of Llanelly and Llangattock both stated that the use of the English language was slowly increasing although "Better instruction in it was necessary." The Curate of Llanelly wrote as follows :—

"Most of the people attend Welsh dissenting places of worship. English services are held at the Parish Church, Welsh in the afternoons, but thinly attended. At Brynmawr there are Baptists, and Primitive Methodist (or Ranters) English services, attended by many people. Strangers are disliked, which is partly due to the prevalence of the Welsh language."

The business of the Brynmawr Board of Health, formed in 1851, was transacted and the Minutes recorded in English. This may have been largely due to the composition of the Board and the predominant influence of the industrialists and local property owners. As late as 1866, when it was necessary to issue circulars giving instructions about the threatened approach of cholera to the inhabitants of the town, 300 were printed in Welsh and 500 in English.

It was not until the period of State education from 1870 onwards and of incursions of new English workers into the collieries after 1880 that English gradually became the language in general use by all sections of the population. By the end of the nineteenth century even chapels, such as Rehoboth, of strong Welsh tradition and membership, found their attendances adversely affected by the use of Welsh, and were obliged to hold some services in English. The proportion of persons of English origin probably increased also after 1880, and at the 1894 Sunday Schools' Walking only 1,180 persons from chapels of Welsh tradition as against 1,700 from chapels of English tradition took part in the demonstration.

Some features which have their bearing on the building up of community life in a cosmopolitan town such as Brynmawr are revealed by the study of these facts. The constant splitting off into new religious groupings and the building of new chapels is a symptom of a certain narrowness and rigidity of intellectual conviction, which allows of little latitude for individual differences in outlook or tolerance of variations in thought or conduct. Hence rebels or pioneers are thrust outside the fold, both in religion and politics, and social groups tend to be antagonistic rather than co-operative.

Again, the suspicious attitude to strangers and "foreigners" mentioned by the Curate of Llanelly persists, even though the language barrier has been broken down. This attitude is now linked up with strong local attachments, which make at once for the stability of the community and for a somewhat parochial outlook, and thus influence relationships both with neighbouring communities and with the outside world.

Since the industrial fringe of the county would account for the greatest fluctuations of population, a study of the birthplaces of the inhabitants of Brecknockshire should throw some light on changes in the origins of population in Brynmawr itself. Appendix I at the end of the chapter gives statistics for 1871, 1881 and 1891, thus covering the dates when both the effects of the depression in the iron trade and the beginnings of the boom period in coal-mining would be reflected in Census statistics.

The period 1871–1891 is notable for an outward migration of persons born in Brecknockshire owing to depression both in the iron industry and in agriculture,—in 1891, only approximately 56 per cent of the persons born in Brecknockshire actually lived in it—and for the commencement of a further incursion of colliery workers especially from Monmouthshire and from various parts of England. As a result the balance between English and Welsh and between the industrial and agricultural population was further tilted in favour of the English and industrial elements.

During the decade 1881–1891, coal-mining was expanding at an unprecedented rate especially in Monmouthshire and Glamorganshire. One result was a decrease in the numbers of workers resident in Brecknockshire whose native homes were in Glamorganshire and other South Wales Counties, and an increase in the use of the southern parts of Breconshire, notably Brynmawr and Llanelly Parish, as a dormitory town for workers in the Monmouthshire collieries. The population of Brynmawr increased by over 1,000 in the decade. If the figures for Brecknockshire can be accepted as a guide to the changes in the Brynmawr population, it would seem that the main influx of new workers at this period, apart from immigrants from over the border of Monmouthshire, came from the

West Midland area of Gloucestershire, Herefordshire, Shropshire, Staffordshire, Worcestershire, and Warwickshire, with smaller increases from the North Midland coal-mining counties, from Cheshire, Lancashire, and Yorkshire, the Northern counties, North Wales, where the lead-mining industry was declining, and from London.[1]

About the middle of the century, following on the potato famine in Ireland, came an Irish influx into South Wales. In Brynmawr this was marked by the building of the Roman Catholic Church in 1863, and also of a Roman Catholic School. A religious element entirely alien from that of any to be found in the Nonconformist sects was thus introduced into the life of the town. Most of the Irish residents in Breconshire first sought work in the iron works and owing to the fact that these closed or declined, a considerable number of them left the county between 1871 and 1891. In 1882 there were 58 children in the Catholic School. It is said that the different social customs and outlook on life of the Irish caused many of the brawls for which Brynmawr was noted in the mid-century, and it is probable that the disturbances attending St. Patrick's Day celebrations and joviality gave such offence to sober Nonconformists that they would find it difficult to accept the newcomers as part of the community.

The building of Bailey Street Congregational Church in 1876 marked an incursion of Scotch residents into the district. These were apparently unaffected by the depression, as the number of males among the Scotch inhabitants of the County of Brecknockshire remained almost stable from 1871 to 1891. It should be noted that few, if any, of the Scotch in Brynmawr worked in the mines or iron works, and that the reason of their coming to the town was their recognition of its geographical suitability as a trading centre. Most of them established themselves as travelling drapers, trading not so much in Brynmawr itself as in the surrounding valleys, but living in the town and using it as their base.

Like the Scotch, the Jews recognised the trading possibilities of Brynmawr, and between 1891 and 1911, it is estimated

[1] See Appendix I at end of Chapter.

E

locally that about fifty Jewish families settled there. Many of them built up successful businesses, and acquired considerable wealth. In 1894, the new Market Hall was let for a Jewish wedding, which appears to have been celebrated with great festivities. Later a Synagogue was built. Since the War, however, many of the Jews have left the town and in 1931 only fifteen families remained.

While the constant fluctuations in the proportions of English and Welsh and the presence of both races from a very early date have led to a process of assimilation, and apparently to the impressing of certain Welsh characteristics on the English immigrants, the Scotch, Irish and Jews have not merged in the general life of the town. The Scotch differ less in religious outlook than do the other two races and also play a part in administrative affairs, but still maintain their own traditions and distinctive occupation. Neither Irish nor Jews take part in administration, although the Irish are for the most part engaged in the mines, and are thus not separated from the bulk of the population occupationally.

The presence of these small racially distinct communities is thus to some extent a barrier to a complete fusion in the larger community, but, in so far as the various racial groups mingle in social life, enriches and widens the possible basis of a common culture; economically, the trading sections have certainly helped to bring prosperity to the town and have proved a stable element in recent years of depression.

From 1891 to 1921, the Census returns show a continuous growth of population in Brynmawr with a further period of increase by immigration between 1901 and 1911. During the War period there were very great fluctuations in population due to the effects of enlistment on the one hand and to the entry of new workers for munitions and coal mines on the other. Figures obtained through the local Survey in 1929 as to length of residence, show that the bulk of the older non-natives now resident in the town entered it during this period and were drawn in almost equal proportions from adjacent mining areas, which would not be noticeably alien in tradition, and from distant parts of England.

After the temporary and partial recovery of the coal-mining industry in 1923–1924 yet another wave of immigration followed, representing for the most part a movement from neighbouring parts of the Coalfield, although a few of the younger men were still drawn from more distant areas. Since 1925, as will be seen by the following graph, there has been a much steeper decline in population than ever before experienced, owing to the failure both of coal-mining and steel works

BRYNMAWR. INWARD AND OUTWARD MIGRATION 1921 – 1931.

OUTWARD MIGRATION

INWARD MIGRATION

1921		1921
1922	16	1922
1923	32	1923
1924	121	1924
1925	77	1925
1926	234	1926
1927	136	1927
1928	597	1928
1929	241	1929
1930	272	1930
1931	201	1931

FIGURES FROM REGISTRAR GENERAL'S ANNUAL POPULATION ESTIMATE

to afford sufficient openings for employment for Brynmawr men.

The contemporaneous influx of Welsh and English immigrants which has been a constant feature in the history of Brynmawr, has thus persisted up to the present time. What have been the effects of the constant coming and going during the last century and a quarter? It is now almost impossible to ascertain in what proportions the Welsh and English stocks are present. Periods of industrial depression have caused emigration of the original inhabitants, while periods of sudden industrial development have brought in influxes of both Welsh and English workers. The effects of these influxes have to some extent been counterbalanced by the intermarriage of the young male workers with local girls, and in some cases the former have obtained a stake in the community by the acquisition of house-property by marriage. Assimilation of the newcomers has been helped in this way, and the community has set its stamp on English as well as Welsh inhabitants.

The local tradition has thus been maintained unbroken and a certain stability of interest has been built up, which has continued even in the recent deep depression. The figures with regard to transfer outside the distressed areas and return to Brynmawr show that the town is still regarded as a home base by the young men and girls who have been forced to leave it to seek a livelihood elsewhere.

The survey of population made locally at the end of 1929 revealed the fact that seven-eighths of the total population were born in the town.[1] The racial origins of these native inhabitants are to a great extent mixed, and, while Welsh temperamental and physical characteristics are noticeable, the predominance of the English industrial leaders and the anglicisation of education since 1870 have resulted in the loss of the Welsh traditional culture.

During the last thirty years the bulk of the immigrants have been drawn from neighbouring colliery districts and have gone into the mines. On the other hand, many of the immigrants from distant parts of England have been attached to other occupations, and have either gone into business on their own account or found work as skilled craftsmen. Very few have come from agricultural areas of late years, although agricultural counties such as Herefordshire, Brecknockshire and Radnorshire contributed a considerable proportion of the earlier immigration in the nineteenth century. The traditions of the present inhabitants, whether native or non-native, are thus predominantly industrial.

[1] See Appendix II for percentages of natives and non-natives in the various age-groups.

The diagram below shows the occupations which the immigrant males are now following:—

BRYNMAWR. Occupations of 489 Non – Natives.

36	General or unskilled Labourers.
40	Clerks, Shop-Assistants, Agents.
53	Shopkeepers, Independent Craftsmen.
54	Public Employees, Professional Workers.
75	Skilled Craftsmen in employment.
231	Mine Workers.

When we consider the amount of unemployment among natives and non-natives respectively in recent times of distress it appears that a larger proportion of the non-natives than of the natives have retained their employment. Thus, the proportion of unemployed natives to the total natives in all occupations is ·52, while the proportion of unemployed *non-natives* to the total *non-natives* in all occupations is only ·34. The relative position in the mines is similar, although in both cases the proportions of unemployment are higher. Taking the native miners, ·75 of the total are out of work, while only ·55 of the non-natives are unemployed.[1]

[1] See Appendix III.

Other considerations than those of capability are, of course, factors in determining which miners are likely to lose their work in times of depression. The place of work and the way in which the waiting list for places in the mines is made up may to some extent neutralise the effect of comparative efficiency on the chances of employment of the individual worker. In spite of this, the difference between the ratio of unemployed natives and non-natives both in the mines and taking all occupations together, is very striking. That it is not due to differences in the proportions of the various age-groups is proved by the fact that the proportion of non-natives over forty years of age and therefore most subject to unemployment is actually higher (·58 of all non-natives) than that of the natives over 40 years of age to all natives which is ·39.

Brynmawr appears, therefore, to have benefited by the immigration of persons of a relatively high degree of initiative and employability into the town.

Students of the South Wales Coalfield[1] have noted the marked capacity of the native Welsh population to impress their characteristics on newcomers from over the English border. In Brynmawr, as elsewhere in English-speaking industrial districts of South Wales, it is difficult to discriminate between the descendants of the original Welsh stock and of early immigrants from England. Certain physical characteristics persist, but in emotional tone and attitude to social, political and religious questions, the mark of the community is more apparent than that of the race. In the first generation of immigrants the fusion of traditions is often incomplete and the prior attachments to the original home may persist for many years. Obscurely seen yet none the less important, racial tendencies may be at work in their children and in the generations which follow; nevertheless, moderating or even running counter to these tendencies, are the influences of climate, scenery, local traditions, occupations and customs, all the attachments, standards and values which

---

[1] See, for instance, *Report of the Commission of Enquiry into Industrial Unrest* (No. 7 Division).

are common to the community and distinctive of it. Only indeed by the encircling atmosphere of a common physical and spiritual environment, can the paralysing effects of uprooting from the native soil and the sense of inner conflict and impotence which comes where allegiance to national cultures is divided, be counteracted. In the cosmopolitan industrial areas of South Wales, the community, as foster-mother, has a special part to play.

APPENDIX I

TABLE SHOWING SOME OF PRINCIPAL BIRTHPLACES OF RESIDENTS IN BRECKNOCKSHIRE IN 1871, 1881 AND 1891

(*Extracted from Census Volumes*)

	1871		1881		1891	
	Male	*Female*	*Male*	*Female*	*Male*	*Female*
Total Inhabitants of Brecknockshire .	29,928	29,973	28,861	28,885	28,509	28,522
Birthplace:						
Brecknockshire .	20,022	20,597	19,525	19,801	18,548	19,060
Monmouthshire .	1,380	1,499	1,365	1,422	1,608	1,717
All parts of Wales and Monmouthshire (including Brecknockshire) . .	26,033	26,997	25,295	25,964	24,398	25,282
West Midlands (Comprising Gloucestershire Herefordshire Staffordshire Shropshire Worcestershire Warwickshire) .	1,732	1,406	1,675	1,385	1,965	1,638
Wiltshire Dorset Devon Cornwall Somerset . .	804	464	621	471	610	466
London . .	183	135	180	171	194	221
Ireland . .	325	239	263	181	196	112
Scotland . .	116	109	116	87	118	85

APPENDIX II

POPULATION OF BRYNMAWR SHOWING

(1) AGES
(2) NUMBER OF PERSONS NATIVES OF BRYNMAWR
(3) NUMBER OF PERSONS NOT NATIVES OF BRYNMAWR
(4) PERCENTAGE OF NATIVES AND NON-NATIVES

Ages	Population of Brynmawr		Natives of Brynmawr		Not Natives of Brynmawr		Percentage of Natives		Percentage of Non-Natives	
	M	F	M	F	M	F	M	F	M	F
Over 65 Years	201	177	177	151	24	26	88·05	85·31	11·94	14·68
Between 40 and 65 Years	1147	1009	885	801	262	208	77·15	79·37	22·84	20·61
Between 30 and 40 Years	589	608	456	498	133	110	77·41	81·9	22·57	18·09
Between 18 and 30 Years	623	511	557	465	66	46	89·40	90·99	10·59	9·0
Between 14 and 18 Years	211	237	205	225	6	12	97·15	94·93	2·84	5·06
Between 5 and 14 Years	835	765	796	737	39	28	95·31	96·33	4·67	3·66
Under 5 Years	280	267	271	262	9	5	96·78	98·1	3·21	1·86
TOTALS .	3886	3574	3347	3139	539	435	86·13	87·82	13·84	12·17

TOTAL POPULATION OF BRYNMAWR 1929   Males   3886
Females   3574

TOTAL   7460

POPULATION 1931 CENSUS . . . Males   3775
Females   3472

TOTAL   7247

APPENDIX III

	Total Number of Natives in all Occupations	Total Number of Natives Unemployed	Total Number of Non-Natives in all Occupations	Total Number of Non-Natives Unemployed	Total Number Natives (Miners) in Occupation	Total Number Natives (Miners) Unemployed	Total Non-Natives (Miners) in Occupation	Total Non-Native Miners Unemployed	Proportion of Unemployed
Natives	2,005	1,033	—	—	—	—	—	—	·52
Non-Natives	—	—	489	169	—	—	—	—	·34
Native Miners	—	—	—	—	1,030	773	—	—	·75
Non-Native Miners	—	—	—	—	—	—	231	126	·55

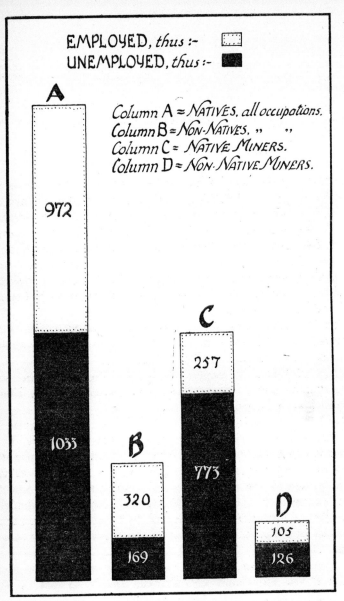

EMPLOYED, *thus* :-
UNEMPLOYED, *thus* :-

A

Column A = *NATIVES, all occupations.*
Column B = *NON-NATIVES,* „ „
Column C = *NATIVE MINERS.*
Column D = *NON-NATIVE MINERS.*

972

1033

C

257

B

773

320

169

D

105

126

CHAPTER V

INDUSTRIAL RELATIONSHIPS AND COMMUNITY LIFE

INDUSTRIAL relationships not only have economic effects in production and distribution, but also affect the quality of life in the individual and in the community. The industrial unrest in the South Wales Coalfield has been shown to spring partly from social causes;[1] it also reacts on social relationships.

Since the district along the outcrop was among the first to be developed industrially in South Wales, it should provide a field for study of those causes of industrial unrest which have their origins in past history.

The Commissioners for Wales and Monmouthshire, who enquired into the question in 1917, remarked that misunderstanding and friction tended to arise when managers and officials who had no experience of the Welsh outlook and temperament and no knowledge of the traditions of the Welsh Coalfield were introduced.

As has been said, the early iron works and collieries in the Brynmawr district, as elsewhere in Monmouthshire, were almost all owned and developed by English or Scotch employers, while the first workers were mainly Welsh. Strikes over the truck system arose as early as 1801, 1810 and 1816, and in 1830 all the collieries in the Western Valleys of Monmouthshire struck. A chain of "Union Clubs" was established from Swansea and Neath in the West to Pontypool and Brynmawr in the East.

It does not appear, however, that the original Welsh workers initiated the movement of industrial revolt. Probably the

[1] See *Report of the Commission of Enquiry into Industrial Unrest* (No. 7 Division, Published 1917).

difference in outlook between the Ironmasters and the English immigrants was as marked in some ways as was the difference between them and the Welsh workers from the moorlands. Richard Crawshay, the "Iron King," complained that "inflammatory tracts" were circulating among the workers from Derbyshire and Staffordshire, who had already known Unions in their native places, and there are other indications of the active part played by the English workers in the early attempts at combination against the masters.

The struggle had a more than local significance for the workers, for the "Friendly Society of Coalmining" decided in 1831 to send a delegate to attend a colliers' meeting at Bolton, where it was decided to affiliate to the Association for the Protection of Labour which had been formed in the north of England in the same year. An organiser, named Twiss, came to South Wales from the North of England to solidify the organisation.

Such evidence as is available goes to show that the revolt of the workers at this early stage was a class-conscious movement of similar nature and origin to that which was taking place in England; how far it was aggravated by the temperamental and traditional difference of outlook of Welsh workers and English owners it is difficult to estimate.

The struggle was a violent one; the military were called in again and again by the employers, and the workers in their turn, with the law and organised religion both against them, resorted more and more to secret terrorist methods. The ardent spirits of the movement organised themselves as "Scotch Cattle" and, disguised with blackened faces, sallied forth at night to paint the sign of the red Bull's Head on the doors of blacklegs, and sometimes, as at Nantyglo during the strike of 1832, to raid their houses, destroy their furniture and beat the inhabitants. Even the house of the manager who had introduced the blacklegs was stoned, and neither military nor the heavy rewards offered for information as to the identity of the ringleaders sufficed to quell the workers.

The far-reaching nature of the employers' power over the lives and intimate concerns of the workers made the issue of the struggle of direct importance to their families and to all in the community. To be forced to procure goods at the Company Shop at prices 20 to 30 per cent dearer than those charged by the private tradesmen was a grievance which the women as well as the men understood. Moreover, in these early days women and children took a large share in the actual work of the mines. In other ways the employers allowed their workers little personal freedom. Even such children as attended the Works' Schools at Nantyglo found that their parents' Nonconformist views did not prevent their being beaten if they failed to learn their catechism or attend the Parish Church at Blaina on Sunday mornings. Yet the Sunday School children of Brynmawr went annually for an outing in Crawshay Bailey's trams drawn by one of his famous engines and in an autocratic fashion the employers were ready to work for the well-being of the community, as was shown by Henry Bailey's energy in agitating for a Board of Health for Brynmawr after the cholera outbreak of 1847.

What were the effects of the intense and violent industrial struggle on the growing community? The workers could not but have admired the organising ability and initiative of their masters. The native workmen in particular, who had known the district or a similar surrounding one in the days when the minerals were unused and the land supported only a scanty population of farm workers, must have marvelled at the energy which had changed their landscape with such rapidity.

Seen from the orthodox point of view of the surrounding clergy and magistrates, the town "presented a frightful picture." In evidence given before the Royal Commission of Enquiry into the State of Education in Wales, in 1847, the "immoral and corrupt state of what is generally termed the Hilly District, more especially the locality designated as Brynmawr" was described with horror by more than one witness. "The elements necessary to produce a contented, well-disposed and orderly community" were said not to be in Brynmawr, with its "dense population" and many licensed public-houses and beer-houses. Bouts of drunkenness lasting from Saturday to Monday or even Tuesday night as long as wages were high, "strife, jealousy, bickerings, assaults, grumblings, oaths and profane language," characterised the town. On the other hand, "Disaffection and sedition" were said to have subsided since the last Chartist movement, since the people "Have seen the error of their ways and felt the effects of insubordination."

Probably the violent character of the struggle with the masters as well as the secret conspiracies, terrorism and suspicions of spies and blacklegs, and the constant incoming of new workers, had all conduced to bring about this state of affairs. Yet the picture must have been one-sided; the habit of mutual loyalty, the pursuit of common interests, the contact with the industrial and political movements in the wider world, even the discussions in the public-houses, centring round the personality of the masters and the struggles of workers in other parts, and the fact that the geographical position of Brynmawr made it a meeting place for the workers of the district, must have provided some education in affairs and in social life.

The master against the worker, organised religion against the Union Club, and, linked with that opposition in the minds of the orthodox, the chapel against the public-house, marked dividing elements in the community. Yet the mere fact of living together in such close contact and the common dependence of almost all sections on iron works and colliery meant that common interests were being built up, and the community with all its associations and attachments was becoming a force in the life of all its members.

In the years of depression in the iron industry before the coal exporting phase and the era of steel had well set in, a new period of industrial revolt commenced. Up to this period the masters, if foreigners, were yet individual human beings who lived near their men and could be approached face to face. The story of a spontaneous and successful one-day strike against Crawshay Bailey told by an old Brynmawr miner who took part in it illustrates this point. Here was no fighting with shadows in the shape of absentee owners or unknown shareholders, but a straightforward struggle in which the individual character of master and man and their personal reactions were important factors. As a result of this brief strike the miners succeeded in preventing a reduction in their wages.

"In 1853, Crawshay Bailey gave notice that there was to be a five per cent reduction in the wages of the miners, ironstone workers, and the limestone workers. None of the men knew of this suggested reduction until they went to work next morning, and the rumour that there was no work spread rapidly. A crowd of men then went to the manager's office to see what it was all about, and was greeted on the steps of the office by James Allen (the manager) who asked: 'Why have you not gone to work, as usual, you rodneys?' The men wanted to see Crawshay Bailey, but they were told that he had gone to Newport. The men thought to cheer themselves up in readiness for their encounter with Crawshay Bailey, of whom they were rather afraid, so they dispersed to different public-houses for a quart of beer.

"At about 4 p.m. the same day, the news flew round that the master had returned and that he wanted to see the men down at the office at once. A crowd of men trooped down once more and Crawshay Bailey was waiting for them on the office steps. He at once, in a loud voice, started shouting at the men. He called them scamps and rodneys, etc., and kept hitting the floor with his staff to give emphasis to his words. All the men stood silent, but one man, a trifle braver than the rest, stepped forward and spoke to Crawshay Bailey on behalf of the men, demanding their rights, and said that what they wanted was an increase in wages, not a reduction, as the price of coal and iron was increasing. The poor miner collapsed after he had made his statement and after a long silence, Crawshay Bailey, in a terrible voice, asked if anyone else would like to say anything. To everyone's surprise a young lad stepped forward and, when asked what he had to say, he repeated the statement that the other man had made. Crawshay then told the miners and the ironstone workers that they were to go back to work on the following day, but the limestone workers were told to remain behind as he had something to say to them."

With the coming of the limited company and the amalgamation of collieries[1] the industrial struggle took on a more impersonal character, and the building up of a permanent and complicated organisation of a national character tended to obscure the human nature of the issues involved in the movement of industrial revolt. The sale to a limited company

[1] See, for example, the unification of the interests of the Ebbw Vale Iron and Steel Company and those of the Colliery Companies in the Western Monmouthshire Valley.

of the Nantyglo Works by Messrs. J. and C. Bailey in 1870 marked the beginning of a new epoch with a new kind of leadership in the Brynmawr district.

In 1870 the South Wales Union Lodge of Coalminers was formed and in 1871, 1873 and 1875 there were strikes and lockouts. The pioneer members of the Union lodges had to suffer both unpopularity and material hardships. Although they paid the large subscription of a shilling a week out of their scanty wages, the Union Lodge had only about £10 as funds in the three months' strike of 1871 and the sufferings of the men and their families were great until help to the extent of ten shillings a week was brought from London to members of the Federation. It is interesting to note that even at this early period, communal feeding of children in soup kitchens held in an old schoolroom at Brynmawr was practised. There was acute local controversy over such questions as the Sliding Scale Agreement and the establishment of the Conciliation Board, payment for small coal (still a cause of local dispute) and methods of weighing the coal extracted.

During the South Wales Iron Strike of 1873, most of the collieries in the district around Brynmawr were idle owing to the failure of demand for coal at the iron works, and once again an organiser from England, Mr. Thomas Halliday, was employed to work up Union membership. Four lodges of coalminers sprang up in Brynmawr, holding their meetings, as had the Secret Union Clubs of earlier days, in public-houses. Their total strength was only about one hundred men and for the next few years the members found it hard to stimulate widespread interest, although Brynmawr and Blaina were considered to be strongholds of the Union movement.

Men from the Forest of Dean and elsewhere, who knew nothing of the history and ideals of Unionism, came in to work in the new collieries at Blaina, and nearly smashed the movement. This difficulty owing to immigrant workers from districts with no Union traditions has occurred again and again and even caused trouble in recent times during and immediately after the War. Industrial differences such as

F

these must have been a force militating against the assimilation of the new-comers into the community life.

The workers were not only suspicious of the employers, who were believed to combine together in such practices as marking the references of Union men with secret signs, and of new-comers, but also even of their own leaders who came among them from England. It is a significant fact that there is still a tradition that the temporary failure of Unionism in the district after the Iron Strike was due to the misappropriation of Union Funds by one of the leaders.

Discipline also was built up only slowly, and local differences of opinion were frequent. The story of the part played by Brynmawr in the Hauliers' Strike of 1893 and of the fierce fight with the Ebbw Vale men is given below in the words of an old Brynmawr miner :—

"Mr. Thomas Richards, the late President of the Miners' Federation of Great Britain, was then the miners' agent of the Ebbw Vale district. The day the hauliers' strike came, a huge meeting was held on the Church Field, commonly called 'Little Waen,' Brynmawr. The Brynmawr Trade Union leaders invited Mr. Thomas Richards to the meeting, with a view to influencing him to bring his men out on strike (Ebbw Vale district) in support of the Brynmawr and district workers. Mr. Thomas Richards told the mass meeting that he would not bring his men out in support. He reminded the meeting that their actions were illegal according to the Sliding Scale Agreement. They were, under the terms of the existing agreement, obliged to give one month's notice, which they had not done, consequently he could not support them in their action. Mr. Richards advised them to go back to work on the old terms, and then, if they desired, they could give a month's notice to terminate the existing contracts and agreements. The meeting, however, rejected this advice, and the strike commenced in real earnest. As a result of the broken contract the employers initiated proceedings against the men for Breach of Contract. The cases were to be heard at the Tredegar Police Court and on the day of the court contingents of strikers from Blaenavon, Abertillery, Blaina and Brynmawr numbering in all about 2,000 marched over to the Tredegar Police Court headed by three bands. The men used to march about the district headed by a band, and one young man carried two loaves of bread and a herring on a stick in front of the band. On the first occasion at the Tredegar Police Court the cases were adjourned. On the way back the demonstrators besieged the pit heads at Ebbw Vale and stripped the horses. They stopped the ironworkers working and there were plenty of free fights because the Ebbw Vale Company had provided their men with wooden clubs. It had reached such a stage that the

Ebbw Vale people wore badges on their arms. If a person did not wear a badge the Ebbw Valians would club him unmercifully, thinking he was a stranger.

The Police Court decision was given against the hauliers and the employers were awarded damages, but some of the employers did not press for the payment of the damages awarded to them, through the influence of deputations of workmen promising that it would never happen again.

A man by the name of Snellgrove was the chief agitator in the hauliers' question, and when it was suggested to the men that they should go back to work there were hoots of derision. The hauliers' strike lasted six weeks and eventually the workmen returned to their employment on the old terms."

It is interesting to note as an example of the persistence of inter-community strife between Ebbw Vale and Brynmawr that even as recently as the 1911 Railway Strike, the Ebbw Vale men came over to loot Brynmawr, and that local patriotism, assisted by the astuteness of the Sergeant of Police, who enlisted the Brynmawr men, who were likely to make trouble, as leaders of the defence, caused the Brynmawr people to chase them back over the mountain.

Year after year disputes between workers and employers occurred over wages, alleged victimisation, payment of train-fares to and from work and conditions of safety in the mines, and the relative power of the two sides gradually changed. While between 1873 and 1888 men were obliged to attend a certain place of worship or a certain public-house before they could obtain employment, by the end of the War, owing to the exigencies of the time, the growth of Trade Union organisation and the determined spirit of the workers, they had so established their status in the mines that the Federation officials were consulted on such matters as the allocation of working places, the promotion of men from one grade to the other and countless other details of colliery administration.

By this time, however, the injustices and oppressions of the past had bitten so deep into men's memories and minds that the workers could not bring themselves to believe in the good faith or good will of the employer. The period of expansion of trade in the mining industry from 1908 to 1913 was marked by constant strikes in the Blaina district, where one of the collieries later became known as "Little Moscow."

The men were conscious of the power of the strike weapon and determined to win what they thought was their fair share of the proceeds of the industry. They succeeded in obtaining a higher district rate than elsewhere, and at the same time took an active interest in the national struggle, although the Brynmawr workers for a time were at variance with Blaina over the question of joining the National Federation. So rooted was their distrust of the employers that even in recent times of depression, when the interests of the men in the neighbouring district of Blaenavon seemed to demand concession of the demand to revert to the Three Shift system temporarily in order to keep up their quota, they could not believe that sinister motives did not underlie the employers' suggestion, and refused almost unanimously to agree to it. From the employers' point of view the intractable and unreasonable attitude of the men often appears to be one of the causes of their present difficulties.

The workers have learnt, too, to distrust the employers' influence over their own members who are promoted to become minor officials and are apt to believe that a man who "takes the lamp" and becomes a fireman or overman soon becomes a "petty boss" and adopts the owners' point of view.

The valley organisation of the Miners' Federation means that Brynmawr men while working in different localities belong to four different District Lodges, of which Blaina and the Western Valley Lodge is the most "advanced." They are thus open to different views as to Trade Union methods and aims, but, in spite of variation in shades of opinion, the conception of class-warfare holds the field and the life of Brynmawr has been permeated through and through with the bitterness engendered in the industrial struggle. So far-reaching are the effects of this that it is difficult for the workers to believe that any employer, inside or outside the mining industry, can have disinterested motives, or that foremen and others in responsible positions can be fairminded and well disposed to those who are under their supervision. With unemployment also, the ideals of brotherhood and mutual self-sacrifice which influenced the early Unionists have to some extent given way to cynicism, and the motive of individual self-interest is now often put forward as the main reason for continued membership of the Federation.

Trade Unionism, however, plays another and more constructive part in the life of the mining community. From the first the Union has discharged certain Friendly Society functions, and the workers have learnt to practise thrift and mutual self-help through the Union organisation. By voluntary deductions from their wages at an agreed rate in the pound they provide Hospital treatment for themselves and their families, retain a doctor for their wives and children, sometimes help to maintain a Welfare Fund and a Sick Fund, and undertake other benevolent work for their members. A striking example of this conscious use of their power for the common good is provided by the formation in 1930 of a Nursing Association for Clydach and Llanelly Hill, the work of which is mainly financed by voluntary deductions at the collieries on the poundage system.[1] The work of the various institutions is to a great extent governed by representative Committees of the miners, whose deliberations are marked by common-sense, shrewdness and a real desire for the common good. The lodges thus help to build up in their members a spirit of neighbourliness and independence and also provide a training in the practical conduct of affairs which must be of advantage to the community as a whole.

Through the Trades and Labour Council and the Miners' Welfare Committee and through their close connection with the political movement, which will be described later, they exercise a great influence on the life of the community in many other directions.

[1] A grant is also obtained from the County Council in return for certain public health services undertaken by the Nurses.

CHAPTER VI

LOCAL ADMINISTRATION AND THE POLITICAL MOVEMENT

THE Breconshire gentry who gave evidence of the "frightful state" of the morals of Brynmawr in 1847 made no mention of the probable connection between this and the lack of the elementary conditions of decency, comfort and good health from which many of the workers suffered. The town had sprung up haphazard at the bidding of industry; it was perhaps less fortunate than Clydach and Nantyglo in that the employers did not live within its bounds and had therefore less personal knowledge of its condition and needs and less incentive to remedy obvious evils. The workers coming in from different areas with different traditions had no common ideal of what was desirable or even essential for the promotion of public health.

There was no town sewerage, scavenging or water system, but the inhabitants drew their water from numerous wells, some of which were seriously polluted. Under such primitive conditions, outbreaks of disease were to be expected, and in 1847 there was a bad epidemic of cholera. In 1849, an "Enquiry into the Sewerage, Drainage, Supply of Water, and the Sanitary Conditions of the Town of Brynmawr in the County of Brecon," was made by a Superintending Inspector to the Board of Health. Even in those days of primitive ideas of the requisites of public health, conditions in Brynmawr seem to have been exceptionally bad, since the Inspector wrote:—

"It is scarcely within the power of pen or pencil to convey to the apprehension of those who are dependent upon such sources of information, an adequate idea of the condition of the cottage tenements which constitute the town, as they presented themselves to my examination during the visit."

The Inspector recommended that a Board of Health should be formed to remedy these evils and, owing largely to the initiative and organising ability of Mr. Henry Bailey, this was done in 1851. The Board was one of the first twenty-one in England and Wales and the first three in Wales to be elected. Brynmawr thus owed its position as a pioneer town in public health administration to one of the industrialists who had helped to bring it into being. The first members also included the proprietor of the Market Hall and property owners, such as Mr. Blewitt and Mr. Hitchman, who had already built and given their names to parts of it.

The Board set to work with great energy. It found that most of the wells could not profitably be put into a state of repair. A water system was therefore devised, although from that time until now the problem of securing an adequate and pure supply has never been wholly solved, and in exceptionally dry weather people still "Besiege the springs and wells all day long." The condition of the town was improved by the employment of a man to sweep the main streets, requiring the owners of property to put roads and highways in repair, by street-levelling at the public expense, by penalising persons who deposited "filth or rubbish" in the roads, and by efforts to educate the public generally in town cleanliness. Permission was sought from the Duke of Beaufort as ground landlord to tip rubbish at suitable spots, street-lighting was attempted, a cemetery was provided and steps were taken to restrict and finally prohibit burials in the old and overcrowded chapel burial grounds. A sewerage system was installed, and, here perhaps, the early start made by the Board was not altogether an advantage, as the science of sanitary engineering had not made great strides, and complaints were constantly received from persons who stated that sewers leaked or discharged near their houses or polluted their water supply. The inhabitants of the neighbouring parish of Llanelly in particular objected to the discharge of the Brynmawr sewage into the Clydach river, and, after this was rectified, to the contamination of springs and wells by leakages of faulty pipes, to which the constant presence of typhoid in Clydach was attributed. This grievance recurred at intervals up to 1925 when the new Sewage Disposal Works were installed; even now the memory of deaths from typhoid and the mental attitude then engendered are not without effects on the relationships of the two communities.

In all these matters, as well as in such questions as street-hawking and the complaints arising out of the constant visits of travelling showmen, the Board seems to have acted promptly and, considering the pioneer character of their work, efficiently under the guidance of their first Chairman, Mr. Henry Bailey. Possibly the autocratic methods by which the great industrial pioneers had developed the natural resources of the district were carried into the work of local administration. At any rate, the first four years of work were not wholly without disagreements and difficulties. In 1855 Mr. Bailey resigned, and his place as chairman was taken by Mr. Jayne, another representative of the great industrial employers of the district.

The early attitude of the Board to any signs of revolt among the workers seems to have reflected the predominant influence of the employing class. In 1853, the year of the spontaneous one-day strike already described, the Board passed a resolution unanimously expressing their extreme regret at "the appearance of riot and disturbances that have just begun to manifest themselves among the workmen of this place," and sent a deputation to the Justices of the Peace entreating them to take "such steps as may to them seem fit to quell the same and guard against a recurrence."

The ratepayers generally do not seem to have been wholly enamoured of their zealous new Board, which was in advance of public opinion in many ways. Public meetings were held and deputations of ratepayers asked that the rates should be kept as low as possible; individuals contested their liability to pay rates and asked to be allowed not to take the new water supply and not to be forced to construct communications with the main sewers. Irregularities and informalities on the part of the Board were alleged and a complaint was sent to the General Board of Health, which resulted in an official visit from an Inspector, greatly to the anger of the Local Board, which in its turn sent up a formal protest at the way in which its authority was being brought into contempt and discontent was fostered among the ratepayers. The inhabitants of Clydach Dingle protested, as they still do at intervals, against having to pay for benefits which they did not receive, and in a spirited way wrote direct to the General Board on the subject. Some inhabitants of the town even moved away rather than pay the rates, although the general district rate was only one shilling in 1852 and fell to eight pence in 1854, a small water rate being levied in addition.

In spite of the difficulties, due to lack of appreciation of the necessity of public health measures on the part of the community and possibly to the fact that the technical knowledge at the disposal of the Board in its first few years was hardly equal to its zeal, its work continued to grow, as the life of the town found expression in new activities.

Gasworks, boot factory, foundry, brickworks, slaughterhouses and market offered employment and trade, and the records of the Board reflected the consciousness of the growing importance of Brynmawr, which was present in the community as a whole, and also the growing appreciation of the possible power and influence of an elected local body. Even as early as 1852 a memorial was signed by twenty-three tradesmen and other inhabitants asking the Board to "use their influence" to prevent the abandonment of the railway from Blaina to Nantyglo, and in 1855 the Board set forth the "many advantages" which would attend the moving of the County Court to Brynmawr, owing to the large population living in and near the town, the central position, and the fact that it had its "Proper representative body" elected by the inhabitants and able to express public opinion.

The Board was not only firm in its attitude to discontented ratepayers but also endeavoured to act with impartiality; tradesmen, whatever their importance as substantial property owners, and even members of the Board itself, and the great surrounding industrialists, were dealt with impartially when their interests clashed with those of the community or threatened to interfere with the prestige or authority of the elected body. Thus, the owner of the Market Hall, himself a member of the Board, was severely taken to task when he neglected to submit plans of his suggested new building. Tradesmen and other occupiers of property in Beaufort Street were reminded that it was "only fair" that they should do what was necessary to put the footpath in repair at their own expense and not out of the general rates. A suggestion by Messrs. J. and C. Bailey that their rates should be remitted in return for their undertaking the upkeep of Bailey Street was countered by the taking over of the maintenance of the latter by the Board. In 1876 the Board showed also that it was not neglectful of the interests of the workers of Brynmawr by urging the railway company to allow cheap travelling facilities to the Brynmawr men employed at the Ebbw Vale Works, and also asking the Ebbw Vale Company to exert its influence on their behalf.

The industrial employers were not the only feudal powers in the neighbourhood. The Duke of Beaufort was the ground landlord of the town and communication between the local Board and the Agent for the Beaufort Estate was constant and on the part of the Board ceremonious and deferential. The naming of new streets, the replacement of name boards of streets, the arrangements with the gas company, the provision of sites for the tipping of rubbish, the adoption of certain streets as highways, the appointment of a "respectable person" as Town Crier in place of one who offended the ears of the religious by "profane language," the site for a new chapel and the vexed question of the disposal of sewage all came partially under the Duke's jurisdiction, and in addition, application was made to him from time to time for financial help in town improvements which could not be carried out at the expense of the ratepayers. Relations with the Estate Office were friendly and substantial help was given to the town by the Duke in various ways. In spite of the growing spirit of revolt in industry, there remained a certain feeling of feudal loyalty to the landowners and the rare visits of the Duke to Brynmawr were occasions of pomp and public interest. Even in 1931, it was possible for Trade Union and Labour leaders to refer publicly to Brynmawr as "One of His Grace's townships." Possibly the town with its predominantly mining population feels the lack of that outlet for the imagination in colour and pageantry which royalty and aristocracy provide on state occasions for the country at large.

In 1860, Mr. Hicks, a tradesman who had also founded a factory which grew to considerable size, became Chairman of the Board and for the next thirty or forty years the control of town affairs was almost exclusively in the hands of the comparatively small local employers, property owners and tradesmen, rather than of the iron masters and colliery proprietors on a large scale whose industrial interests centred in the area just outside the town.

The years between 1860 and the formation of the Urban District in 1894 witnessed various epidemics of Cholera, Smallpox and Typhoid, with Government pressure on the town to provide an Isolation Hospital—in 1932 still not an accomplished fact—troubles about the water supply, disagreements with Llanelly Parish, and government enquiries in 1872 and 1876 about the connection of typhoid with the sewage system. The Reports of the Brynmawr Medical Officer of Health constantly draw attention to the need for facilities for the isolation and treatment of infectious diseases, to the overcrowded and insanitary conditions in lodging houses and to other abuses, including some nuisances created by the local Authority itself in the tipping of refuse. As late as 1897 he wrote:—"I wish to draw attention to the very unsatisfactory state of Twyncynghordy Road. The refuse from the town is tipped in it, as I am informed for the purpose of 'forming a road.' If such is the intent it is futile, as vegetables in all stages of decomposition and empty lobster tins are scarcely suitable material to form a road." From which statement, it appears that public opinion with regard to town cleanliness and health had perhaps still further advances to make.

Probably Brynmawr is still influenced both by the low standards of public cleanliness in the unsightly and untidy

colliery towns all around as well as by the traditional carelessness of the essentials of public health. From time to time the
Board of Health and District Council have tried to discourage
the indiscriminate tipping of ashes and rubbish and the litter-
ing of the streets, and to inculcate higher standards of town
cleanliness. In the long run, however, only general education
in public health can achieve improvements of this kind, and
the standards of the elected body cannot be permanently far
in advance of those of the mass of the citizens. Probably only
an awakening of the sense of community obligation and civic
pride together with the growth of knowledge will lead to lasting
and universal improvement.

Some defects of early building and sanitary engineering
afford excuses for low standards to-day. In the old and narrow
central streets the drain for slop-water is often in the street
channel; and too often dirty water is not emptied carefully
down the drain, but is thrown broadcast over the streets to
the danger and discomfort of the passers-by. A further
nuisance and danger to public health is involved by the method
of disposal of ashes and house-refuse. In certain parts, where
open spaces are available and where the District Council
collect rubbish infrequently or not at all, this is tipped out
by the householders without regard to appearance or health.
Even where this does not happen, the bye-law requiring that
ashes and rubbish should be contained in a covered receptacle
so that the pavement and road may be kept clean, is almost
universally disregarded. Instead of covered ashbins, receptacles
of every size and shape, boxes, baskets, buckets, old baths,
most of which are themselves candidates for the ash heap,
are placed out on the pavement to await collection by the
town lorry; sheep, dogs, mountain ponies, and children or
pedestrians knock these over constantly and the frequent high
winds blow the contents over road and pavement. Possibly,
if the ash-men were allowed to fetch a bin from private
property, more householders might be induced to obtain a
properly covered one; as it is, there is always a likelihood of
these being knocked about when left on the edge of the streets.
In this, as in other matters, co-operation between the local

Authority and the enlightened tenants and house owners is needed to bring about a general effort to preserve and improve the amenities of the community.

Brynmawr also lacks some of the machinery of public health. As has been seen, it has no Isolation Hospital and, except for a recent arrangement with the County Council as regards smallpox cases, makes no provision for the admission of persons suffering from infectious diseases to Hospitals maintained by other Authorities. Recent suggestions with regard to the provision of a School Treatment Centre, Ante-Natal Clinic, Open-Air School, provision for more thorough street cleaning, and other needs have been shelved owing to the financial straits of the County Council. Owing to the same need for economy the Brynmawr Medical Officer of Health is a part time officer only, and the District Council expect their Surveyor to combine with his own duties those of Sanitary Inspector.

Many of the difficulties with regard to Public Health provision are due partly to parsimony in more prosperous times, or undue care for the financial interests of the ratepayers when the welfare of the community demanded wise expenditure. To remedy the existing evils probably both public opinion must be aroused and the financial difficulties with regard, for instance, to payment of full-time officers be met by an extension of local Government boundaries.

It has been seen that Brynmawr, placed on the borders of Monmouthshire and Breconshire, had historical links in both directions. Both its religious and industrial development drew much from Nantyglo. It sought the help of Nantyglo and Blaina in obtaining the extension of the Railway Line from Nantyglo to Brynmawr, the Brynmawr market attracted buyers from the Western as well as Eastern Valley and cheap railway tickets were issued on Market days. When the provision of an Isolation Hospital was under consideration a suggestion was put forward for joint action with Nantyglo, and later on, in 1909, the advisability of joining with the Western Valleys (Monmouthshire) Sewage Board was forcibly pointed out by a Government Inspector, advocated, with a promise of substantial help by the Beaufort Estate, and only dismissed from motives of short-sighted economy on the part of the Brynmawr Council.

On the other hand, agricultural produce from the districts to the north of Brynmawr was the mainstay of the Brynmawr market; the town was in the Breconshire electoral area, and part of Llanelly Parish was joined with Brynmawr in the Petty Sessional Division. The interests of Brynmawr were thus divided and the relative closeness of its link with Breconshire and, in particular, Llanelly Parish, as opposed to Monmouthshire and the industrial areas to the south of it, is still a cause of discussion. In 1885 and the succeeding years, when the question of local Government Boundaries was under discussion, the Board was firmly of opinion that the whole of the Brynmawr area should remain in Breconshire, and this was finally arranged, while for Poor Law purposes the portion of Brynmawr which was in the Parish of Aberystruth was transferred from the Union of Bedwellty (Monmouthshire) to that of Crickhowell (Breconshire).

Since the local Government Act of 1929, the question of the boundaries of Brynmawr has again become a subject of controversy, and it is interesting to note that Brynmawr, despite its reactions to the critical attitude of agricultural Breconshire, still feels that its attachments should be with it rather than with Monmouthshire. It is unfortunate, therefore, that the influence of controversies supposedly dead and buried and a somewhat narrow view of local interest have so far prevented the putting forward of a scheme of amalgamation with part of the rural district to the north of the town, which would bring about a wider area of local government.

The establishment in 1894 of the Urban District Council in the place of the Board of Health coincided with the beginning of the direct influence of the workers on town affairs, and in that year a miner was for the first time elected as a member of the local Government body. The point of view of the organised workers began to come to the fore in Council meetings from that time onwards. In the following year it was resolved as a result of a letter from the Secretary of the

Tin Plate Workers' Association that as far as possible hands thrown out of employment in consequence of the stoppage of Tin Plate Mills at Nantyglo and Blaina should be employed on works of improvement in the district.   In the same year the Trade Union rate of wages of 3s. 4d. per day for a week of fifty-four hours was adopted by the Council for its able-bodied labourers.   Trade Union influence thus began to play an increasing part directly and indirectly in town administration.

In the early days of the New Unionism, which commenced in the 'seventies, the education of the leaders both on the academic side and in practical affairs was largely drawn from the Chapel and Sunday School, and, despite the traditional opposition of organised religion and the movement of industrial revolt, the Band of Hope and other social organisations of the Chapels provided the chief training ground of the workers. The idealism and enthusiasm fostered in these spheres found new expression in the brotherhood, loyalty and mutual self-sacrifice which, in spite of many failures, inspired the early Trade Union Movement.   It is probable that the general outlook of John Thomas, the Clerk to the Board of Health and Urban District Council for sixty years, strict Noncon-formist and pioneer and enthusiastic in the causes of education, temperance and social progress, was not so very different from those of the first miner representative of the town.

With the growing up of a generation educated in the Elementary Schools and with the dissemination of the political and economic theories formulated by the Fabian Society and of the later theories of the Independent Labour Party, both Trade Unionism and the political outlook of the workers changed.   Liberalism was ousted by a definitely class-con-scious and separatist creed, and the belief of the Unions in the political movement—varying in degree from time to time— was expressed in the attempt to secure political dominance in local as well as national government.   During and after the War, speakers from England and Scotland visited Brynmawr and did much to introduce more "advanced" political and industrial ideas.   To-day the composition both of the Urban

District Council and of the Brynmawr representatives on the Breconshire County Council is largely determined by party politics, and is at present predominantly Labour. The Trade Union lodges have direct representation on the Trades and Labour Council, through which they nominate candidates for the local Government Bodies.

Two results of great importance in the life of Brynmawr spring from the control of local affairs by one political Party.

The class-conscious outlook tends to make the welfare of the community as such appear less important than the welfare of a section of it, and the minority both in the Council and in the town get little consideration and chance of self-expression.

This majority rule and bias of course obtained equally in the early days when the employing interest was predominant, but the effects of it are accentuated under a Labour regime owing to the underlying theory which is the basis of both political and industrial democracy as understood in South Wales. The ultimate authority of the individual is assumed to involve his immediate authority even on points of detail and the mass meeting of the lodge or party send delegates, whose course of action is predetermined, rather than free representatives, to Conference or Council. Thus, in Brynmawr, any points of special interest on the Agendas of the District Council are considered by the Labour Party *before* the Council meets, and subsequent discussions in the Council in which the minority point of view or that of the individual independent member is put forth, cannot affect the decisions already taken by the mandated Labour Councillors.

In practice, of course, the officials of the Trade Union and the Executive or unofficial leaders of the Labour Party tend to wield power and exert an influence out of all proportion to their members, and the "Voice of the people" tends to become an echo of that of the expert or popular leader. This in its turn sometimes brings with it the evils of demagoguery and corruption and there is a danger that the ideals of the political movement may be turned to cynical self-seeking.

Perhaps the final argument against party politics or class dominations in the local government of a town like Brynmawr lies in the multiplicity of mutual interests and of pioneer adventures and experiments which the healthy life of the community involves. Such common interests and individual or group efforts are lost sight of, or crushed out of existence where expression is only possible through the party machine and only the party point of view gains a hearing. It would indeed be paradoxical if in Brynmawr, the home of industrial and political revolt against the oppression of the many by the one, the success of the movement should involve the loss of the fullest life both for the individual and the community.

G

CHAPTER VII

HOUSING

THE rapid growth of population owing to successive influxes of workers from outside Brynmawr meant that houses also sprang up rapidly and without any conscious planning. Fortunately the intersecting tramroads built for industrial purposes provided a skeleton town-plan,[1] as the workers' dwellings, apart from those in outlying districts such as Clydach Dingle, where the iron-ore industry of the town was concentrated, naturally grew up along the existing tracks. The streets tended, therefore, to be at right angles to one another, and the town escaped the monotony and congestion of the ribbon-like neighbouring settlements along the narrow valleys to the south and west. The situation on a spacious plateau allowed of subsequent expansion on all sides and of a central square, as well as of the use of outlying land for gardens, allotments and recreation grounds. Hence a centre for community life as well as means of outdoor recreation and spare time occupation were available.

Unlike the industrial settlements of Nantyglo, Beaufort, Blaenavon, and to a lesser degree Clydach, where the iron works were actually situated, the dormitory town of Brynmawr owed little in the way of building enterprise to the great employers. Individual workers built their own cottages here and there along the tramroads in the very early days, and shortly afterwards tradesmen who, like the workers, were attracted by the central position of the town, began to build courts and rows of houses as a commercial speculation. Later

[1] See Map of Tramroads on following page.

still, thrifty workers, who built their own cottage, invested
what was left of their savings in the building of an additional
cottage which was inhabited by a married member of their
family or let to a fellow-worker, and speculative builders put
up rows of houses.

Thus the tied cottage belonging to the employers has
never been a feature of Brynmawr life, and in consequence
of this labour has been mobile and workers have been able

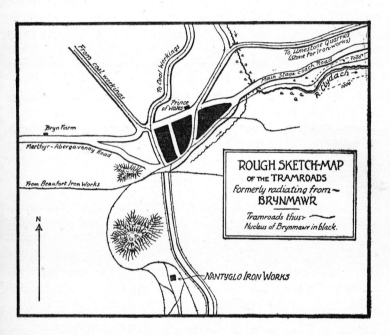

ROUGH SKETCH-MAP
of the TRAMROADS
Formerly radiating from
BRYNMAWR

Tramroads thus
Nucleus of Brynmawr in black.

to move from one colliery to another within travelling distance
from Brynmawr in the search for work in bad times. Another
consequence has been an accentuation of the importance of
the trading element in the community by their ownership
of house property, and a tightening of their bond with the
fortunes of the iron and coal industries on the success of which
the payment of their rent depends. Both tradesmen and
workmen owners of cottages have a stake in the community,

which has had effects on the strength of their attachments
to it and on their attitude to local government questions
and especially to rating. In addition, the workmen who own
a cottage are tied to the town in bad times by the fact that
their savings are invested in fixed property and that they are
unable to realise them at times when employment is at a low
ebb and ready money is scarce. The importance of this factor
in binding unemployed miners to the distressed areas is considerable. Maps 1 and 2 at the end of the Chapter show the
extent to which house property in Brynmawr is owned by
Brynmawr residents, and the extent of owner-occupiership
of houses.

Building in Brynmawr seems to have kept pace with the
growth of population throughout the nineteenth century.
Both in 1811, 1821 and 1831 the houses in Llanelly Parish
were almost equal to the number of resident families,[1] while
between 1831 and 1841, when the population of the Parish
increased by an amount exceeding the whole increase in the
previous thirty years, the number of houses built was also
unprecedentedly great.[2] In 1861, when the industry of the
district was declining, there were actually 127 uninhabited
houses, and in 1881 at the end of the period of depression
prior to the expansion of the coal-mining industry, there
were as many as 305 uninhabited houses in the Brynmawr
Petty Sessional Division. A separate house for each family
has thus been the normal condition in Brynmawr, and this
has been a constant factor in the maintenance of family
solidarity and self-sufficiency.[3]

[1] In 1811 the number of inhabited houses in Llanelly Parish was only four
less than the number of families, while in 1822 the numbers were exactly
equal. In Llangattock Parish the position was not quite so favourable and
building proceeded less rapidly. Thus in 1822 there were 303 houses inhabited
by 372 families. At the same time a number of houses were uninhabited
probably owing to the swift transfer from agricultural to industrial occupations of residents in this parish, which no doubt led to some migration
from those parts of it which were most remote from the iron-ore ground and
the Iron Works. (See Census Volumes for Breconshire for 1811 and 1822.)

[2] See Census Volumes for Breconshire 1811 to 1921 for numbers of inhabited
and uninhabited houses in Llanelly Parish and Brynmawr. The areas for
which statistics are given varied at different census periods and are thus
not strictly comparable throughout.

[3] See Map on following page.

Before 1821	1801 1821	1821 1841	1841 1851	1851 1861	1861 1871	1871 1881	1881 1891	1891 1901

BRYNMAWR

DEVELOPMENT
1800~1930

1921
1930

[To face page 86

The types of property built at different dates reflect the economic conditions prevailing in the community. To the original farms and shepherds' cottages further cottages and a few shops and inns, including the important Coaching Inn, the Griffin Hotel, were added prior to 1830. In the period of industrial and trading prosperity between 1830 and 1840 were added not only cottages, but the shops in the present main street, and two important chapels. The next decade brought three more Chapels, the British and Foreign School, and some larger houses. Between 1860 and 1880 there was less building of cottage property, but the railway station and all the present elementary school buildings were erected. With renewed industrial prosperity and the growth of the town as a trading centre from 1880 onwards a wide new street was added with substantially built cottages on each side; existing shops were re-modelled and others were built, together with a new Market Hall and the Secondary School. In the first decade of the twentieth century, the town was extended on its eastern side by the building of several new streets of artisans' houses of a type very superior to the older cottage property, and by a further addition of shops between the railway station and the Market Square. The higher standard of wages and comfort among the workers was thus reflected in the kind of houses built for their use. Many of the houses built at this period were erected by Building Societies formed for the purpose, through which a number of residents, both business men and miners, invested their savings in house property. Since 1920, there has been practically no private building, but under official pressure the District Council built one hundred and fifty houses on the outskirts of the town. These were of a good type with gardens and bathrooms, but were built at a very high price, and are now a financial burden rather than a source of revenue to the town. The almost parallel growth of houses and population up to 1910 is a striking illustration of the general optimistic outlook with regard to the prosperity of industry and the stability of the community.

Early development was largely within the central area,

along narrow parallel streets running between the tramroads
at the upper and lower levels of the town, intersected by
the main shopping street. The result was a congestion of
population in the Central Ward, where the density per acre
was 84·7 in 1921.[1] Within this congested central area the
cottage-property is now nearly all a hundred years old or
more, and is of a very poor type. The cottages are small,
ill-lighted and ill-ventilated by small windows; some of them
are back-to-back and very few of them have damp-courses.
(The latter are also lacking in most of the more recently
built and larger houses in the town.) Many of the living
rooms open straight on to the street, and a number of them
have only a common open yard without garden at the back
or front. The workers are thus deprived of the possibility
of adding to their diet by growing their own vegetables.
The majority of the five hundred houses in Brynmawr which
have no separate lavatory accommodation are to be found
in this older central part of the town. Many of them are
also unconnected with the gas mains and are lighted by
paraffin lamps and candles.

The diagram on the next page shows the distribution of
the various types of houses in the various parts of the town.
It will be observed that back-to-back houses number 93;
and constitute a less serious problem numerically than in
many towns which have been built in the early days of the
Industrial Revolution. The houses, which have both back
and front gardens, are for the most part in the Wards outside
the Central portion of the town, and in the main correspond
with those which have bathrooms. The absence of the latter
in a mining community has meant a great addition of work
and much inconvenience to housewives, who have to heat
water for the daily bath which their husbands and sons
usually take in the family living room on their return from
the pit.

Up to 1850, as has been seen, there was no piped water-
supply and the inhabitants had to fetch their water from
wells. This position was remedied by degrees, and to-day

[1] See Census Volume for Breconshire, 1921.

BRYNMAWR. TYPES OF HOUSES.

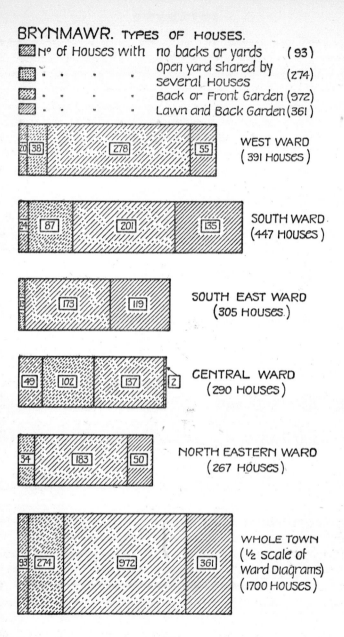

N° of Houses with no backs or yards (93)
" " " open yard shared by several Houses (274)
" " " " Back or Front Garden (972)
" " " " Lawn and Back Garden (361)

WEST WARD (391 HOUSES)
70 | 38 | 278 | 55

SOUTH WARD (447 HOUSES)
24 | 87 | 201 | 135

SOUTH EAST WARD (305 HOUSES)
173 | 119

CENTRAL WARD (290 HOUSES)
49 | 102 | 137 | 2

NORTH EASTERN WARD (267 HOUSES)
34 | 183 | 50

WHOLE TOWN (½ scale of Ward Diagrams) (1700 HOUSES)
93 | 274 | 972 | 361

almost all the houses in the town have a separate water supply. Farms and outlying houses in Clydach Dingle and other outskirts of the town are still without water-taps. About one hundred of these outlying houses are also without connection with the town sewers, owing to their isolated position.

In the actual size of dwellings as denoted by the number of rooms, Brynmawr compares favourably with some other mining areas such, for instance, as Tyneside. The majority of the houses are of the four-to-five roomed type, the average number of rooms per dwelling according to the 1921 Census being 4·79. Since 1921, the average has been increased by the building of 150 new houses by the Urban District Council all of which have three bedrooms, and either two or three rooms, including a small kitchen, but excluding the bathroom which all possess, downstairs.

ROOMS PER DWELLING. 1921 CENSUS

	Dwellings occupied by non-private families	Vacant	of 1–3 rooms	4–5 rooms	6–8 rooms	9 or more rooms	Total Rooms
Undivided Private Houses (1,446) . .	1	10	216	776	432	22	6,748
Shops (135) .	—	2	10	57	54	14	820
Others (10) .	1	—	3	2	4	1	68
TOTAL: (1,591)	2	12	229	835	490	37	7,638

On the other hand the distribution of families among the houses of various sizes meant that, in 1921, 960 persons, or twelve per cent of the total private family population lived more than two persons to a room and were thus overcrowded according to the Census definition.

The average number of rooms per person were ·95.

The position with regard to family overcrowding or houses structurally divided but occupied by more than one family was also unsatisfactory, as there were 1·12 families per dwelling. This position was largely due not to any longstanding deficiency in houses but to the fact that the normal increase in dwelling-houses to meet increase in demand was not maintained between 1911 and 1921 owing to the effects of the War. As many as 178 houses were occupied in 1921 by two or more families. By 1931, owing to the building of the Council houses and the effects of migration from the district, the position as regards family overcrowding was distinctly better, and the houses occupied by more than one family were reduced from 178 to 137.[1] The number of houses occupied by more than two families was very few. On the other hand, many of the unemployed men living even in the smaller type of house have been obliged to take a lodger and a good deal of social overcrowding exists.

During the last ten years, neither the local Authority nor the private speculative builder has been in a position to remedy the overcrowding of families and persons. Between 1921 and 1931 only six houses have been built by private enterprise, while 36 houses have been closed as unfit for human habitation, some of these being demolished and five of them subsequently repaired or reconstructed. The situation was altered, however, in 1933, and in the early part of this year the local Authority put forward a scheme for the erection of fifty new houses. If this is sanctioned and put into operation it should not only relieve overcrowding, but also make it possible to insist on a higher standard of reasonable repair and lead to some of the houses now occupied being condemned.

The development of Brynmawr has been largely influenced by the policy of the ground landlord, the Duke of Beaufort. From the start, the Beaufort Estate Agent has allowed land to be taken up for building purposes at very reasonable terms, usually on a ninety-nine years' lease, and has also aided the town by giving facilities in the use of land for tipping purposes, and other common needs. At first certain roads were maintained by the Estate. Whenever conditions warranted it, the Estate Office has brought pressure to bear to ensure that buildings were kept in a good state of repair, and has made this a condition of renewing leases. Under present conditions, at a time when the majority of leases in the older part of the town are running out, landlords and

[1] Brynmawr Survey figures.

owner-occupiers find it very difficult to fulfil the conditions
of renewal with regard to repairs, and as there is little market
for cottage property (in spite of a shortage in the supply
of houses in a state fit for human habitation) houses of the
older type can be acquired for very low sums.

The following report on some of these houses has been made
by an Officer of the Welsh Town Planning Trust:—

"As regards a number of houses in the town it appears that all those
inspected were in a very bad state of repair, the tenants living under
the worst possible conditions. The roofs are leaking badly, the external
walls are damp, windows are too small, and in many cases the woodwork so decayed that the windows would not open. In a few houses
the sculleries do not contain windows, and one block of seven or eight
houses contain only two dilapidated w.c.'s, the drains from which are
defective."

Estimates were also given of the cost of repairing and
reconditioning such houses, including "repairs to roofs,
inserting new and larger windows, providing new fascia
guttering and water-pipes, rendering of external walls, repairing chimneys, clearing and re-instating drains, and providing
proper w.c. drains." It was suggested that back-to-back
houses under one roof might be converted into one decent
dwelling, and a description was given of typical houses which
are uninhabitable without extensive repairs:—

"Two of the houses on the corner of the block referred to on the main
road, have had roofs completely stripped with only a few rafters,
3 x 1¼. The internal walls have collapsed and very little of the floor
and joists could be sandwiched. The window frames are all quite
rotten; the external walls and window openings, however, are in quite
a good condition, and the bedrooms are better than in the other houses.
If these buildings are tackled for reconditioning, it is estimated that
the cost will be at least £140 each."

The extraordinarily bad state of repair of the cottage
property of Brynmawr is the worst feature of the housing
situation there. It is due in the first place to the age of the
cottages and their method of construction without proper
provision against damp, to the nature of the climate with
its heavy rains and periodical gales, rendering frequent attention to roofs essential and to the financial effects of the last

ten years of unemployment and poor trade. The discomfort and injury to health due to leaking roofs through which the rain drips on to the beds and floor, and to walls which ooze with dampness, can be imagined. It is significant that rheumatic troubles come next in order of numerical importance to influenza, bronchitis and other diseases of the respiratory system, in the claims for sickness benefits made on the four principal Approved Societies between 1920 and 1929.

During the course of the local Survey, a special study has been made of the correlation of tuberculosis with bad housing and overcrowding conditions, and poverty. This disease accounts for a considerable proportion of the illness and deaths in the town. It is impossible to isolate the various factors which conduce to it, but a detailed study of all the cases notified in a number of selected streets between 1919 and 1929 shows that in 53·60 per cent of them bad housing or overcrowding with or without poverty was present.[1] There were a considerable number of recurring cases in the same house, and a study of these indicates the importance of overcrowding especially of sleeping accommodation as a factor facilitating infection in the home. This was present in twenty-three of the forty-four recurring cases which were notified from twenty houses. In one of the older streets containing a large proportion of back-to-back houses with very small, airless rooms, little access to sun, and leaking roof and walls oozing with damp, as many as seventeen cases were notified from the twenty-nine houses in the street. It requires little imagination to realise the human suffering and danger to human life occasioned by the prolonged serious illness of a member of a family living in such a house. In one such case one of the two small bedrooms was given up to a dying girl, while the father and mother and six other children crowded into the second bedroom and the living room (used also as a bedroom). It is not to be wondered at that two other children contracted the disease, and that two out of the three infected children died within two years. One of these went to Sanatorium for a few months, but returned home to die after a few

[1] See Appendix III for an analysis of cases.

weeks, during which he slept and lived in the airless and damp family living room in which the family food was cooked and the family meals served. Other cases of the same nature could be quoted, where one member or another of the family was notified as suffering with tuberculosis and isolation or even separate sleeping accommodation was impossible to arrange. In such cases, efforts to transfer the family to a better and less overcrowded house have failed owing to the pressure on housing accommodation and the fact that so large a proportion of the cottages in the town are of the same type and in an equally bad state of repair.

The problem of the poor type of house in a bad state of repair is of course accentuated by that of the bad tenant. Generally speaking standards of pride in the home are high in Brynmawr. The miner who has struggled to save sufficient to buy or build his own cottage makes an effort to keep it in repair and even to improve it. The local custom of colour-washing the outside of the houses is declining but still gives some of them that "neat and cheerful appearance" which Archdeacon Coxe noted in the neighbourhood more than a century ago. Incredible labour has been put into the improvement of the soil by some of the outlying cottagers with large gardens or little holdings of land, and the housewives continue to give many poorly designed cottages an air of cheerfulness and comfort, to which the polished brasses which still linger in the homes of the older people, and the large fires banked up day and night, contribute.

Many even of the unemployed men regard their rent as the first charge on their income, and as a rule it is the honest and independent tenants together with the house-owners who bestow the most care on house and garden. There are many other men who habitually leave their rent unpaid for long periods, and such financially bad tenants often show the same carelessness of other people's property in their management of house and garden. Their irresponsible habits render it difficult for owners to do necessary repairs or to pay their rates. In this way they play their part in the process of self-destruction of the social structure. In a community which needs to make the most of all its available assets they are destructive forces and enemies of the public good.

The new Council houses provide many instances of this anti-social behaviour on the part of the tenants. The policy of the Council itself in allowing some tenants to avoid payment of rents, and ceasing to enforce by-laws with regard to the preservation of common amenities, although possibly inspired by sympathy with the unemployed, has played its part in this process.[1] Untidy and uncultivated gardens, disfigured by ramshackle sheds, and used as a run for fowls and geese, which are a pest to striving neighbours, are far too common on the Council Housing Estate. Until public standards of care for house and garden are raised, the appearance of the town will continue to deteriorate and will react unfavourably on its prospects as a trading and residential centre. So, too, every derelict shop with rotting and unpainted doors and window frames is a menace to the prospects of its struggling neighbours, who still strive to attract custom to the town.

Since the population of Brynmawr is declining and the coal-mining industry offers no hope of employment on its former scale, it might be considered that efforts to improve the housing position by reconditioning old houses or building new ones have no economic justification. To accept this assumption is to acquiesce in the process of drifting to decay. The substantial, though poorly-designed, houses and shops of Brynmawr, its traditional pride in house-ownership, and its town plan are part of its economic assets. Owing to financial straits and to neglect and apathy on the part of some residents, they are daily declining in value. As conditions of damp and disrepair grow worse, one housewife after another slackens the struggle, and health, family relationships and self-respect inevitably suffer. As a result, the population must gradually become less employable, and the town less attractive to trade and industry. The economic as well as the social self-preservation of the

---

[1] Between 1926 and 1929 the arrears of rent on the Council houses rose from approximately £414 to approximately £2,885. By March, 1932, they had risen further to £4,200.

community demands that the rot should be stopped. Psychologically, traditions of family unity, self-respect and ambition, the use of leisure and the prevalent conception of real values are all bound up with standards of housing and with the separate occupation of a house by one family.

The number of structurally sound houses complying with the standard suggested as the minimum by the Ministry of Health falls so short of the actual number of houses returned in the Census volumes that even when the probable continued decline in population during the next few years is taken into consideration, some scheme of reconditioning old property and of building new houses is essential if the people are to live under conditions approaching those necessary for human welfare and the capital already invested in house-property is not to lose all value.

Reconditioning would appear to be a feasible proposition and if undertaken at an early date might salvage much property which would otherwise become worthless. With the co-operation of the ground landlord, which would probably be forthcoming through the Beaufort Estate Office, it should be possible to acquire suitable houses at low rates, and to repair and adapt them in the manner suggested by the expert officer of the Welsh Housing and Town Planning Trust, whose remarks have already been quoted, at a total cost which would not involve the imposition of high rents. The formation of a Public Utility Society to undertake this work, as has been done at Birmingham and elsewhere, together with the scheme of building already put forward by the Local Authority would do much towards solving the housing problem in Brynmawr, and would probably evoke local sympathy and help, as the effort would be in accordance with the traditions of the town.

Brynmawr: Property owned by persons living in and outside Brynmawr 1930

■ Property owned by people living outside

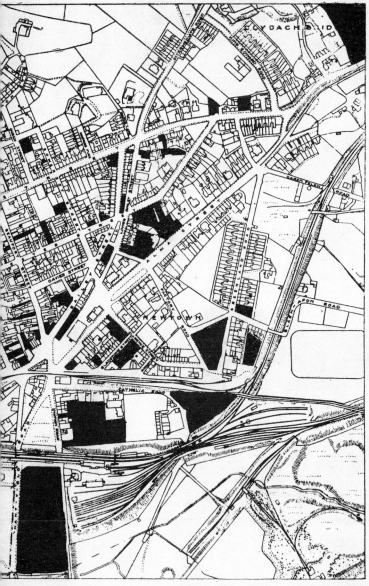

[*To face page* 96

BRYNMAWR,
1930
Owner Occupiers :–

Tenant Occupiers :–

[To face page 96

BAD HOUSING, OVERCROWDING AND POVERTY IN RELATION TO TUBERCULOSIS

SIX SELECTED STREETS

	Notification	Percentage of Total Notifications	Deaths	Percentage of Deaths to Notifications
Constitutional (including possible human infection) .	27	27·83	19	70·37
Constitutional Bad Housing .	6	6·18	2	33·3
Constitutional Poverty . .	13	13·40	5	38·46
Constitutional Overcrowding .	20	20·61	4	20·0
Constitutional Bad Housing Overcrowding .	6	6·18	2	33·3
Constitutional Bad Housing Poverty . .	3	3·09	1	33·3
Constitutional Overcrowding Poverty . .	14	14·43	6	42·85
Constitutional Bad Housing Overcrowding Poverty . .	3	3·09	2	66·66
No Particulars .	5	5·15	1	20·0
TOTAL . .	97	100·0	42	43·29

TWO CONTROLLING STREETS

	Notification	Percentage of Total Notifications	Deaths	Percentage of Deaths to Notifications
Constitutional .	8	100	1	12·5
TOTAL . .	8	100	1	12·5

CHAPTER VIII

THE influence of transport and communications upon trade is apparent throughout the history of Brynmawr. From its early days it was brought into touch with the outside world by the fact that the coach-road from Merthyr to Abergavenny, which was used by Nelson on his way from Pembroke Dockyard to the north, ran through its site and horses were changed at the Grand Stand there. Very soon an important Coaching Inn grew up to cater for travellers along the main road. This road has remained the shortest route from England to the South Wales Coalfield and has thus brought traders and goods through Brynmawr.

The tramroads leading to the iron works and other rough local roads also passed through the town and along them came Breconshire farmers bringing produce for sale to the Company Shops and to the residents of both Brynmawr and Nantyglo. The greatest bulk of trade in farm produce in the early days, however, appears to have come from West Wales. Carriers from Cardiganshire and West Carmarthenshire brought dressed pigs and casks of butter to the "hills" of South Wales, and every week the open-sided, red "Cardy" carts drawn by the free-stepping, light brown "Cardy" horses might have been seen in strings of ten or twelve on their way from Teivy-side through Brecon and Llangynidr to the Company Shop at Nantyglo.

The potential trading value of communication between the industrial area of South Wales and the agricultural districts of Mid- and West-Wales was thus partially exploited even at this early date. The road used, however, was both poor and devious, and the full benefits which might result from bringing the two areas into close touch have not yet been realised owing to the lack of a direct Mid-Wales road.[1] Such a road, passing through Brynmawr at the head of the mining valleys of Monmouthshire would be of great advantage both to Wales generally and to the town itself as a trading centre.

The early shopkeepers in Brynmawr found their trade somewhat restricted by the competition of the Company Shops at Clydach, Llanelly Hill and Nantyglo, and from about 1840 onwards in Brynmawr itself. Although the Truck Acts of 1817 and 1820 made payment in kind illegal, the fact that wages were drawn in money only once in six or eight weeks and also that debt at the Company Shop was recognised as a kind of security for continued employment, made it difficult for the workmen to trade elsewhere. It is interesting to note that William Crawshay of Cyfartha, who did not make use of the Truck System, estimated in 1860 that it gave his competitors "A clear advantage of 10 per cent or two shillings in the pound upon all amounts incurred for labour"; while the men claimed in 1830 that the goods in the Company Shops throughout South Wales were from 20 to 30 per cent dearer than in any other shops in adjacent market towns.

Complaints by the workmen's wives on the score of inferior food and goods were frequent[2] and the effort of a few workers between 1860 and 1870 to start a Co-operative shop in opposition to the Company Shop is a sign of the intense discontent which the system aroused in Brynmawr. Unfortunately hard times, shortage of capital, and paucity of customers brought this independent local experiment to an end after seven years. A branch of the Blaina Co-operative Society's Stores took its place.

Long before this experiment, private shopkeepers had built up substantial businesses in the town, drawing their customers from those workers not directly employed in the

---

[1] The route of the proposed road is indicated on the Map on Page 17.
[2] See *Old South Wales Iron Works*, by John Lloyd.

H

iron works and from farmers, farm labourers and the limestone quarries in the surrounding districts. As early as 1827,
a Brynmawr shopkeeper was able to lend the substantial
sum of £700 for the building of Rehoboth Chapel, and by
1850, the line of shops in the present main street was almost
complete, and the trade of the town must have been considerable.

Up to about 1870, Welsh is said to have been the usual
language in commercial circles; it appears, therefore, that
many of the shopkeepers were of Welsh stock and probably
as a class they would be more homogeneous in origin and
tradition than was the industrial section of the community.
The fact that their trading connection was their means of
livelihood and that many of them owned and built property
in the town would also bind them to it, and render them a
comparatively stable element even in times of depression.
Such records and memories as are available with regard to
earlier generations of tradesmen reveal them as hard-working,
enterprising and religious,—although one or two of them are
remembered as exceptions in not being "professing Christians"
—somewhat secretive about their financial affairs, some of
them preferring even to go to Abergavenny rather than use
a local bank, but capable of generosity in such matters as
provision for education and also in private benevolence. It
is noteworthy that one or two of them seem to have been
in sympathy with the Chartist Movement, although as a rule
their point of view was opposed to the more violent movements of revolt, as was perhaps to be expected in property
owners with a distinct interest in the good order and quiet
of the town. They were proud of the rising prosperity of
Brynmawr, convinced of its importance, and eager for its
prestige as a trading centre.

As has been seen, they played a great part in town administration until recently. In the days of the Board of Health,
indeed, there was a provision that members must qualify
by being rated for the relief of the poor at a minimum of
£15 per year, or have property to the value of £500; this,
in itself, meant that the shopkeepers and innkeepers, of whom

there were as many as 57 in 1847, and 65 in 1881, would constitute the bulk of the persons eligible for membership.

In the 'eighties and 'nineties many of them remodelled their shops, which had previously been of the old-fashioned front-parlour type, and the gunpowder explosion in a grocer's shop in 1870, as well as two great fires in 1898 caused further rebuilding and modernising of the shopping street.   Shops such as the "Yard Shop" and "Toppe Shoppe" became noted throughout the neighbourhood and drew customers from considerable distances by their enterprise and quality and range of goods.

As early as 1844 a Market Hall was built and after various alterations was replaced by a new and larger hall in 1894. The trade done in the Market was largely wholesale, but in addition several local shopkeepers had stalls there, and applications for places in the market were received from as far afield as Sheffield.   Christmas poultry fairs were held in the hall, and stock fairs on the adjoining ground.   The comfort of the country buyers and sellers was catered for by an enterprising Brynmawr tradesman who provided meals for them on the premises.   The importance of the Market to the town was so fully recognised that the Board of Health continually pressed for special Saturday market fares from Blaenavon, Blaina, Abertillery and even as far afield as Aberbeeg, and in 1889, the rights of the Market Company were bought out by the town.   The new hall was built at the public expense and was opened by a civic ceremony and lunch to which two hundred guests were invited.

Railway extensions were desired by the traders urgently for the purposes of their own businesses as well as from the point of view of the Market and the Board of Health, which was largely dominated by the trading interests, and later the Chamber of Trade pressed them continuously on the Railway Companies.   There seems to have been no doubt in the minds of the Brynmawr residents throughout the nineteenth century that additional travelling facilities would bring shoppers to the town rather than attract them from it.   By 1862 Brynmawr had its own railway station and was connected by rail with

Abergavenny and the North and shortly afterwards with
Nantybwch and Rhymney Bridge and Blaenavon and the
Eastern Valleys, but the line up the Western Valley from
Newport was not extended from Nantyglo to Brynmawr
until 1905. So exasperated were the traders of Brynmawr
by the delay, which they felt to be a grave disadvantage in
view of the expanding trade of the town, that in 1877 they
met the Bristol merchants, from whom they purchased their
goods, with a view to arranging for them to be conveyed
via Cardiff instead of by the Monmouthshire Railway and
Canal Company which had hitherto brought them to
Newport.

Despite the disadvantage of this "missing link" of about
two miles of railway line, the position of Brynmawr at the
head of the valleys and the fact that it possessed what was
said to be the best hotel in the district, the nearest rivals
being at Merthyr and Newport, brought to it both private
and commercial travellers. Both the Griffin Hotel, which
had formerly been the headquarters of the stage-coach and
still kept its pre-eminence, and the less famous Mitre sent
buses to meet trains at Brynmawr and Nantyglo stations;
commercial travellers would stay at the Griffin for considerable
periods, returning nightly, after working their day's round
some miles afield, to enjoy the music of the harpist, "Will
the Herring," so called on account of his excessive thinness,
and the hospitality of the landlord, Mr. Richard Wain. The
latter was a figure in the life of Brynmawr; he was a member
of the Board of Health, at the meetings of which he championed
the cause of the fairs, which some of the members wished
to discontinue; as a "sporting man" who was addicted to
horse-racing, he enclosed a piece of land named Wain's Park
where races and other sports were held.

In addition to its use by commercial travellers, Brynmawr
has served since the decade 1870-1880 as a centre for travelling
drapers, most of whom do a credit trade stretching some
distances into the Eastern and Western (Monmouthshire)
Valleys and into the Rhymney and Tredegar Valleys. The
first of these credit drapers was a Scotchman who came to

the town after having served an apprenticeship at Newport, at the end of which he was given the connection which he had worked up in the Brynmawr district. He, in his turn, took on other apprentices until the town became the centre for a very substantial trade, penetrating to lonely farm-houses, hamlets, and villages in the mountains as well as to the industrial areas. The country-side indeed offered special opportunities for this kind of trade, depending for its success on enterprise in seeking out customers as well as on commercial ability, and the appearance of the "packie" with his bundle must often have been an exciting social event in the isolated places which they visited. A little later than the Scotch credit drapers came a number of Jewish travelling drapers, who utilised the central position and good road and rail communications to establish a cash trade on similar lines. Thus a source of considerable wealth was brought into the community without very much additional competition with the local shops since, as a rule, though living and consequently spending much of their income in Brynmawr, the travelling drapers find their customers almost entirely outside it. A further extension of the area from which the local shops might draw their customers has been brought about by the growth of motor transport. Owing to this, life in the little villages, and lonely mountain farms and cottages has been revolutionised. Instead of infrequent trains to be caught at a railway station often some distance away, hourly or even half-hourly buses could be picked up anywhere along the main roads, and in the villages often at the very house-door. Villages which before had no means of communication were linked up, and the market town of Brynmawr could be reached with ease as often as business or amusement tempted the people to seek it.

One effect has been to draw a certain amount of custom from the village shops of Clydach to the bigger towns, but Brynmawr has not monopolised the custom thus transferred, and both Abergavenny and the towns beyond Brynmawr in the opposite directions are now used to some extent by shoppers from the rural district.

The reason for this lies partly in the fact that the bus services which have Brynmawr as their centre or pass through it only commenced to operate in 1922, and their development has coincided with the period of intense industrial depression, during which the financial resources of the shopkeepers have been severely strained and the Brynmawr shops have thus become less attractive. Yet road traffic has brought increased trade to the Market, which is no longer wholesale, and which now attracts not only sellers and buyers from the neighbouring country but traders from such distant parts as Hereford, Monmouth, Taff Wells, Merthyr, Porth, Pontypridd, Cardiff, Aberdare and even Manchester and Liverpool. Lorries, vans and private cars bring in drapery, sweets, china, boots, second-hand clothing and ironmongery in addition to meat, fish and country produce. Much of the stock offered for sale is of poor quality, and some of the meat and fish in particular might not always be passed as fit for human consumption, if the finances and hygienic standards of the town were such as to ensure regular official inspection. The second-hand clothes and some other goods are sold by auction, and the space outside the Market Hall where sellers and buyers congregate every Saturday morning in great numbers is a scene of bustle, noise and excitement.

Such developments of markets, which were formerly designed for the exchange of local farm produce, are common in centrally placed mining towns of South Wales, and the eagerness to buy the cheap goods offered is partly a symptom of diminished family resources owing to prolonged unemployment. Many of the shopkeepers complain of unfair competition by market traders, who do not pay rates, and no longer think of the Market as an asset to the town, but as a rival to their own business. Yet it is the general experience that trade begets trade, and it is hardly credible that, given good value and an enterprising attempt to attract custom, the weekly influx of shoppers should not bring some additional custom to the local shops. In particular, it is to be expected that country folk, who have few alternative shopping facilities in their home villages, would spend a little of their income in the

Brynmawr shops when once they have travelled there to visit the market. If the shopkeepers are correct in their assertion that this does not happen, the reason must be sought for not only in the market itself.

A census of customers taken by a number of shopkeepers on Market days appears to bear out the contention that the shops do not attract the market customers. Moreover, it appears to be a fact that some inhabitants of the rural district actually travel *through* and change buses at Brynmawr in order to shop in Ebbw Vale and Abertillery. Yet they would scarcely wish to spend the extra time and money involved in a journey through the town if equal attractions were forthcoming there. Again, while local patriotism and ties of friendship would naturally induce Brynmawr residents to shop in the town, many of them even now take their custom elsewhere.

What, then, has caused the reversal of the customary assumption that Brynmawr, owing to its unique central position, benefits by any extension of travelling facilities? The town has a considerable variety and number of shops[1] and commerce and finance still come second on the list of occupations from the point of view of employment capacity. There has, in fact, been no decrease in the number of persons engaged in commerce since the onset of the depression in 1921, although the numbers of persons attached to mining and all other occupations have diminished. There are thus practically the same number of persons who endeavour to make a livelihood by selling to a diminishing population with a very much smaller purchasing power than in the days when the mines were flourishing.

Brynmawr shopkeepers are faced both by the special difficulties due to the depressed state of industry in South Wales and by the other difficulties which to-day beset the small private tradesmen everywhere. With smaller turnover and profits are coupled depletion of capital and diminished ability to replenish stocks. The tradition by which the unemployed workers fall back on the family tradesmen in times of industrial

[1] See Appendix I at end of Chapter.

depression has meant that large debts have been accumulated, and, while the powers of resistance and stability and solidarity of the community as a whole have thus been increased, the strain on the shopkeepers has been severe, and of late years many of them have been obliged to give up business or have been declared bankrupt.[1] In 1932, empty shops and derelict buildings in the main shopping streets are one of the most striking signs of economic depression in Brynmawr as elsewhere in South Wales.

The shopkeepers who remain in business are for the most part natives of the town—only one-twentieth of them were born elsewhere—and in many cases have inherited old-established businesses which have been handed down from father to son or passed without break of tradition to a former apprentice. They tend, therefore, to be somewhat local and conservative in outlook. Many of them are drawing heavily on the resources accumulated in previous times of mining prosperity and good trade, and a natural reluctance to deplete their capital more than is necessary to enable them to carry on has led them to reduce their stocks and to offer less variety and range of goods than in former years.

A certain amount of trade is ensured by family connections and habit, and by the indebtedness of their mining customers. Where trade is declining all around, these personal ties are not sufficient, and the psychological effects of a pessimistic attitude are not such as to enable shopkeepers to compete with counter attractions elsewhere. While they wait for the turning of the tide, advertisement, shopping by post and more enterprising rivals gradually steal their old customers from them. Even the old-established local inhabitants and the families of fellow-tradesmen complain that drapery, millinery and clothing of all kinds, as well as certain articles of food cost more in Brynmawr than in Abertillery and Ebbw Vale, that certain goods are unobtainable in the town and that the local shops offer little choice of goods.

The amount of money spent by Brynmawr inhabitants

---

[1] Between 1921 and 1931, thirteen tradesmen have filed petitions and eight have been obliged to close down owing to trade depression.

outside the town is shown by the number of combined shopping and amusement tickets to neighbouring towns issued on the railways.[1] It is a result partly of the enforced quest for the cheapest article in such large shops as Woolworth's and other cheap stores, and partly of lack of enterprise on the part of Brynmawr shopkeepers.

Closely connected with the question of the goods and services offered by the shops is the provision of other attractions such as public amenities and recreational facilities. Thus, when the " Talkies " were installed the number of persons taking cheap railway tickets to the neighbouring towns decreased and the local shops no doubt derived some benefit from the fact that the inhabitants were no longer tempted out of the town by superior provision for amusement elsewhere. Similarly, the period when Brynmawr attracted the inhabitants of other districts to it by debates, lectures and Town Eisteddfod, coincided with the period of greatest trading prosperity. While ease and cheapness of travelling have now permanently altered the position, in that greater centres of trade, recreation and population, such as Cardiff and Newport, have been placed within access of many who could not have frequented them in former days, distance is still an important factor, and the main problem of the Brynmawr tradesmen as regards competition from outside is due to the attractions of the neighbouring towns which have no natural advantages in the shape of superior amenities.

Some of these attractions are created by the combined efforts of the shopkeepers themselves. Abertillery and Ebbw Vale have been sufficiently energetic to organise shopping weeks and Carnivals while the pessimistic and apathetic outlook of Brynmawr traders allows the Chamber of Trade to languish and the geographical advantages of the town to remain unused owing to lack of advertisement. Owing to

---

[1] From November, 1928, to March, 1930, an average of 300 persons per week took advantage of the combined railway and cinema tickets to Abertillery. About 500 persons per week, excluding workmen, travelled by rail to Ebbw Vale for shopping and other purposes. In addition on Fridays and Saturdays considerable numbers of persons travel from Brynmawr to both places by 'bus.

political differences their influence in local government affairs is now not great, yet such questions as town amenities and perhaps especially street lighting by electricity[1] bear indirectly on their trading fortunes, and a determined effort to lead public opinion on such points might not be without effect. The depression of industry, which is more persistent in its effects in Brynmawr than in neighbouring towns, which are nearer to the mines now being worked, calls for added enterprise and effort on the part of the Brynmawr traders if they are to maintain their position. In fact, mere maintenance of the existing position is impossible. Either an attempt must be made to re-capture trade or the process of drifting down the stream will inevitably be accelerated. Hence psychological factors are even more important to-day than economic ones.

The second set of difficulties which have to be faced are those due to the competition of multiple shops and large stores. Within the town the small private tradesman has little competition of this kind to fear. There are only two multiple boot dealers, a butcher, a provision merchant and a cheap store dealing in boots, drapery and china and glass. The greater financial resources, powers of buying advantageously and contact with up-to-date methods in the outside world of the multiple shops in the surrounding towns form part of their advantages, and thus help to draw custom from Brynmawr. Against such factors and against the attraction of the large, well-lighted shops with striking window dressing displays and other advertising facilities the small private trader in Brynmawr as elsewhere can set the individual attention, personal knowledge of his customers' tastes and needs, and freedom to cater for them without restriction which the larger shops, managed by a salaried employee under the supervision of a non-local inspector finds it more difficult to attain. As a counterweight to advertisement and display, he offers his personal service. Thus the methods of selling in small

[1] Electricity is now being brought to the town by the Shropshire, Staffordshire and Worcestershire Electricity Supply Company and, if the shopkeepers take advantage of it, should do much to increase the attractiveness of their shops.

private shops must be the exact opposite of those in such stores as Woolworth's, where goods are expected to "sell themselves" by their cheapness and variety and the girl shop-assistants have little more to do than watch the articles for sale, make them up into parcels when sold, and demand and receive the proper price from the customer.

To such family businesses, not only the personality of the owner and his connections with the locality, but the quality of the assistants whom they employ are all important. From this point of view it is unfortunate that Brynmawr shares in the general tendency observable in South Wales to econo-mise in this time of depression by substituting adolescent for adult shop-employees. The young boy or girl, untrained and inexperienced, who is employed at low wages varying from 3s. to 10s. a week and who is often dismissed as soon as he reaches the insurable age, is unable to give just that dis-tinctive service which would enable his employer to keep his place in the world of commerce.

From the wider point of view of the community the em-ployment of considerable numbers of young people in blind-alley posts at "pocket-money" rates of wages means that commerce, while maintaining and even increasing its numerical employment capacity, is really to some extent parasitic on other industries and even on the State, since parents dependent on Unemployment benefit are least able to demand good conditions of employment and training or prospects for their children.

Owing to its geographical position, Brynmawr is ideally situated not only as a centre of retail trade, but for the pur-pose of wholesale distribution. It is now served both by the Great Western and by the London, Midland and Scottish Railways. It is the headquarters of a Bus Service covering the surrounding industrial and agricultural districts, and is well served by long distance buses, which link it up with the main towns of England and Wales. Its road connections, except with Mid-Wales, are excellent, and there is actually a considerable saving of mileage by road and rail in bringing goods from the Midlands or from North or South England to the South Wales Coalfields via Brynmawr as compared with any other route.[1]

The importance of a site where roads converge at the head of a number of valleys is great in South Wales, where trade is normally hindered by the difficulties of inter-valley communication. Moreover, within a radius of six miles there is a population of over 85,000 with easy access to Brynmawr. The advantages of this central position in the midst of a thickly populated area have been recognised by the four great oil and petrol companies, all of which have established depots in the town and use it as a base for distribution to the surrounding areas. At present, however, only two wholesale distributive firms have recognised its possibilities as a centre, and it may be that one avenue for renewed prosperity will lie in development along these lines. It should also be possible to develop the town further as a centre for wholesale as well as retail distribution of market garden produce by fostering fruit and vegetable growing in the fertile valley of the Usk only five miles away. At present the needs of Brynmawr and of the industrial valleys of Monmouthshire are met by bringing in agricultural, market garden and dairy produce, as well as poultry and eggs from very long distances.[2]

In yet another way, transport facilities and natural surroundings may be used to serve trade. As early as 1880, some of the Brynmawr shopkeepers, realising the advantages which the natural beauty of the adjacent district of the Clydach Valley might bring to the town, co-operated in an attempt to popularise the neighbourhood as a holiday resort. Local poets wrote of the beauties of the Valley and, in an article in the *Freemasons' Chronicle* in 1884, the district is described as "A locality of surpassing beauty, with its shady nooks, bold precipitous hills, its clear rippling streams, its waterfalls, and rapids, and above all things, that best of all medicines, a pure, bracing air." Recently the idea has been revived and is still under consideration.

[1] See Appendix II at end of Chapter.
[2] See Appendix III.

Not only do road and rail communications facilitate commerce but the latter in its turn is responsible for a considerable proportion of their business. Apart from coal, goods for the retail shops constitute the main portion of the general merchandise received by the railway company at Brynmawr. Provision for grocers, flour for bakers, livestock for butchers and the slaughterhouse, greengrocery, ale, and hay and straw for tradesmen with horses, are the most important items. The employment capacity of the railways is therefore bound up with the trading fortunes of Brynmawr to a greater extent than ever before, since the coal forwarded decreased by about fifty per cent between 1922 and 1928. In addition some of the lighter goods for the shops are brought long distances by road, and again contribute to the prosperity of the transport industry and its power to employ men regularly in the country generally, although in this case the weight of goods carried does not, as in the case of the railways, directly affect the employment of local men.

Trade and commerce have an importance then which is not confined to the interests of the shopkeepers themselves, but reacts on other occupations and on the general outlook of adults and adolescents as regards employment and the power of the workers to maintain their footing during times of industrial distress. Hence the trading element has a special part to play in the mining communities of South Wales where the predominance of the coal industry throughout a large area and the difficulties of communication owing to the separation of the narrow thickly-populated valleys by wild and lonely mountain ranges, have tended to narrow the outlook, and to produce an attitude of mind which is distinctive from that of workers in areas where occupations are numerous and varied in character.[1]

In such communities it is chiefly through the trading section that a different point of view is brought to bear on social and economic questions, and that wider interests can be introduced.

---

[1] See Report of Commission of Enquiry into Industrial Unrest. (No. 7 Division.)

How far this function is discharged depends largely on the closeness of social cohesion. One of the difficulties in bringing about a healthy community in which there is a mixture of ideas and a realisation of the common interests of all sections of the population is usually to be found in the fact that occupational divisions tend to be somewhat rigid, and that the families of persons engaged in the different grades of occupation do not mix socially.

In Brynmawr, as in many other Welsh mining towns, this difficulty is less acute than in some English towns. There are, of course, differences of interests and modes of life to be seen in the shopkeepers and professional men as against the miners and other manual workers. On the other hand, it is not unusual for a miner to leave the colliery to take up some occupation which usually carries a higher social standing. At the present time in Brynmawr there are six business men who were originally miners, together with seven drapers who at one time worked in the mines.

There seems to be no bar to the children of industrial workers entering either commerce or the professions, and a considerable number of them are now teachers in Brynmawr. Since there are no private schools, the majority of the tradesmen's children attend the Elementary Schools until they are old enough to enter the Secondary School, where again they mingle with the children of miners and other wage earners; thus, the presence of teachers drawn from miners' homes must tend to make for social cohesion between the two sections. On the other hand, it is noticeable that there is no case of the child of a business man entering the mines, and both socially and politically there is a certain cleavage between the manual workers and the trading and professional section of the community. An example of this underlying antagonism was afforded after the 1931 General Election, when the defeat of the Labour candidate was attributed to the action of the shopkeepers, and some of the workers threatened to boycott the local shops and transfer their custom to Ebbw Vale.

The failure of the mining industry to provide employment for the population of Brynmawr renders it essential for the town to develop on other lines. One of its greatest assets is its geographical position. Its communications are also excellent, although a mid-Wales road is lacking and a few minor local road improvements linking up the town with neighbouring villages such as Llanelly Hill would probably divert trade from elsewhere. Of all the means of livelihood open to it in the past apart from mining, trading has proved the most successful and, in spite of depression in adjoining areas, there is still a sufficient population within easy reach of the town to make a return to its past importance as a shopping centre possible and also to offer opportunities for distribution on wholesale lines. To bring this about, an effort to improve the amenities of the town so that it may once more offer attractions to visitors, co-operation among the traders, and the maintenance of the tradition of efficient personal service, enterprise and good value for money, are essential.

APPENDIX I

ANALYSIS OF BUSINESS FIRMS ACCORDING TO NATURE OF TRADE

Trade	Number
Bakers	3
Boot Makers or Boot Repairers	8
Builders and Carpenters	13
Butchers	12
Chemists	3
Cinema Proprietors	1
Coal Merchants	5
Commission Agents	3
Grocers and Confectioners	27
Corn Stores	2
Travelling Drapers	32
Drapers and Outfitters	16
Fish Fryers	3
Green-Grocers	6
Furniture	2
Garage Proprietors	5
General Dealers and Ironmongers	9
Hair Dressers, Tobacconists and Newsagents	7
Ice-Cream Shops	2
Jewellers	1
Milkmen	6
Painters	5
Publicans	38
Saddlers	1
Tailors	2
Printers	2
Miners' Bus Owners	5
Various Small Businesses	28
TOTAL	247

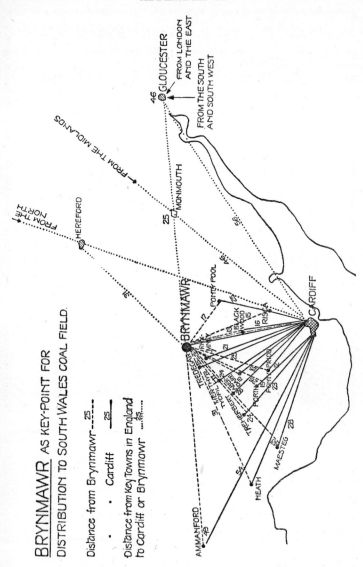

BRYNMAWR AS KEY-POINT FOR
DISTRIBUTION TO SOUTH WALES COAL FIELD.

Distance from Brynmawr ---25
· Cardiff ——25
Distance from key Towns in England
to Cardiff or Brynmawr 25

IMPORTATION OF
FOOD SUPPLIES
1930
BRYNMAWR

REFERENCES

■ *Provisions for Grocery Shops. (Bacon. Eggs, Sugar, Tea, Jam, Flour.)*
▲ *Fruit & Veg.ˢ (home grown).*
♠ *dᵒ (foreign).*
● *Dairy produce, (Eggs, butter, poultry, other than foreign.)*
✝ *Meat, livestock, fish.*
▲ *Milk.*
♣ *Ale.*

CHAPTER IX

RELIGIOUS AND CULTURAL INFLUENCES

THE "Boom, boom" of the bitterns upon the Brecon Beacons is not very many miles from Brynmawr; Abergavenny with its famous Cymreigyddion, the starting point of the Welsh literary Renaissance, is nearer still; Carnhuanawc, famous preacher, orator, historian of Wales and maker of harps, was born near Builth in Breconshire and for a time was curate of Llanelly Parish. The furnaces of Nantyglo were nearer still and right in the heart of the early Brynmawr was the hymn singing of austere Nonconformist congregations and the sermons of their preachers. What kind of culture has been born from this strange medley of influences? What qualities of mind and character, what skill in making beautiful objects fitted for the use and pleasure of man, are likely to be evolved in this industrial and cosmopolitan community on the fringe of a country once full of peasant arts?

The culture of a people may be compared to the bloom on the fruit or the dust on the butterfly's wing; it is the final effluence of the life within, a mysterious compound of mind, aspiration and physical well-being. Yet it is not wholly individual, but comes through the inter-relationships of man, attaining its glory through contact and right and generous living together. Often a cultural renaissance has preceded and inspired a revival of political or national idealism, as though fullness and harmony of life demanded a new form, bursting through the constricting bonds of the old organisation and the too narrow ideas of government. The individual genius is then but the pioneer who lights the dormant spark

117

in the lives of countless others or the first wave in a tide which cannot be stayed.

Carnhuanawc, or the Rev. Thomas Price, represents the flowering of the culture of the Welsh fireside and countryside. Born in 1787 in a lonely farmhouse with thatched roof, he spoke Welsh from his infancy, but in the village dame-school learnt to read both English and Welsh, and in the circle around the fireside listened to the songs and stories of country folk, heard the poetry of the Welsh bards recited, and rejoiced if a harper chanced to visit his home. Natural beauty of mountain and valley kindled his imagination and the ruins of old buildings excited his curiosity. He handled the carpenter's tools in the cottages and watched and imitated the village blacksmith at his work. Music and musical instruments delighted him and he became so skilled as a harp-maker that he was asked to help in the construction of a harp which was presented to the Prince of Wales. He studied and wrote about the Welsh language and Welsh history, and became a famous speaker at literary Societies and eisteddfodau. His mode of life was simple and he was commonly clothed in home-spun cloth woven by the village weaver.

The old peasant culture of rural Wales was not, however, confined to its great exponents, and it is significant that the daughter of Carnhuanawc's housekeeper and servant sat down and played his favourite harp-tunes while waiting to be summoned to clear his tea-table on the day of his death. Such cultural interests as music and craftsmanship were the common heritage of the Welsh villagers of all occupations and grades of society. They were in a large measure due to the vitality of the creative instinct, rather than the fruits of knowledge or book-learning, although they depended also on inherited aptitudes and the passing on of traditional skill.

Such a culture has two foes to fear, materialism with its preoccupation with the means of existence, and an artificial division of the physical and spiritual sides of man's life. The former appears to deaden the creative spirit, while the latter, though it may produce a culture of its own, so narrows the outlook that its achievements tend always to be confined to a section and cannot form the basis of a common culture such as that of the old rural Wales.

Brynmawr has had to contend with both these dangers in the evolution of its life as a community. It was from the first the melting-pot of peoples, the meeting-place of conflicting traditions and ideas. The clashes were too sudden and frequent for immediate fusion, and, as has been seen, there is still no unity nor complete interpenetration of the various groups, which maintain to a great extent their religious, occupational and civic isolation. Its problem, as that of countless industrial settlements up and down the South Wales Coalfield, is how to achieve so much intensity of common purpose and unity of ideas as will provide the depth and richness of soil from which culture may spring. If this can be attained, the fierce and ardent life of democracy, grafted into peasant stock and religious force of character, together with the magical and soul-stirring quality of natural beauty in mountain and valley, may flower in a culture of a new and startling kind.

The early ironmasters and their workers frankly came to the district for materialistic ends and in the struggle against nature and the clash of opposing factions, cultural interests must have sunk into the background. That they did not altogether die is shown by chance references to harpists and singers such as the Chartist innkeeper of Nantyglo. Little regard was paid to natural beauty in the exploitation of iron-ore and coal and the countryside was soon blackened by ill-shaped and unsightly tips. Fortunately, Brynmawr itself owing to its position on the extreme edge of the mining area has never been disfigured by smoking chimneys and colliery tips in its very midst. Nevertheless colliery traditions have undoubtedly lowered the standards of beauty and order in the community as a whole and the tipping of household refuse in public places, which continues to-day, as well as the erection of hideous sewage pipes above a lovely waterfall in the Clydach Valley by the local government body, are evidences of private and public insensibility to aesthetic claims.

The predominance of the economic outlook in employers and workers alike has been an even greater bar to the growth of a common culture. Class divisions and animosities, a sense of insecurity and instability, do not make for that quietness of spirit out of which a culture of everyday life can spring. Moreover, of late years, the growth of a Marxian point of view based on the interpretation of all activities of the human spirit as expressions of material or economic forces, has undoubtedly narrowed the outlook of some of the workers. Unemployment and the uncertainty of even the bare means of existence have contributed to the same materialistic outlook.

From the start, however, materialism was not allowed to monopolise the field. The first force to oppose it was the traditional love of craftsmanship and skill of the early peasant workers. In their new occupational surroundings, pride in efficiency and skilful manipulation of their material still prevailed. Not only in the building of the uncemented stone arches in the mines, which still stand the strain of water and weight of mineral, but in the actual hewing of the coal and the timbering of their " places " in the mines, the pride of craftsmanship found expression. Until a few years ago competitions in timbering were still part of the programme of sports and exhibitions in Brynmawr. Now, the use of mechanical coal-cutters, the practice of sharing " places " with men employed on alternate shifts which was introduced during the War, " speeding up " of work, and perhaps above all the growth of hostility between officials and men, have done much to prevent the craftsman spirit from finding expression in the mines. Moreover, the predominant part played by the mining industry and the comparatively high wages paid to boys on entering it,[1] have prevented the population from seeking outlets in other skilled work, and apprenticeship to a trade or craft is seldom sought by parents or boys.

Not only craftsmanship, but religion entered early into

[1] The total wage per *shift* of boys aged 16, 17, 18, 19 and 20 years employed in the mines is 3/11, 4/5, 4/10, 5/3 and 5/9.

the lives and thoughts of the workers. The building of chapels by the successive waves of immigrants has already been described. Periodical religious revivals in 1828, 1839, 1849 and 1859, and recently in 1904 brought in new members and afforded outlets for emotion and the dramatic instinct. The Church meetings and the Brethren's meetings, the Sunday Schools, Children's choirs and Bands of Hope, became the means of a closely knit social life centring round the chapels. Meanwhile, a common standard of morality, narrow but honest, was built up and out of common efforts for social reform in the causes of temperance and education, a sense of loyalty and comradeship was evolved. In the singing of hymns and sacred 'Books' the cultural side of life was expressed, while the reading of the Bible and the study of the lives of Welsh preachers such as Howell Harris and John Penry, provided a common literary and theological knowledge, which was the material for discussion and debate. Throughout the nineteenth century nonconformity was predominant in Brynmawr. It was not until 1872 that the Church in Wales at last achieved a separate building of a permanent kind in the town; in this it was helped substantially by a last gift from Crawshay Bailey, who had previously succeeded in bringing about his own plan for a Church on the borders of Nantyglo and Brynmawr to serve both places, despite the wishes of Bishops, Archdeacons and parish Clergy! In 1875 Brynmawr became a separate ecclesiastical parish. Nonconformists still formed an overwhelming majority of the population, however, and when the question of dis-establishment came to the fore in Wales, Brynmawr shared in the general enthusiasm for the cause. The controversy, in fact, afforded a rallying ground for the fighting spirit in the Free Churches, and the appeal to revolt against apparent injustice and coercion stirred in the members the traditional reactions, which in the industrial sphere, resulted in the success of the Trade Union Movement. Meetings were frequent, and both ministers—notably those of the Congregational Church—and laymen were assiduous in propaganda. There is no doubt that the appeal of organised religion was increased for the

time being by the fact that dis-establishment afforded a
rallying-ground, brought the different Nonconformist bodies
together for common action, and introduced a political element into religious life.

Thus, in spite of divisions of nationality and theology, in
the Free Churches a community within a community was
built up and towards the end of the nineteenth century it
seemed that owing to the influence of religious idealism a
common culture was once more evolved. Even the leaders of
the workers were still largely influenced by the chapels[1]
where they received education and training in affairs, and were
not yet divided from the rest of the community by the idea
of class warfare; language was ceasing to be a separating
factor as English more and more gained the day; and there
were even signs of broadening of outlook with regard to
legitimate means of amusement and recreation.

Thus in the late 'eighties, the 'nineties and the beginning of
the twentieth century, a multiplicity of cultural interests were
to be found in Brynmawr. Music, as always, took the first
place. The connection of Welsh music with the chapels has
been close since the predominance of nonconformity, and, as
David Jenkins of Trecastle said, secular music played little
part in the life of the community in the nineteenth century.
"No musician could get a footing in Wales unless he was a
religious man in sympathy with religious work." Thus in
Brynmawr an agnostic musician found his means of expression
in sacred music. The influence of Calvinistic Methodism
"imparted a gloomy character to the hymns and through
them to the tunes." The music sung by male voice choirs,
and at psalmody festivals and at eisteddfodau, was thus
somewhat restricted in scope, and lacked the breadth of
human interest and direct human appeal of the folk music,
which sprang from the people in pre-Nonconformist days. At
the same time the existence of numerous musical societies
helped to keep alive and stimulate a passion for excellence

[1] At a Census taken by the Sunday School Union on a particular Sunday
in 1882 it was found that nearly three-fifths of the total population of all
ages attended Chapel, and nearly three-quarters attended Sunday School.

in musical performances within the bounds imposed by custom and popular taste. Not only Chapel Choirs, and the
Annual Sunday Schools' Walking provided outlets for musical
talent, but there were weekly concerts of the Harmonic
Society, Glee Parties, Sunday Sacred Concerts, in the new
Market Hall, which had been opened by a grand concert and
luncheon in 1894, and an Annual Eisteddfod.

In addition to concerts, dancing and theatrical performances took place in the Market Hall, though the stricter
chapel-goers still denounced them as ungodly. The leader
of the Dramatic Society gained permission to put up an
illuminated description on the gas light in front of the en-
trance of the Old Market Hall in 1892, and in 1894 the Primitive Methodists themselves gave a "Golden Hair Perform-
ance." Balls were allowed if arranged by "Committees of
approved respectability." There was also a Voluntary Reading
Room Committee and at a public meeting in 1896 the Council
were asked to provide a Reading Room and Library, to
adopt the provisions of the Public Libraries Act and "to use
all other effectual means to secure this much needed means
of education and character." In the early years of the twentieth century a Mutual Improvement Society flourished and
debates and lectures were well attended. An Annual
Flower Show and Timbering Competitions proved that the
influences of nature and regard for craftsmanship were not yet
dead.

Unfortunately the fusion of the various sections of the
community was not yet deep enough to stand the strain
of War-time changes in population and the growth of political
and industrial class-consciousness, and of materialism fostered by unemployment. With the coming of dis-establishment,
nonconformity ceased to make a political appeal and political
interest was diverted to other and more revolutionary causes.
Moreover a new generation of industrial leaders had grown up
who derived their education from the State Schools instead
of the Chapels and their ideals from spheres outside that of
organised religion. Both the Church in Wales, now grown
enormously in membership and prestige in Brynmawr, and

the various Free Churches continue to influence the lives of many workers,[1] but their theology no longer commands universal adherence, and for the time being perhaps some of their old rallying power is lost. Some of their members, who should be well qualified to judge, believe that they would still respond generously and gladly to a call upon them to take the lead in self-sacrifice for an ideal.

It may be noted in passing that while there is now a considerable amount of co-operation among the old-established Free Churches and even considerable friendliness with the Church in Wales, of late years new sects of a more emotional character have sprung up, which are more divergent in views and less willing to co-operate with the older denominations.[2] This recurrent tendency to split off makes a common basis of social and cultural interests difficult even within the sphere of religious influence. In 1932, Brynmawr is once more a community in the melting pot of ideas, divided into warring or non-co-operative sections and without the basis for a common culture.

Substantial as was the proportion of the population actively attached to the religious bodies at the height of their power and persistent as is their influence, nonconformity at all times in Brynmawr has drawn a dividing line between certain sections of the community. The one section found the centre of its social life in the public-house and in the vivid life of the streets, the disorderly shows and fairs, and the travelling theatres, which made Brynmawr so exciting and fascinating a place for the young or the ungodly. The workers in this section even looked for patronage or influence when seeking employment among those who frequented the same public-house. To the other section, the chapel was the centre of social intercourse and any help or influence needed was looked for

---

[1] See Tables in Appendix I at end of Chapter VI for membership of chapels, Sunday-schools and religious organisations. The proportion of the population on the church rolls or known as "attenders" in 1932 was 70·94. At a house to house enquiry made by a body not connected with the religious organisations of the town in 1929, 86 per cent of the families in the town claimed to belong to a religious denomination.

[2] For example, the Spiritualists, Penticostals and Apostolics are all bodies which took root in Brynmawr after 1914.

among its members. Since the economic depression set in, there has been a change in the habits of the more boisterous section of the population, and, even if it is true that the influence of the chapel is fading, it has achieved its desire to see the end of excessive drinking and brawling for which Brynmawr was once notorious up and down the valleys. In 1930, although there were still 40 public-houses and beer-houses in the town—as against 65 in 1881—there were only four convictions for drunkenness.

What part has organised education played in the evolution of cultural interests? In this sphere nonconformity was again the pioneer in Brynmawr, although at Nantyglo and Clydach the Works Schools opened by the employers were conducted by the National Society on the principles of the Established Church. The first schools opened in Brynmawr were held in cottages and in one or two of the Chapels and were conducted by lay preachers or Ministers. The Chapels early realised their responsibility as regards the provision of education, and before 1847 a British and Foreign Society School had been opened at their initiative. The initial cost was met by voluntary subscriptions and by a voluntary levy on themselves made by the five leading chapels. Dame-schools and a "finishing" school kept by the wife of a watch and clock-maker also existed before the Education Act of 1870, together with a Roman Catholic Day School opened in 1863, following on a period of Irish immigration into the town. There were also Night-Schools, the pupils of which were said to be so zealous that they were "discovered in the mines in the dinner-hour working equations with chalk on the shovel blades."

Probably more important and far-reaching in influence than any of the Day Schools were the Sunday Schools, which were open to all irrespective of age and creed, and which throughout Wales attracted *adult* workers in large numbers. Desire to read the Bible on the part of the scholars and enthusiasm for 'The Salvation of Souls' were the origin of the voluntary educational movement of the eighteenth and nineteenth centuries in Wales, and the idealistic and non-utilitarian motive, the use of whatever was the native language of the scholars attached to the respective chapels, the connection through the Chapel with efforts at social reform and with the familiar social intercourse of the congregation, made them powerful forces in the life of nation and community.

Nonconformist opinion in Brynmawr under the leadership of Mr. John Thomas, was strongly in favour of the adoption of the Education Act in 1870, and the Board School was built in place of the Old British and Foreign School in 1876. The Head Master of the British School was transferred to the new School. In the previous year the Church in Wales made a belated effort at denominational education by building a Church School. In 1897, again largely owing to the zeal of the Nonconformist chapels, which raised a large proportion of the sum needed, a Secondary School was opened.

In 1930, approximately 1,700 children attended school in Brynmawr, of whom 260 were Secondary School scholars.[1] Although some of the latter came from outside the town the percentage of Brynmawr children receiving the advantages of a Secondary education is high, being 20 per thousand of the population of the town, or ten per cent of the total school population, as against 15 per thousand of the population for Breconshire and only 9·1 per thousand for the County Boroughs in England. This is partly due to the large proportion of free places[2] and partly to the fact that there are no private schools in Brynmawr. The educational system is therefore very democratic.

One of the results of the establishment of the Board Schools and of compulsory education was to hasten the disappearance of the Welsh language, and at present Welsh plays no part in education except as an optional subject at the Secondary

[1] See Appendix II at end of Chapter for distribution of School population and proposals for re-organisation in order to carry out the recommendations of the Hadow Report.

[2] In view of the industrial conditions in the mining districts, the Breconshire Education Committee have for some years obtained sanction from the Board of Education to award free places in the County Schools in excess of the fifty per cent of the number of admissions in the previous school year allowed under the regulations of the Board.

School. The break in the cultural traditions of the Welsh part of the population and their divorce from their national literature and history were no doubt accentuated in this way, although the process of anglicisation had already set in. At present, education in Brynmawr cannot be said to foster or derive inspiration from the Welsh national traditional culture, although in view of the origins of a large part of the population, such inspiration would undoubtedly vitalise and enrich the life of the community.

It is difficult to estimate the effects of the State educational system on the life of Brynmawr. Perhaps the advantages of free and all-embracing education are counter-balanced by lack of roots in an ideal dear to the people as a whole. Undenominational education is, after all, a negative idea, unless it is linked with a clear conception of the purpose of education. The capacity for enthusiasm and idealism inherent in the Welsh people might well become an incalculably great force in the right building of the community if it were once more inspired and guided in youth by the inculcation of a common ideal.

Many of the teachers have strong individual ideals and by force of character and integrity exert a great personal influence both on the children and on the quality of community life. Most of them are local[1] and some come from miners' homes. Thus they are able to understand the temperaments and peculiar difficulties of their pupils as no 'foreigner' could do; on the other hand, they have had little contact with new ideas and methods in the educational world and nearly half of the assistants in the Elementary Schools are uncertificated.[2] There tends, therefore, to be a strong conservative and local bias in the actual teaching, although enterprising individual Heads and Assistants from time to time act as pioneers of new methods and ideals in education.

[1] At the time of the Survey in 1930, 40 out of the 44 assistant teachers in Elementary Schools were local. Only 2 were trained outside Wales; only 4 had experience outside Wales and only 8 had experience in other parts of Wales.

[2] In 1930, 21 out of 44.

Although there are now Manual Training Centres and Domestic Economy Centres they have so far not succeeded in rekindling the craftsman spirit in the community, perhaps because they have been almost entirely divorced from any contact with a local occupation demanding a high measure of skill and training.

The School Medical Service has done much to raise standards of cleanliness in the school-children and through them in the homes; but the percentage of the children found to need medical attention treatment who actually receive it is still not satisfactory.

This is probably partly a symptom of the lack of real understanding of the aims and methods of the schools which is found in the parents and community generally. While the individual parent is treated courteously and sympathetically by the teacher, he or she, in Brynmawr as in many other places, is looked on as outside the mysteries of education, and the old intimate contact of education and the people, which was so characteristic of the Welsh Sunday School, has been lost.

This mutual failure of the people and the schools to conceive of education as springing out of the life of the community and answering its intimate needs is shown by the decline of interest in continued education since the mining depression. It is perhaps natural that the formerly well attended classes in mining technology should cease to attract when so large a proportion of the mining population are unemployed, but the almost complete lack of interest in craftsmanship, especially on the part of the boys who have recently left school—only one boy between the age of 14 and 18 attended the Evening Classes in Woodwork, and only three girls attended the Dressmaking Class in the Session 1929–30, and the abandonment of Classes in subjects such as literature and history owing to lack of numbers year after year, are perhaps proofs of the failure of the State education to stimulate cultural interests in the community at large. This failure is as much a reflection on the community as on the school system; taken together with the general assumption that a secondary school education is mainly an avenue to entry to the teaching profession[1] and with the undue emphasis placed on examination results by the parents of children in the Secondary School, it denotes a materialistic conception of life. It is even widely suggested by lay persons outside the educational system as well as by some teachers that the only way to make continued education popular is to give it a commercial basis, institute terminal examinations and issue certificates to the students.

It is significant too that of late years voluntary provision of further education for adults has attracted very few people. Classes in music have been successfully organised by the Teachers' Association in conjunction with the University Extension Movement, and W.E.A. Classes in English Literature and Political Science have maintained a precarious existence. The Central Labour College has also arranged classes in economics which have persisted for some years. The prevailing interest of the workers, apart from music, appears to be the study of economics, and here political bias tends to make it a dividing factor in the community life rather than an element in a common culture.

Organised education whether voluntary or publicly provided only too faithfully reflects the financial straits, witnessed by poor and old buildings and by the lack of qualifications of many of the teachers, and the preoccupation of the community by the struggle for material existence which is common throughout the distressed areas. In recreation, the queues awaiting the opening of the Cinema, the crowds assembling to watch football matches, the prevalence of betting, and, on the other

---

[1] The following Table shows the proportions of boys and girls who left the Secondary School between 1927 and 1929 who went on to train for the teaching profession in local schools or at colleges:—

	Boys	Girls
Training for Teaching in local schools or colleges	30	25
Employed locally	29	11
Employed outside District	8	13
Known to be unemployed	2	15
Family left District	5	10
Pupils from homes outside District . . .	5	10
Total	79	84

hand, the paucity of books in the town library, the abandonment of the town Eisteddfod and of the old Mutual Instruction Society, the lack of any building for use solely as a cultural centre in the town, tell a tale of a community, in which excitement and gregarious and non-creative amusements have taken the place of creative enjoyments and mutual emulation in the making of beauty and song, craft and oratory.

There is, however, a brighter side to the picture. Despite political bitterness and occupational cleavages, all sections of the population unite in work for the local Hospital, and by association in such organisations as the Moose, the Oddfellows and the 'Buffs', many still find a means of expressing ideals of brotherhood, as well as certain codes of conduct and social ideals. There is still also an appreciation of oratory in a popular preacher or speaker and an intellectual keenness in discussion which is common to all classes. The numerous glee-parties, Male Voice Choirs and other choirs which spring up are evidences of the persistent love of song, and of the desire to *do* as well as to play the part of spectator, which is a sign of enduring vitality and the fountain of all native culture.

Equally, important, perhaps, are the common preoccupation with home and family, the warmth and colour in human relationships, the intense attachment to the place, proved by the constant return of emigrants from it, and the habit of mind which constantly turns to the contemplation of the primitive and universal facts of human life. The ceremonial service beside the body of the dead in the home itself on the night before the funeral, the long funeral processions, winding along the narrow valleys or up the steep main street, the intense conviction of the dignity and claims of death, could not persist in a community wholly given up to artificial and material values.

Brynmawr, apparently so disintegrated, has an underlying common life. Yet neither nonconformity, organised education, nor the movement of revolt has proved sufficiently wide to form the basis of a community culture, flowering in the inner ordering of individual lives and social relationships, in the

knowledge and appreciation of beauty, and in skill in creating
it. Perhaps out of distress of body and soul, some common
ideal and philosophy related to the origins and make-up of
the people will be evolved, which will include the expression
of beauty in and through the material, and so fuse the diverse
elements in a common but distinctive culture.

K

APPENDIX I

MEMBERSHIP OF RELIGIOUS AND SOCIAL ORGANISATIONS

TOTAL POPULATION

Adult Church Members (including Adult Sunday School Members and Members of Guilds)	2,310
Sunday School Members (other than Adults) . . .	1,868
Members of Social Organisations attached to Churches (e.g. Bands of Hope, Clubs, Children's Choirs, Junior Endeavour, etc.):	
(a) Children of School age	392
(b) Boys 14–18 years	126
(c) Girls 14–18 years	160
Members of other Social Organisations:	
(a) Adults (See following page)	
(b) Children of School Age	60
(c) Boys 14–18 years	56
(d) Girls 14–18 years	25
FAMILIES ATTACHED TO VARIOUS DENOMINATIONS (1929):	
Congregational	449
Baptists	427
Church in Wales	361
Calvinistic Methodists	237
Roman Catholics	95
Wesleyans	93
Salvation Army	23
Pentecostals	17
Jews	14
Apostolics	10
Spiritualists	5
Plymouth Brethren	4
Society of Friends	3
Claiming Membership of no Denomination or making no return on Survey Form	256
Total Families	1,994

APPENDIX Iᴀ

ADULTS CONNECTED WITH SOCIAL ORGANISATIONS OTHER THAN THOSE CONNECTED WITH THE CHURCHES

Organisation	*Number of Adults*
Town Band	26
Territorial Association . . .	96
Brynmawr and District Canine Society	150 (includes men and women)
Sheep Dog Trials Committee . .	25
Poultry Association . . .	60 (approximately)
Soccer Club . . . from 20 to 30	
Bowls Club	73
Rugby Football Club vary from 35 to 60	
Cricket Club . . . from 35 to 50	
St. John Ambulance Brigade .	55
British Legion	230 men; 50 women
Breconia Glee Men . . .	18
Brynmawr County School Association of Past Students . . .	200 (approximately)
"Rover" Section of Boy Scouts .	16
Institute	209
League of Nations Union . .	100 (approximately)

DISTRIBUTION of SCHOOL POPULATION . April: 1932

COUNTY SCHOOL, (330).
Children from Darenfelen, Clydach, Gilwern & Cefn Coed, mix! 156.
and from BRYNMAWR, 174 mixed

COUNCIL SCHOOLS :-
(960)

Infants _ _ _ _ _ _ _ 288

Girls _ _ _ _ _ _ _ _ _ _ _ 319

Boys _ _ _ _ _ _ _ _ _ 353

CHURCH OF ENGLAND SCHOOLS :-
Infants _ _ _ _ _ _ _ _ _ _ 118
Mixed _ _ _ _ _ _ _ _ _ _ 246

CHURCH OF ROME SCHOOL : 83.

To meet the recommendations of the Hadow Report as far as need for economy will permit, a scheme for re-organisation based on mixed departments for infants under 7 years of age, junior boys and girls from 7 to 11 years, and senior boys and girls from 11 years upwards in the place of the present Departments will be adopted at the Council School from August, 1933, onwards. The Church and Catholic Schools will not be affected by the re-organisation.

CHAPTER X

EXTENT AND EFFECTS OF UNEMPLOYMENT

IT has already been seen that the local mineral resources of Brynmawr are not likely again to afford any considerable amount of employment. The town also suffers from more general causes of depression such as the substitution of bituminous by anthracite coal for smelting and export purposes, and of oil for coal fuel on the part of the great shipping lines and the Navy, the lack of cohesion on the part of the colliery owners, the discovery of new Coalfields abroad and of new forms of power in areas which formerly constituted part of the South Wales markets, and the movement of the steel industries to the ports as well as competition by new foreign steel centres.

The extent to which Brynmawr men have come to depend on employment at some distance from their homes is shown by the diagram on the following page. In 1921, 2,046 out of 3,230 persons, or 63 per cent of the total occupied Brynmawr residents worked outside the Urban District. Up to that time, it may be said that capable colliery workers from Brynmawr had no difficulty in obtaining employment. Wages were comparatively high and it is said locally that Brynmawr and Blaina colliers had "Money to burn." Since 1921 Brynmawr has constituted a permanent 'pocket of unemployment,' and at the lowest point of the unemployment figures for the Brynmawr Employment Exchange area[1] from July, 1923 to

[1] The Brynmawr Exchange area includes Brynmawr, Clydach and Llanelly Hill, and part of Beaufort and Nantyglo. It is estimated that the Brynmawr men constitute 60 per cent of the total numbers on the live registers.

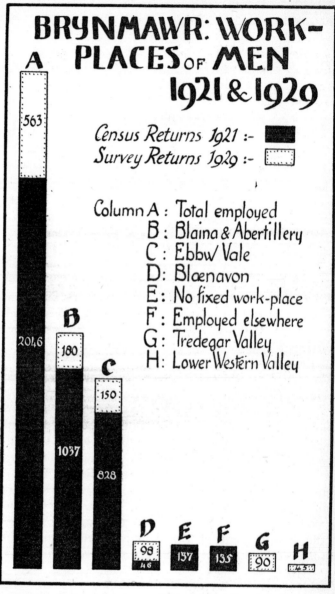

BRYNMAWR: WORK-PLACES OF MEN 1921 & 1929

Census Returns *1921* :-
Survey Returns *1929* :-

Column A : Total employed
B : Blaina & Abertillery
C : Ebbw Vale
D : Blænavon
E : No fixed work-place
F : Employed elsewhere
G : Tredegar Valley
H : Lower Western Valley

A 563 / 2046

B 180 / 1037

C 150 / 828

D 98 / 46

E 137

F 135

G 90

H

136

April, 1924, when the effects of the strike of the German colliers during the occupation of the Ruhr were felt in South Wales, the number of unemployed men living in Brynmawr constituted approximately 10 per cent of the insurable population.

Since the second half of 1924, with the exception of a slight temporary improvement in the first few months of 1926, the position has been considerably worse. The graph on page 13 shows the trend of unemployment in the Brynmawr Exchange area from 1921 to 1931. Men from Brynmawr sought employment in more distant collieries, such as those in the Tredegar district, only to be displaced by local men living in houses owned by the Colliery Companies as the mining depression grew more general in South Wales. The town has in fact been at a great disadvantage owing to its position as a dormitory area, and in view of the fact that there is a permanent surplus of miners in the South Wales Coalfield as a whole, it is unlikely that the position as regards colliery employment for Brynmawr men will improve to a substantial degree. In July, 1932, in spite of some temporary schemes for work, the unemployment figures for the Brynmawr Employment Exchange area were higher than they had been since January, 1927, when the after effects of the prolonged stoppage of the mining industry were most acutely felt in the Brynmawr district.[1]

The outstanding features of unemployment in Brynmawr are the length of periods of consecutive unemployment of a large proportion of the men, constituting a different kind of economic and psychological problem from that of casual or short-period unemployment and the preponderance of men over forty years of age who have been out of work for such long periods that they are unlikely to be reabsorbed in the mines. At the other end of the age scale are a considerable number of youths from 14–18 years of age who have never had even temporary employment and who are fast losing

---

[1] In January, 1927, there were 1,898 men wholly unemployed and 97 "temporarily stopped," the latter being men who had been out of work less than six weeks. In July, 1932, the wholly unemployed men numbered 1,669, while the "temporarily stopped" were as many as 252, making a total of 1,921 as compared with 1,995 at the previous peak of unemployment.

their employability. The Table below illustrates these points.[1]
Such prolonged unemployment results in the exhaustion
of savings and family resources, so that it becomes difficult
to do more than lead a hand-to-mouth existence with no
provision for sickness or other family emergency or for the
replacement of household articles or even clothing. Moreover
the apparent lack of grounds for hope for any improvement
in the mining industry or elsewhere is bound to lead to des-
pondency, bitterness and apathy in the minds of many of
the men.

While some effects of unemployment are general, individual
men and their families of course react to it in different ways,
and out of some six hundred families normally dependent on
unemployment benefit probably no two have precisely the
same attitude to life and circumstances. Certain habits of
thought and action are enforced by these circumstances. The
unemployed man must register twice a week at the Exchange;
he must draw his "pay" there on Friday; if he has been out
of work for some time, each Friday he will have a short period
of sickening anxiety lest the clerk should single him out and
tell him that he is to be sent to the "Court of Referees"; then

[1] POPULATION SHOWING PERIOD OF UNEMPLOYMENT
IN YEARS AND AGE-GROUPS

	LENGTH OF UNEMPLOYMENT					
Age	Unemployed under 2 Years	Unemployed 2–3 Years	Unemployed 3–4 Years	Unemployed 4–5 Years	Unemployed 5 or more Years	Totals
Over 65 Years	6	19	12	23	72	132
40–65 Years	77	99	107	104	143	530
30–40 Years	49	64	54	40	25	232
18–30 Years	77	51	52	24		204
14–18 Years	17					17
Never been Employed 14–18 Years	87					87
TOTALS	313	233	225	191	240	1,202

will follow a few days' consequent dread lest his benefit should be stopped and he be cast on to the Poor Law, have to do "task work," for his maintenance, and take home less to his family in return for it. Having received his "pay," duly contributed his "penny" to the Unemployed Lodge of the Miners' Federation, and conversed with his fellow unemployed, he returns home. There, his wife awaits his return in order that she may do the weekly shopping, and in many cases almost all his unemployment pay, with the exception of a little pocket-money for "fags" goes straight to her.

So far, there is similarity of practice, but beneath the surface this similarity does not reign. One man will approach the Exchange with impatience and bitterness at his dependence and impotency to help himself; one in a mood to find causes of complaint and irritation with the officials; one with growing apathy, and no conscious feeling except when his pay is threatened; one again with each visit feels the need for a change in the economic and social system; his political consciousness is inflamed, and he will fumble in his mind for an alternative, or shout the current formulae at the next "unemployed" or "party" meeting according to his mental outlook and capacity.

Visits to the Exchange at most take up part of two half-days in the week. For the rest, some men stand aimlessly on the Market Square or at the street corners, content apparently with a passive animal existence, or with the hour-long observation of passers-by, varied by an occasional whiff at a cigarette. Others work on allotment or garden, tend fowls or pigs, or do carpentry in their backyard or kitchen, making sideboards out of orange boxes stained brown with permanganate of potash, while their wives cook and tend the children in a restricted space around the fireplace, uncomplaining because they realise the necessity of providing some occupation for their husbands in order to keep them even moderately content. Some few attend classes on Political Economy or Industrial History; more talk or listen at frequent meetings of "Unemployed Lodges" or the Trades and Labour Council, where grievances can be ventilated and pent-up bitterness find vent. Others again stroll "down the valley" or sit on the banks in groups when the sun is warm. On wet days the Miners' Institute offers papers and a shelter, although shop doors and street corners satisfy many. At nights, there are the pictures, and the long queues outside the "Picture House" probably account for more of the "pocket-money" of the unemployed than do the public-house, although the "Clubs" are said to do good business all day long. In a drab and empty existence the "pictures" provide some colour and excitement if little food for thought.

In these and other ways the unemployed man drags out his time and, whether he expresses it lucidly or not, in almost every individual there is an abiding sense of waste of life.

Here, then are some universal effects of unemployment. First, the fact of *financial dependence*, with recurrent crises when the means of existence are threatened and all that the individual can do is to pit his advocate against the representatives of the State, and, secondly, the sense of waste, the realisation that energy, capacity and strength are ebbing away unused, owing to causes scarcely to be known and *certainly not to be controlled by the individual*.

Dependence, unfulfilled capacity, the sense of impotency, must generate an abnormal and unhealthy atmosphere in the community where they are prevalent.

The Miners' Federation has recognised the probable danger to its prestige and authority and also to the wage-standards of its employed members which would result if unemployed men were allowed to remain outside its ranks. In return for a nominal weekly payment of a penny the unemployed man can therefore retain his full financial membership with all the consequent social benefits to himself and his family. Through the "Unemployed Lodge" attached to his District Organisation, he therefore exercises some influence on Federation Policy. On the other hand, he is outside the day-to-day concerns of the mining industry, and, especially if he lives some distance from the colliery to which he was formerly attached, cannot maintain very close contact with his employed fellow-workers.

Unemployment also tends to involve some weakening of the relationship with the other groups which play their part in communal life. If the individual unemployed man is of the governing political persuasion, joint meetings of the Trades and Labour Council and the Labour Party offer him an opportunity to take part in local politics. Here again, unemployment and its direct and indirect effects tend to occupy a large part in the discussions. Elected representatives, as well as the practical policy they put forward, tend to be judged by the amount of work on the roads they can offer to the unemployed, the distribution to individual men of opportunities for "getting stamps," scales of relief, enforced "repayment of relief on loan" and similar immediate concerns. It is not without dust and heat that the local government representative wins and keeps his garland of popular esteem. There are of course a number of " politically conscious" unemployed, who judge affairs from a less narrow point of view, hold fast to what they conceive to be the guiding principles of the Trade Union and Labour Movement, and if they are less noisy in their meetings, have the courage of their convictions when they speak. Unfortunately, some of these are disheartened by the seeming failure of the many to keep their political ideals and either withdraw from active participation in local government or are left behind by the noisy demagogues. Comparatively few become communists and set out boldly to achieve a new social and economic order through revolution.

For the mass of the unemployed, local politics in South Wales only concentrate their thoughts more firmly on the material problems of their existence. "Vote Labour, and put an end to poverty, misery, and Courts of Referees" is the popular slogan, not "Stand together and assert the value of man and his right and duty to express himself by work."

Perhaps it is in this degradation of local politics more than in anything else that the loss of the higher non-material values which has been accelerated by prolonged and massed unemployment is most easily apparent.

In the prevailing attitude to the State and local public
authority, dependence on unemployment benefit has accentuated certain features. It is a man's right to *take* from the
State, not his duty and privilege to *serve* it; it may indeed
come to be considered morally wrong to give any service
voluntarily—even if it only is to act as Honorary Secretary
to a Children's Canteen Committee—for which the State might
pay. It is right on the other hand to take one's dues, if one can
get them, from the State and pay them over to the voluntary
organisation which comes to one's aid and which presumably
has less unlimited resources. This of course is an attitude not
restricted to the unemployed, but it has certainly become more
prevalent with the breakdown of family independence.

Nor are these assumptions with regard to the relationships
of State and individual necessarily morally wrong. The danger
is that in discarding conceptions which may be out of date or
need restatement, certain permanent moral values such as
disinterested service for a cause wider than self or family,
may also be thrown aside unconsciously.

Wales is said to be the land of chapels, and in most Welsh
villages and towns the social life of the people is firmly linked
with their religious organisations. Chapel going is an ingrained
habit with many unemployed, but there is no doubt that some
disillusionment with the teaching of the religious bodies has
resulted from unemployment. Many chapels can no longer
afford to maintain a minister, and some men speak bitterly
of the failure of ministers formerly respected to live up to their
teaching and offer to take a bare maintenance grant rather
than move on from their church to more prosperous places
which can still pay the usual salary. In Brynmawr there were
in 1931 only four ministers (outside the Church of England in
Wales) for thirteen churches representing various denominations and even these served several churches spread over
a large district. While the children are still sent to Sunday
School, there are many unemployed parents who count
organised religion as one more of the "values" which has not
stood the test of poverty and economic insecurity.

The tragedy of unemployment in the distressed areas

chiefly consists not in material want but in the loss of belief
in these non-material values which differentiate man from the
animal. Social provision has ensured that the people shall not
starve, or go naked, or without shelter, although they undoubtedly lack much even of material goods. Compared with some
of the pioneers in the workers' movement of a hundred or even
fifty years ago they are materially well off, but mentally and
spiritually some of them are bankrupt. Trade Unionism,
politics, and even religion have failed to lift their preoccupations from the level of mere existence, and since they have lost
the habit of expressing themselves in daily work, they are
almost prepared to believe that all they really want is security
of existence, maintenance, rather than opportunity to live
and develop all their powers in action.

Varied though the individual and family habits and reactions to unemployment are, one general statement can be made
of the unemployed homes in the mining areas of South Wales.
With remarkably few exceptions, the bond of parental pride
and affection has held firm. It expresses itself in diverse ways,
not all of which are good, but which represent the various levels
of family life and relationships. In some instances the old
ambition of the collier to make his son a teacher holds good,
and the whole family cheerfully goes short when necessary
in order to give his boy a college career and to keep him
decently clothed during it. It has not been the custom in
mining communities in South Wales to send away young boys
and girls to work, and the loss of home training and influence
during the years of adolescence may well be feared by careful
parents. It is a real test of unselfish affection and courage on
their part when they meet the present situation by sending
away their boys of 14 and 15 years of age when some chance
of training or permanent employment offers. Many are now
making this sacrifice, although others with less enlightened
affection prefer to keep them idle at home rather than risk
the chance of their being homesick or less well-cared for in
the outside world. Some will go further in sentimental weakness
and encourage them to give up prospects of skill and independence on the whim of the moment rather than see them

temporarily homesick or let them suspect that home and the family resources, scanty though they are, are not open to them at will. Even where parents and boys are anxious for their transfer, the opportunities for placing them in suitable employment are few and far between, and many promising and enterprising lads perforce remain idle in Brynmawr.

Family feeling rather than family enlightenment and common sense represents the element common to all, but in a surprisingly large number of instances ambition for the children remains a real force where years of unemployment have left the father without much hope of any improvement in his personal prospects. Were this not the case, the effects of unemployment on the morale of the young would be even more serious than they are. The extent to which natural initiative and energy are wasted in boys just leaving school is shown by the fact that out of 292 boys leaving the elementary schools in Brynmawr between 1926 and 1929, 74 obtained no employment, while 98 obtained local blind-alley work as errand boys, etc., 45 going on to work outside the distressed areas and 68 to Secondary Schools.

It must be remembered, too, that many of these boys passed their school years in homes in which the father and elder brother were unemployed, and in any event were members of a community in which unemployment was rife, and the atmosphere full of disillusionment and bitterness. It is not to be wondered at that some of the 87 youths between the ages of 14 and 18, who in 1929 had never been employed, show signs of lack of discipline and, in the absence of a spur to their ambition in the form of openings for their future career, can hardly be persuaded to take an interest in further education even on the craftsman side, while they tend also, as elsewhere, to lose touch with religious organisations at this age, and so are largely without a stimulus for their natural idealisms and enthusiasms of adolescence. It is remarkable under such circumstances that there are so few cases of actual conflict with the law. That the human material to be found in the youth of Brynmawr is good is shown by the success with which

these boys who have been transferred to training and employment outside the distressed areas have adjusted themselves to
new conditions of industry and social life. The good reports
which they have earned as apprentices and trainees seem to
prove that the craftsman spirit is dormant only and can be
re-awakened in Brynmawr.[1]

Older youths and adults have on the whole been less successful in adapting themselves to conditions outside South Wales.
Steeped in the atmosphere of a largely one-industried community, sensitive to the charge of disloyalty to their fellows in
seeking or accepting work in areas where there is already local
unemployment, suffering from that deep and almost uncon-
trollable " hiraeth " or attachment to their home mountains or
valleys which seems rooted in the temperament of the Welsh,
they find it incredibly difficult to settle down in the alien
atmosphere of English towns. For these and other reasons,
the policy of transfer to work outside the distressed areas has
been only partially successful. Between the period commenc-
ing January, 1928, when it was inaugurated, and the end of
April, 1932, 597 persons from the area of the Brynmawr
Employment Exchange have been placed in employment in
other districts; of these only 240 or considerably less than
half are still away. In addition 334 young men under the age
of thirty have been sent to Transfer Instructional Centres
or Government Instructional Factories, and from thence
placed in employment, and of these only 80 or less than a
quarter are still away. Only 39 families have been officially
assisted to remove from the district.

It seems, therefore, that the policy of transfer is only a
very limited solution to the difficulty created by the "permanent pocket" of unemployment in Brynmawr. Moreover, it has scarcely affected the men over 40 years of age,
and it is these, as has been seen, who constitute the larger
proportion of the men suffering from prolonged periods of
consecutive unemployment. The vast majority of these men

[1] Part of the foregoing section has been reproduced from a pamphlet on
"Social Work in the Families of the Unemployed" as a study in preparation
for the Second International Conference on Social Work, 1932, by Hilda
Jennings and Peter Scott.

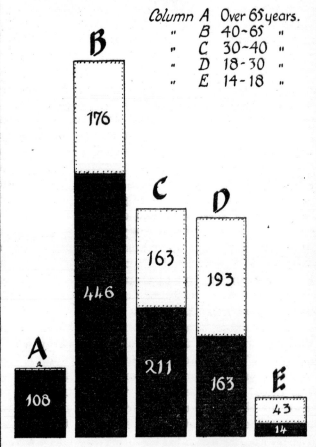

AGE GROUPS OF EMPLOYED AND UNEMPLOYED MINERS.

Figures taken from Survey made at end of 1929.

EMPLOYED, thus :—
UNEMPLOYED, thus :—

Column A   Over 65 years.
    "   B   40~65   "
    "   C   30~40   "
    "   D   18~30   "
    "   E   14~18   "

B   176   446

C   163   211

D   193   163

A   108

E   43   14

are attached to the mining industry, and the diagram on the opposite page shows the proportions of employment and unemployment among miners in the various age-groups. The Tables contained in Appendix I and Appendix II give percentages of unemployment and periods of unemployment in the same age-groups both among miners and in all other insurable occupations.

It will be noted from these tables that 62 per cent of the men employed in the mining industry were unemployed when the survey enquiry was made at the end of 1929, and that 56·45 per cent of all the unemployed miners had been out of work over two years consecutively. In the age-group 40–65 years the percentage of men in the mining industry who had been unemployed for over two years was as high as 67·96, and in other occupations as high as 60·71.

What are the prospects of these men over forty years of age who are unlikely to return to their normal occupation of mining? Obviously they will be most difficult to train for any new skilled occupation, and as unskilled workers, they will have little chance of transfer to permanent employment in other areas. Yet very few of them have any skill or experience outside the mining industry. In 1929, 95·95 per cent of all the men in the industry, whether employed or not, could lay claim to no alternative occupation except that of labourer. Only 1·13 per cent claimed to be skilled workers outside the mines, and only ·43 per cent had any experience of work on the land. The following Table gives the exact numbers as well as the percentages claiming knowledge of alternative occupations of any kind:—

ALTERNATIVE OCCUPATIONS OF MINERS

Alternative Occupations of Men attached to Mining Industry	Number	Percentage of men having experience of Alternative Occupations
Labourers	1352	95·95
Skilled Workers	16	1·13
Semi-Skilled	18	1·27
Business	17	1·20
Land Workers	6	·43
TOTALS	1409	99·98

L

The position is similar in the business, clerical and skilled workers' groups; some men even in these groups have for a time worked in the mines, and the majority of them have no second string to their bow when their employment is affected directly or indirectly by the mining depression.[1] Thus the predominant part played by mining in the life of the community and the lack of alternative industries with a nucleus of skilled workers are again emphasised.

How then are the evil effects of unemployment to be counteracted? The temperament, to some extent determined by racial origins, and the historical attachments of the population, together with the state of industry elsewhere, prevent a successful policy of wholesale transfer. Existing alternative occupations in Brynmawr itself are insufficient. The old traditions of craftsmanship have been lost. Government Training Centres affect only the younger men and even for them, in many cases have not led on to permanent absorption in industry. Where then is Brynmawr to turn for an outlet for the energies of the 600 boys who will leave school between 1932 and 1938, or for a means to the renewed independence and self-respect of the four or five hundred miners over 40 years of age who are not likely to be reabsorbed in the mines? How, moreover, are the non-material values to be restored to their due place in the minds and lives of men embittered and disillusioned by long years of unemployment and dependence?

Unless the community can find in the qualities of its members, in its common traditions, natural advantages and historical links some answer for these questions, it seems unlikely that it can for long continue to exist.

[1] See Appendix III.

APPENDIX I

PERCENTAGES OF EMPLOYMENT IN MINING AND IN ALL OTHER OCCUPATIONS AT THE END OF 1929

MINERS

Ages (Years)	Number of Miners in Occupation	Number Employed	Percentage Employed	Number Unemployed	Percentage Unemployed
40–65 .	622	176	28·29	446	71·7
30–40 .	374	163	43·58	211	56·41
18–30 .	356	193	54·2	163	45·78
14–18 .	57	43	75·43	14	24·56
TOTALS .	1409	575	—	834	—

Total Number of Miners under 65 years of age in Occupation . 1,409
Percentage Unemployed . . . . 59·17
Percentage Employed . . . . 40·79

ALL OTHER OCCUPATIONS

Ages (Years)	Number of Persons in all Insurable Occupations Excluding Miners	Number Employed	Percentage Employed	Number Unemployed	Percentage Unemployed
40–65 .	292	208	71·23	84	28·79
30–40 .	139	118	84·8	21	15·1
18–30 .	237	196	82·7	41	17·21
14–18 .	164	74	45·1	90	54·81
TOTAL .	832	596	—	236	—

Total Number in all Insurable Occupations excluding Miners . 832
Percentage Employed . . . . 71·63
Percentage Unemployed . . . . 28·36

APPENDIX II

MINING OCCUPATION

Ages (Years)	Total Unemployed	Unemployed under 2 years	Percentage Unemployment under 2 years	Total Unemployed over 2 years and under 4 years	Percentage over 2 years and under 4 years	Total Unemployed over 4 years	Percentage over 4 years
40–65 .	446	143	32·06	175	39·27	128	28·69
30–40 .	211	102	48·34	87	41·23	20	10·42
18–30 .	163	102	62·57	61	37·42	—	—
14–18 .	14	14	100	—	—	—	—
TOTALS .	834	361	43·29	323	38·72	148	17·98

INSURABLE OCCUPATIONS OTHER THAN MINING

Ages (Years)	Total Number of Unemployed	Number Unemployed under 2 years	Percentage Unemployed under 2 years	Number Unemployed between 2 and 4 years	Percentage Unemployed between 2 and 4 years	Number Unemployed over 4 years	Percentage Unemployed over 4 years	Number never been employed	Percentage never been employed
40–65 .	84	33	39·28	36	42·84	15	17·84	—	—
30–40 .	21	11	52·38	8	38·09	2	2·52	—	—
18–30 .	41	26	63·41	15	36·58	—	—	—	—
14–18 .	90	3	3·3	—	—	—	—	87	96·6
TOTALS	236	73	30·93	59	25·0	17	7·23	87	36·86

APPENDIX III

MALES. ALTERNATIVE OCCUPATIONS

Numbers in Ordinary Occupations	Other Unskilled Occupations	Labourers	Skilled Workers. Carpenters Plasterers Blacksmiths Bootmakers Painters Fitters	Business. Shop-Assistants Butchers Insurance Agents Travellers	Farmers and Gardeners	Motor Drivers	Miners	Clerks
MINERS (1,414) .	10	1,348	16	11	6	6	—	6
SKILLED WORKERS (121) .	1	62	2	3	2	12	10	—
TRANSPORT WORKERS (114) .	4	64	7	8	6	—	16	9
BUSINESS (128) . .	21	42	3	7	7	4	16	18
SEMI-SKILLED (73) . .	5	59	5	1	—	—	—	2
OFFICE WORKERS (60) .	2	10	1	5	—	1	11	—
OTHER OCCUPATIONS (90) .	1	—	—	2	1	1	2	4
TOTAL .	44	1,585	34	37	22	24	55	39

N.B.—Certain persons gave another branch of their ordinary occupation as their alternative, but such occupations have *not* been included in the above return.

CHAPTER XI

PRIVATE AND PUBLIC FINANCE

"Oh, Lord, have mercy upon us
And keep us all alive;
There's round the table nine of us
And only food for five."

MANY times during the history of Brynmawr there must
have been occasion to use this rhyme, which is still handed
down as part of the local tradition. Fluctuations in industrial
prosperity together with constant lock-outs and strikes have
accustomed the people to hard times, and have induced an
outlook at once fatalistic and optimistic. So far, the main
source of income has never failed permanently; and, although
in periods of exceptionally prolonged distress, the younger
men without family responsibilities have migrated, the
married men and the shop-keepers tied to the area have
waited for the turn of the tide, which they believed to be
inevitable.

When in 1921 the period of depression set in, the traditional
reactions to it held good. At first the bulk of the population
waited for the return of prosperity, and there was even some
immigration into the district during the temporary recovery
of 1923 and 1924. After the 1926 dispute, many of the young
men gave up hope of local employment and migrated elsewhere, and from that time onwards the population declined
steeply, and the proportion of older men left behind increased
markedly.

After the considerable savings accumulated during the
previous years of comparatively high mining wages had

been depleted, the unemployed fell back upon the resources of the community and of the nation. The tradesmen, most of whom are private shop-keepers with a long established family connection, played their traditional part in times of distress and gave credit to such an extent that their capital resources, in spite of the previous unprecedented prosperity of the town, were severely strained. Many of the principal grocers had debts amounting to as much as £5,000 by 1929, and the general effect of the industrial depression on the finances of the traders during the last few years is shown by the number of them who have been forced to give up business or have become bankrupt. Some of them have been forced to sell their debts for a small fraction of their value to enterprising persons who have had less compunction in demanding repayment from the workers.

Relief was at first undertaken by efforts on the part of the community, as had been done previously at such times as the 1912 strike. A Town Relief Committee was set up in 1921, and teachers, shop-keepers and others co-operated in providing funds for meals for the children outside the scope of the Provision of Meals Act, and for food for the families of the unemployed, as well as for boots for children and adults. It is estimated that in the year 1921–1922, the need for boots was so great that 1,313 weeks of education were lost by 373 children from this cause alone. In 1926 distress was again acute, and the civic responsibility of the elected body was recognised by the setting up of a Distress Committee by the Urban District Council, and the feeding of adults at a Communal Kitchen. As many as 45,520 meals to adults and 8,164 meals to children under and over school-age were supplied by this Committee. Yet even in this time of acute distress, many families of unemployed men refused to apply for or accept relief. Later on, when town resources were nearly depleted, help was brought in from outside by the Coalfields Distress Committee of the Society of Friends, the town of Worthing, which "adopted" Brynmawr and provided help in the form of clothing, money for food, holidays for children and other necessities, and the Mansion House

Fund. By this time, few families were in a position to meet
any extra strain, or even to replenish clothing and household gear such as bedding and blankets, and the reluctance
to accept help was gradually overcome.

In the meantime, family habits of self-sufficiency were
also changed by the adoption of school-feeding by the
Education Authority, which spent over £2,000 in school
meals in Brynmawr between May, 1926 and February, 1927.
In 1921, 350 families with 909 children were supplied
with school meals; the temporary revival of industry
which followed reduced this number to 98 families, and
led to the closing down of facilities until 1926, when as
many as 236 families with 363 children were again fed in
school.

Reluctance to apply for help from the Poor Law was also
overcome by financial strain, as is shown by the following
table giving the number of persons in the Crickhowell Union
who were relieved on account of unemployment from 1922
to 1930 inclusive.

RELIEF ON ACCOUNT OF UNEMPLOYMENT

Year			Men	Women	Children	Total in receipt of domiciliary relief
1922	.	.	723	677	1,693	3,741
1923	.	.	346	337	902	2,219
1924	.	.	108	106	246	1,072
1925	.	.	101	93	237	1,106
1926	.	.	240	176	431	1,590
1927	.	.	872	658	1,342	3,506
1928	.	.	384	251	478	1,672
1929	.	.	212	150	310	1,225
1930	.	.	239	173	351	1,446

Relief on account of unemployment is given *on loan* and
efforts are made to recover it by instalments from men who
subsequently obtain work. The following table shows the
great amount of debt still outstanding from individuals
and the small amount recovered in the Brynmawr district.

Relief on Loan.	In area of Breconshire Public Assistance Committee	In Brynmawr and Llanelly Hill District
(a) The amount of debts of individual men, who had received relief on loan outstanding on March 31st, 1932	approx. £86,000	approx. £48,000
(b) The amount of loans written off up to that date, as irrecoverable .	approx. £3,000	approx. £1,800
(c) The amount repaid up to 31st March, 1932	£2,058	£260

The present period of industrial distress has thus led to a great change in the habits of mind of the population, and very many families, which would have refused to seek aid either from the rates or from private charitable funds in previous shorter crises, have been driven to depend on it during the last few years.

The main source of income of the unemployed has, however, been unemployment benefit, which under the "transitional" clauses of the Insurance Acts has been prolonged year after year. Benefit, whether statutory or transitional, has come to be considered as a right, and there is no feeling of injury to pride or self-respect in drawing it, such as still lingers on in the minds of the workers with regard to relief from the Poor Rates. In the year ended March 31st, 1929, the large sum of £81,970 was paid out from the Brynmawr Employment Exchange, about 60 per cent of which was drawn by persons actually living in the town of Brynmawr, while only £6,235 was paid by the Guardians to Brynmawr residents. Voluntary relief during the same period amounted to £3,866.

The average weekly income of persons drawing unemployment benefit was as low as £1 0s. 1d. Since then there have been changes in the scale of unemployment benefit, first in the upward direction and since October, 1931, a cut of twenty per cent on the allowance for man and wife. Up to July, 1933, the provisions of the Means Test, owing to sympathetic administration and the general lack of any considerable additional means of existence other than the earnings of adolescent or adult children, had made little practical difference to the unemployed in the Brynmawr area.[1] To some extent this was no doubt due to the failure to distinguish between insurance benefits to which there was a right and the transitional benefits which were in reality a masked form of relief at the national expense. Owing to the prevalent confusion of thought with regard to the principles distinguishing social insurance and relief, there was a natural disinclination on the part of some members of the local Public Assistance Committee to take into account *family* income in determining the needs of individuals applying for transitional benefit, or to reduce payments of transitional benefits to the Public Assistance scale.

Thus the man drawing his income from the Employment Exchange has continued to be better off than the man receiving relief from the rates.[2] Yet even the former has little left over after meeting the primary demands for food and house rent. The diet of many unemployed workers is scanty and unnutritious. At breakfast, tea, and at supper, if taken, it consists mainly of bread and butter and tea. Dinner is the only meal at which meat is eaten, and in most cases this is only freshly cooked on Sundays. Vegetables, also, except where men have allotments are often regarded as Sunday fare. On other days, the remains of the Sunday dinner, bacon, bread and cheese, sausages and faggots, form the menu. Specimen budgets of families of unemployed men in receipt of relief and of unemployment benefit are given at the end of the Chapter.[3]

The fact that until 1931 school meals were supplied to necessitous school children twice a day no doubt prevented

---

[1] See Appendix I.

[2] The scale of relief on loan on account of unemployment adopted by the Breconshire Public Assistance Committee in January, 1933, is 20s. for a man and wife, 23s. for man, wife and child, with an additional 2s. for each additional child up to a maximum of 31s. This was an increase on the amounts previously granted, but was of course still less than the scale of Unemployment Benefit under the Insurance and Transitional Payments Acts. As a direct result of pressure on the Public Assistance Committee to conform to the law in administering the Means Test, the scale of relief was again raised in July, 1933, this time to correspond with that of Unemployment Benefit.

[3] See Appendix II.

them from suffering ill-effects owing to the defects of the home dietary. Since 1931, milk has been substituted for school meals, and this, together with the reduction in unemployment benefit, must have affected the budget of the entire family. Free milk is also given to mothers and babies at the Infant Welfare Centre when the family income is below a certain scale, and the babies on the whole are healthy, although the records at the Infant Welfare Centre show a significant drop in the rate of increase in weight in the babies over six months old from the families of unemployed as compared with those of employed men.

If any member of the household has to suffer from lack of quantity as apart from quality of food it is usually the mother, and it is on her health that poor and insufficient diet seems to have told most. Nurses and other experts agree that the mothers generally now suffer more from debility and have less recuperative power than formerly. Many of them worry about the financial position of the family and this no doubt reacts on their health. The reports of Friendly Society Secretaries seem to point to a tendency on the part of the male members also to remain on the sick list longer than was the case in times when industry was flourishing and it was financially profitable to return to work as soon as possible. Nurses, doctors, Public Assistance officers and other competent observers also agree that the general vitality of men who have been unemployed for a long period is lower, and it is remarked that when such men return to work they find difficulty in standing the strain of heavy manual labour. The effects on the health and physique of the population generally will no doubt be cumulative and can hardly be estimated in full at present.

While food is the first charge on the income of the unemployed man, rent is also an important item. This varies from five shillings to twelve shillings and sixpence, with a few instances below and above these limits. The more independent families keep their rent paid up whatever sacrifice it costs them. Very many others pay it only when the landlord brings pressure to bear. The ownership of house property due to the custom prevalent among the miners of investing their savings in their own houses in the days when wages were comparatively high, now has unforeseen effects. It both tends to tie unemployed men and their families to the depressed areas and in times of great straits when unemployment benefit fails, renders it difficult for them to get Poor Law Relief, since a mortgage of 75 per cent of the value of the house owned is often insisted on. Repairs are also a difficulty for the unemployed houseowner without other resources.

Pride in personal appearance seems little affected by prolonged unemployment. For years the mothers made and remade old clothes, and when sewing parties were introduced as part of Relief Schemes, they took an aesthetic pleasure in fingering and making up "new stuff" even though the garments were not for themselves but for the common stock of the relief centres. At the Annual "Sunday Schools Walking" the children continue to be turned out gay and smart with well-shined boots and some "new" garments to mark the occasion, although before the Relief Committees began to function, little material even for remaking could have remained in many homes. When nothing could be done to make a brave appearance many an unemployed man and his family would remain at home on Sundays rather than show their shabbiness. So hardly do social customs give way to financial stress.

In spite of the depression, a certain amount of luxury spending has continued. There is comparatively little drinking, and the incomes of publicans have been severely affected. Many of them, indeed, assert that they make no profits what ever, and are unable to pay their rates. Betting and gambling in small sums seem, however, to be on the increase, and the two Picture Theatres continue to flourish. Such diversions, together with attendance at football matches within the town and occasionally at long distances, are the main readily available sources of colour and excitement in the empty and monotonous existence of the unemployed. Indeed, while in a short temporary period of unemployment the natural tendency would be to conserve all available resources and to dispense with all luxuries in the form of amusement, where unemployment is continuous and there is no apparent hope of improvement, some means of escape from the prevailing drabness and apathy becomes essential. That such a means of escape is found chiefly in commercialised amusement is perhaps also a natural consequence of the lack of incentive to ambition and of the material outlook induced by insecurity of livelihood and the loss of once-cherished ideals. By the end of 1929, the position had been reached that over 54 per cent of the families of men in insurable occupations were dependent upon relief from rates, taxes and voluntary sources, and income from these sources made up 41·73 per cent of the income of the town apart from the gross incomes of traders and other independent persons. A large part of the population was thus financially parasitic.

The diagrams which follow show the number of men dependent on various occupations and other sources of income. It will be observed from the diagrams on page 162 that in spite of the mining depression the largest number of men employed for any period during the year ended March 31st, 1929, were to be found in the collieries. The average weekly income of the 1,053 miners employed at some time during the year ended March, 1929, however, was only 33s. 8d., a figure well below the legal minimum. This in itself indicates the considerable amount of short-time working during the period, and many of the miners concerned must have drawn unemployment benefit during the year. The mining industry was thus not self-supporting even as regards the men and boys to whom it afforded some employment. When it is considered that fares to and from work averaged three shillings a week and that in addition the miners had to pay various stoppages[1] amounting to half a crown or three shillings, it will be seen that the financial position of the employed miner living in Brynmawr was poor.

[1] In the Eastern and Western (Monmouthshire) Valleys, stoppages, apart from slight local variations, were as follows. Compulsory State Insurance 1s. 4d., Voluntary payments to Hospital and Doctor 6d. in the pound, Payments to checkweigher (by hewers) 1s. In addition the Trade Union subscription amounts to 1s. a week.

Since April 1st, 1931, the rates of wages have again been diminished by the following changes:—

The minimum percentage has been reduced from 28 to 20 above the 1915 standard base rates. The subsistence wage has been reduced from 7s. 10½d. per day in the following manner:—

	Rate per Day	Reduction Per Day
Married Men with Families	7/6	4½d.
Married Men without Families . . .	7/3	7½d.
Single Men with no Dependants . . .	7/-	10½d.

Single men who are the sole supporters of families are paid on the highest scale of 7s. 6d. per day.

Following are instances showing how the men are affected per shift worked:—

	Old Rate	New Rate	Reduction
Colliers and Timbermen (Piece Workers)	8/9½	8/2	7½
Colliers and Timbermen (Day-wage Men)	8/3·84	7/9·6	6·24d
Coal-cutter Men	8/1·9	7/7·8	6·1d
Masons, Pitmen and tonnage Hauliers	8/0	7/6	6

The average wages of transport workers, who came next in number to the miners, were comparatively high, amounting to 62s. 6d. per week, while employees of public bodies earned an average of £3 9s. 8d. per week, and employees in the professions as much as £4 2s. 11d. It is significant of the depressed state of the trade of the town that the shopkeepers employed only 78 persons, apart from their own labour, and that the wage of these commercial employees was lower even than that of the miners, averaging only £1 11s. 7d. per week. This was accounted for largely by the substitution of young boys and girls at low wages for experienced adult employees. Non-salaried professional workers earned an average income of £8 13s. 1d. per week or £450 per year, giving them a net income after paying business

BRYNMAWR. SOURCES OF INCOME

£			
80,000—			

A
PAYMENTS FROM RATES, TAXES AND VOLUNTARY CHARITABLE FUNDS

B
WAGES AND SALARIES

C
NUMBER OF MEN WHOSE INCOMES ARE SHOWN IN B

Bank Staffs; Doctors; Publicans; Shop-keepers and Assist-ants, Sundry Small Craftsmen — 1,500—

Bank Staffs, Doctors, etc. — 1,400—

£3,339
Ministers and Nurses

15 Ministers and Nurses

National Health Insurance and School Meals — 1,300—

£23,092
Public Officials (Police, Postal Workers, Urban District Council Employees, Teaching Staff)

123 Public Officials

Army Allowances £6,516 — 1,200—

Pensions
Widows' } Pensions
Orphans' } £10,588 — 1,100—
Old Age }

128 Transport Workers

Special Coalfields Relief Funds. £8,644 (from total for 17 months).*

Guardians Ordinary Poor Total Relief £2,081

£20,504
Transport Workers — 1,000—

Relief £6,236 | Unemployment Relief £3,153 — 900—

800—

70,000— 700—

1,053

Miners and Steel-

Workers. (Many of

these worked for a

600—

500—

£92,030

Miners' and Steel-

Workers' wages

short period in the

year only.)

£81,970

Unemployment Benefit paid

out from Brynmawr

Exchange

400—

300—

200—

100—

0— 0—

The above figures refer to the year ended March 31st, 1929.
*Relief in cash and kind excluding secondhand clothing.

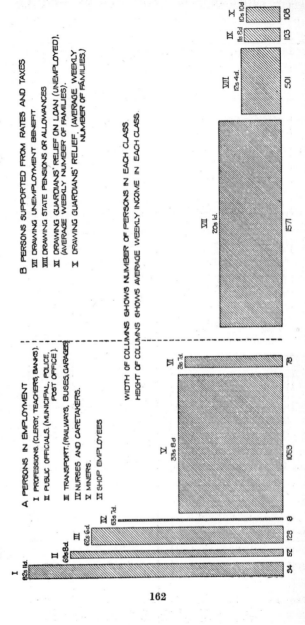

BRYNMAWR : AVERAGE WEEKLY INCOMES FOR YEAR ENDED 31ST MARCH 1929

A PERSONS IN EMPLOYMENT
  I PROFESSIONS. (CLERGY, TEACHERS, BANKS).
  II PUBLIC OFFICIALS. (MUNICIPAL, POLICE,
        POST OFFICE).
  III TRANSPORT. (RAILWAYS, BUSES, GARAGES).
  IV NURSES AND CARETAKERS.
  V MINERS.
  VI SHOP EMPLOYEES

B PERSONS SUPPORTED FROM RATES AND TAXES
  VII DRAWING UNEMPLOYMENT BENEFIT
  VIII DRAWING STATE PENSIONS OR ALLOWANCES
  IX DRAWING GUARDIANS' RELIEF ON LOAN (UNEMPLOYED).
        (AVERAGE WEEKLY NUMBER OF FAMILIES).
  X DRAWING GUARDIANS' RELIEF. (AVERAGE WEEKLY
        NUMBER OF FAMILIES.)

WIDTH OF COLUMNS SHOWS NUMBER OF PERSONS IN EACH CLASS
HEIGHT OF COLUMNS SHOWS AVERAGE WEEKLY INCOME IN EACH CLASS

162

expenses of about £7 a week. The average weekly income of all families outside the trading section in Brynmawr was only £3 2s. 1d.[1]

It was impossible to obtain returns of nett profits from the traders, but a careful estimate of their gross takings was made as part of the financial survey and from this it appears that for the year April, 1928, to March, 1929, these amounted to approximately £340,704 or a weekly average of £6,552 for 183 persons in business on their own account. The average household in Brynmawr, excluding those of traders and persons with private means, had a weekly income of just over £3 a week in 1929 on which from four to five persons had to be maintained. Since then the miners' rate of wages has decreased, and it is probable that the weekly income of the town is lower in 1932 than it was when the financial survey was carried out. Even in 1929, however, little saving was going on, and the average weekly amount put aside in National Savings Certificates and Savings Banks, the two main channels for savings in Brynmawr, was only £185. This amount was practically equalled by withdrawals from savings to meet current special expenses. The nett savings of the population through these two main channels were thus only at the rate of $1\frac{3}{4}$d. in the pound of the total income of the inhabitants. The community was in fact living from hand to mouth, and most of the people found it difficult to put aside even temporarily enough to meet necessary household replacements or expected special demands on their income. Clubs and such primitive expedients as paying some private person to "mind" their money for a few weeks helped some of the housewives to resist the temptation to spend all their small weekly income on day-to-day needs.

From a consideration of all the figures available with regard to the income and expenditure of the community of Brynmawr it seems evident that the savings and investments of all sections are decreasing owing to the long continued drain on

[1] See Appendix III at end of Chapter for summary of financial position of Brynmawr.

M

capital due to the ten years' industrial depression and that
the town itself cannot provide sufficient capital to open out
new avenues of employment. On the other hand, a certain
amount is still being spent in unproductive ways and at
cinemas and shops outside the town and if all sections were
convinced of the possibility of restoring prosperity by a wise
outlay, some combined local effort to produce part of the
necessary means would be possible. An effort to create
community values by the use of voluntary labour such as
that described in a subsequent chapter might also have important financial results.

The public finances of Brynmawr have suffered from the
mining depression equally as much as the private incomes
of the inhabitants. Table IV at the end of the Chapter shows
the enormous increase in the rates during the post-War period.
From a total rate for County, District and Poor Law purposes of 9s. in the financial year ended March 31st, 1914, it
rose to a figure consistently over £1 from the year ended
March, 1921, onwards and in the peak years of distress following the industrial stoppages of 1921 and 1926 was as high
as 28s. 6d. (1922–1923) and 29s. (1927–1928). It now (1931–
1932) stands at 23s.

How has this enormous increase in rates been caused and
how is the burden being met? Changes in social legislation,
in methods of rating and valuation and the transfer to the
County Council of responsibility for certain services, together
with fluctuations in the purchasing power of money must all
be taken into account before conclusions can be drawn from
the figures quoted. The outstanding facts are, however, the
large increase in the cost of poor relief, and the increase in the
cost of education. Appendix V throws light on the cost
to the locality under both headings. The decrease in the
rates for the years 1930–1931 and 1931–1932 is largely due
to the spread-over of the cost of poor relief due to the transfer
of responsibility from the Crickhowell Board of Guardians to
the Breconshire County Council, which has resulted in the
sharing of the burden of the depressed industrial areas by
the agricultural and residential districts. The estimated

product of 1*d.* rate in the various districts of Breconshire is given below.[1]

Name of Authority.	Estimate Product of penny rate.		
	£	s.	d.
Brecon Urban	101	6	4
Brecon Rural	257	6	11
Builth Rural	40	12	11
Builth Urban	33	15	7
Llanwrtyd Urban	15	6	0
Brynmawr Urban	57	0	0
Crickhowell Rural	82	13	11
Hay Urban	22	4	1
Hay Rural	85	12	8
Vaynor and Penderyn Rural . . .	128	2	0
Neath Rural	30	0	0

The study of the figures in Table VI suggests yet another cause for the maintenance of high rates. The amounts collected during the ten years ended March 31st, 1932, have been consistently below the amounts levied and considerable debts both to the County Council for general purposes and to the Board of Guardians and Public Assistance Committee have been accumulated. In order to meet current liabilities and to repay something of the burden of debt, the rates have thus necessarily been raised, and the burden upon those ratepayers who endeavour to meet the demands made upon them is still further aggravated. Yet even apart from rates, tradesmen and small property owners are suffering through the large amounts owing to them for goods and rents, and the publichouse licensees, in common with the tradesmen, are suffering from bad trade. To prosecute those of them who are in default with their rates would in many instances lead to their bankruptcy, as they would be unable to collect the debts owing to them, and their debtors might even be driven to increased recourse to the Public Assistance Committee if unduly pressed to repay. Public and private debts thus react and form a vicious circle which it is difficult to break.

In spite of this difficulty a stricter policy of enforcement of payments has recently been instituted owing to pressure

[1] *Basis for rates in Breconshire,* 1930–31. (*From Abstract of Receipts and Payments of the Breconshire County Council for Financial Year, ended March 31st,* 1931.)

from the Ministry of Health and the Breconshire County Council and a decrease in the difference between the amounts levied and the amounts collected has been brought about in the years 1930–31 and 1931–32. Current demands are thus being met out of income and the outstanding debts are being reduced.[1] An agreement has been entered into between the Breconshire County Council as Public Assistance Authority and the Brynmawr Urban District Council for additional levies towards Poor Law arrears to take place when the county rate falls below a figure which was originally fixed at 13s. 2d. in the pound, but as a result of continued industrial depression was reduced to 12s. in April, 1932.

The combined effects of the spread-over of the cost of Public Assistance and of a stricter policy in the collection of rates and the gradual repayment of debts in respect of past liabilities seem to afford hope of a sustained decrease in rates. Against these factors must be set certain psychological factors due to political conceptions of the functions of the State and Local Government Authorities. Among a large section of the community and of their elected representatives the incidence of taxation, whether local or national, is not taken into consideration, and there is a tendency to consider that public authorities which spend lavishly confer an unmitigated benefit on the electors in that they provide some additional employment and put additional money into circulation by adding to the incomes of those who have the smallest resources. This assumption is fostered by the habit of looking at questions of public finance from a class point of view instead of from that of the general welfare. To a certain extent there is of course an economic justification for using public money

[1] BRYNMAWR URBAN DISTRICT

	Debts Repaid to 31st March, 1932	Equivalent in Rate in £	Debt Outstanding
To County Council for:—			
(a) General Purposes . .	£3,600	2s. 8d.	£3,982
(b) Poor Law . . .	£896	6d.	£10,961
TOTAL	£4,496	3s. 2d.	£14,943

to equalise distribution and so maintain purchasing power. On the other hand with rates at their present level of 23*s.* in the pound, even the nett addition to rent which they involve is a very heavy burden on the small incomes of the unemployed man or the man earning low wages. Thus a rent of 6*s.* is brought up to 11*s.* 1*d.* by the addition of rates, and the housewife who has to cater for two adults and two dependent children on unemployment benefit of 27*s.* 3*d.* may well pause to consider whether under existing circumstances the expenditure of 5*s.* 1*d.* weekly in rates is counterbalanced by the value of the rate-maintained services, however desirable and necessary these may be in normal times. Could the incidence of rating be fully determined and generally understood even in a small community such as Brynmawr, the policy of local government might perhaps be revolutionised as a result of public demand. In this connection it should be noted that the rates per head of the population in the Brynmawr Urban District amounted in the year 1931–32 to £2 15*s.* 10*d.*

An important question for depressed areas such as Brynmawr is the probable effect of the level of rates on industry. It will probably take some years for the debts of the District Council and of the County Council for loans in respect of poor relief[1] to be cleared, and until this is done the rates will necessarily remain higher than would be needed to meet current liabilities. In view of this it might be thought that the establishment of new industries would be handicapped. On the other hand, not only does de-rating materially reduce the importance of rates from the point of view of industry, but lower assessable values and rents may well tip the balance in favour of Brynmawr as against larger and more prosperous centres of population, where the actual rates are lower.[2] Despite this a consistent policy of reduction of debt, leading to public solvency and ultimately to reduced rates would of

[1] On March 31st, 1932, the County Council debts to the Ministry of Health in respect of Goschen loans amounted to £66,007. The sum of £10,156 in respect of such loans had been repaid.
[2] A comparative study of site values and rents in Cardiff and Brynmawr which was made in 1932 by the Plan Committee of the Brynmawr Community Study Council bore out this suggestion.

course be an important factor in the probable success of any plan for new industrial developments.

Although no definite minima with regard to the population and financial capacity of local authorities have been laid down either by the Ministry of Health or the Royal Commission on Local Government in connection with the revision of boundaries under the Local Government Act of 1929, the figures of 10,000 population and £100 as the produce of a penny rate have been suggested by experts in evidence before the Royal Commission and have served as a guide in discussions of revision of boundaries. At present Brynmawr falls below these minima, and it is doubtful whether the present area of the Urban District provides the necessary basis for efficient local government and finance.

As has been seen, suggestions have been made from time to time for amalgamation with either Llanelly Parish or the larger area of the Crickhowell Rural District. If these proposals are considered wholly from a financial point of view, irrespective of the psychological factors which are important elements in good local government and which might prove disruptive forces between the rural and industrial population unless changes of outlook could be brought about in both sides, there is no doubt that the amalgamation of Brynmawr and the whole of the Rural District would be advantageous. The population of Llanelly Parish is largely made up of miners, and has suffered from the same causes as that of Brynmawr. It is true that by the imposition of a special rate amounting to 5s. 1d. spread over two and a half years Llanelly Parish has succeeded in wiping out the whole of its debt to the County Council for poor relief, and by its present policy of enforcement of payment of arrears of rates is gradually clearing its debt for general purposes. On the other hand the produce of a penny rate for the year 1931–32 was only £22 12s. 0d., and this added to the produce of a similar rate in Brynmawr would still be under £100. Moreover, the amalgamation of Brynmawr and Llanelly Parish only would merely mean the addition of one distressed area to another without the inclusion of any broader occupational

basis except in the Gilwern area. Appendix VI gives particulars
of rateable values, debts and outstanding loans in Brynmawr,
Crickhowell Rural District and Llanelly Parish, together
with a table of rates over a period in Llanelly Parish.

A general consideration of the private and public finance
of Brynmawr leads to the conclusion that the public services
necessary for the welfare of the inhabitants can hardly be
maintained and developed without a change of boundaries
and a consequent increase in the rateable value per head
of the population. The presence of a large percentage of
persons who over a long period have remained financially
dependent on the community, the effects of decreased purchasing power and capital resources on the trade of the town,
the difficulty in collecting rates from many inhabitants,
and the burden of private and public debts, call for vigorous
steps to improve the financial position. While strenuous
efforts are now being made to meet current liabilities and to
pay off debts previously incurred, essential developments
such as improvements in the water supply have to be met
by fresh borrowing, and the burden of rates on the community
remains heavy.

Determined efforts by the public authorities to make and
keep the town solvent and a spread-over of the financial
effects of unemployment through an extension of area would
together help to promote the possibility of developing new
means of producing wealth. Public administration and
finance may thus be important factors in any attempt at
reconstruction by which surplus labour may be utilised once
more as a productive asset and the shadow of financial insecurity as well as of unused creative energy be lifted from
the lives and homes of the people.

APPENDIX I

(1) The following Table shows the number of applications received by the Breconshire Public Assistance Committee for transitional benefit between November 12th, 1931, when the provisions of the Means Test came into operation, to May 13th, 1933.

District	Determinations	Allowed Full Scale	Reduced	Disallowed
Brynmawr and Llanelly Hill .	1,336	1,266	55	15
Clydach, Gilwern, and Rural Part of Crickhowell Rural District	414	326	67	21
Brecknock	436	2	386	48
Vaynor and Penderyn .	706	503	166	37
Hay and Talgarth . .	194	5	118	71
Builth	152	32	109	11
Ystradgynlais . . .	570	411	109	50
TOTALS . . .	3,808	2,545	1,010	253

This Table shows the great difference in the effects of the Means Test in the agricultural districts of Brecknock, Hay and Talgarth, and Builth and in the mining districts.

SPECIMEN BUDGETS OF UNEMPLOYED MEN

Average Weekly Expenditure on	BUDGET A Man, Wife and 3 Children, Income from Unemployment Benefit 29/3d.		BUDGET B Man, Wife and 3 Children, Income from Relief on Loan 25/6d.		BUDGET C Man, Wife and 1 Child. Income from Unemployment Benefit 25/3d.	
	s.	d.	s.	d.	s.	d.
Nett Rent (after sub-letting if any)	6	0	4	6	6	6
Fuel and Lighting . .	1	10½	2	0	2	6
Food						
Meat	3	0	2	0	2	0
Fresh Milk . . .		10½ (½ pint daily)	—— (condensed milk from grocer)			10½
Fruit, Vegetables and Fish .	3	3	(vegetables from allotments. No fruit or fish)		2	0
Bread	2	11 (10 small loaves)	4	11½ (17 small loaves)	2	0½
Grocery	7	8	9	6	6	6
Household replacements, Clothing, Pocket-money, Hospital (1d.) and Trade Union Subscriptions .	3	8 (Clothing Club 2/-)	2	6½	2	10
TOTALS . .	£1 9	3	£1 5	6	£1 5	3

APPENDIX III

STATEMENT WITH REGARD TO FINANCE IN BRYNMAWR FOR THE YEAR ENDED MARCH 31st, 1929

BASED ON VERIFIED ENQUIRIES OF FINANCE GROUP OF SURVEY COMMITTEE

	Amount per week			Amount per year			No.
SALARIES AND WAGES OF EMPLOYEES	£	s.	d.	£	s.	d.	
Mines	1,769	16	4	92,030	7	3	1,053
Professions	389	15	2	20,267	10	0	94
Public Bodies . . .	181	0	11	9,414	10	2	52
Transport	400	0	0	20,800	0	0	128
Tradespeople . . .	123	1	9	6,400	10	0	78
Sundries	21	8	8	1,114	9	6	8
	2,885	2	10	150,027	6	11	1,413
ALLOWANCES AND PENSIONS	317	2	4	16,490	2	4	515
GROSS INCOMES							
Professions . . .	95	3	10	4,950	0	0	11
Traders, etc. . . .	6,552	0	0	340,704	0	0	183
Sundries	5	15	5	300	0	0	——
TOTAL	6,652	19	3	345,954	0	0	194
Unemployment Benefit and Relief from Guardians, Mansion House Fund and Society of Friends . . .	1,766	15	4	91,871	16	1	
TOTAL MONEY PAID OUT IN THE TOWN							
Salaries and Wages . .	2,885	2	10	150,027	6	11	
Pensions and Allowances .	317	2	4	16,490	2	4	
Unemployment Benefit and Relief . . .	1,766	15	4	91,871	16	1	
	4,969	0	6	258,389	5	4	
Gross Income . . .	6,652	19	3	345,954	0	0	
GRAND TOTAL . .	11,621	19	9	604,343	5	4	

SAVINGS	Amount per week £ s. d.	Amount per year £ s. d.
National Savings Certificates	88 15 5	4,616 1 0
Savings Banks . . .	96 15 8	5,032 13 6
TOTAL	185 11 1	9,648 14 6
WITHDRAWALS FROM SAVINGS		
National Savings Certificates	39 15 4	2,067 17 8
Savings Banks . . .	130 6 0	6,775 10 0
	170 1 4	8,843 7 8
NETT SAVINGS		
Savings	185 11 1	9,648 14 6
Withdrawals from Savings .	170 1 4	8,843 7 8
TOTAL	15 9 9	805 6 10

	Amount per week £ s. d.	Amount per year £ s. d.
AVERAGE WAGE OF EMPLOYEES		
Mines	1 13 8	87 3 0
Professions	4 2 11	215 12 3
Public Bodies	3 9 8	181 0 11
Transport	3 2 6	162 10 0
Tradespeople	1 11 7	82 3 2
Sundries	2 13 7	139 6 2
Average on Total	2 0 10	106 3 6

	£ s. d.	£ s. d.
Average Gross Income of Traders, etc. .	35 16 1	1,861 15 5
Average Gross Income of Professions .	8 13 1	450 0 0
Average Pensions and Allowances . .	12 4	32 0 5
Average amount received in Unemployment Benefit	1 0 1	52 3 7
Proportion of Unemployment Benefit, etc., to Salaries and Wages, Pensions and Allowances	35·56%	
Proportion of Income of Town Saved .	0·1332%	
Average Income of Brynmawr Households (excluding Traders, etc.) 1,600 . .	3 2 1 per week 161 9 10 per annum	

APPENDIX IV

BRYNMAWR URBAN DISTRICT COUNCIL

Years March 31st	Population[1]	Poor Rate (Including County Purposes)				General District Rate			
		Rateable Value	Rate in £	Amount Levied	Amount Collected	Assessable Value	Rate in £	Amount Levied	Amount Collected
April 1st									
1913–14	7,761	19,744 16 2	6/–	5,821 3 11	5,447 8 6	17,031 19 6	3/–	2,548 12 2	2,525 11 0
1919–20	7,974	19,553 11 8	8/8	8,337 14 7	8,110 2 5	16,901 10 8	5/6	4,646 19 7	4,497 7 4
1920–21	8,120	19,697 8 8	11/–	10,659 5 10	9,906 8 5	17,023 13 5	10/–	8,512 11 1	8,075 18 11
1921–22	8,240	19,839 12 3	17/6	17,076 16 8	12,411 11 10	17,272 3 1	9/6	8,177 16 0	6,754 15 2
1922–23	8,338	19,656 18 3	19/–	18,500 12 1	11,853 9 1	17,962 18 1	9/6	8,323 6 7	6,609 5 8
1923–24	8,460	20,613 14 10	15/6	15,752 7 4	11,624 17 10	18,122 5 7	6/6	5,895 8 7	5,495 3 4
1924–25	8,657	20,454 8 0	13/–	13,165 4 7	10,371 14 0	18,952 2 9	6/–	5,555 3 0	4,472 18 10
1925–26	8,667	20,997 7 9	13/–	13,227 12 4	11,407 1 7	18,636 13 7	5/6	5,050 8 1	5,393 13 5
1926–27	8,515	21,244 15 2	14/4	14,916 1 3	11,081 10 1	18,907 16 0	5/6	5,192 0 3	3,835 5 11
1927–28	8,445	21,503 12 6	21/–	22,074 7 11	14,875 3 10	19,180 9 10	8/–	7,651 11 8	5,198 10 5
1928–29	7,878	21,439 5 6	21/–	22,078 10 4	15,351 2 10	19,185 8 1	7/6	7,197 15 6	5,424 10 10

Years	Population	Rateable Value[2]	General Rate		
			Rate in £	Amount Levied	Amount Collected
1929–30	7,694	19,067	26/6	25,942 3 6	20,981 10 8
1930–31	7,466	18,887	23/6	22,309 17 6	20,353 2 11
1931–32	7,247	18,884	23/–	21,771 16 0	19,295 13 1

[1] These figures are taken from the Registrar General's Estimates of the Population for each Mid-Year from 1913 onwards, with the exception of 1931, for which the Census figure is given.

[2] The effect of De-rating on the Assessable Value of the town was a reduction of £655.

APPENDIX V

EXPENDITURE ON ELEMENTARY EDUCATION IN BRECONSHIRE

(FROM ABSTRACT OF RECEIPTS AND PAYMENTS OF THE
BRECONSHIRE COUNTY COUNCIL FOR FINANCIAL YEARS
ENDED MARCH 31ST, 1931)

Year	Net Expenditure £	Per Child £ s. d.			Grants Per Child £ s. d.			Rates Per Child £ s. d.		
1918–1919	57,673	6	4	5	3	3	3	3	1	2
1919–1920	78,436	8	13	6	5	1	11	3	11	7
1920–1921	92,974	10	5	11	6	9	8	3	16	3
1921–1922	97,266	10	17	3	6	11	3	4	6	0
1922–1923	94,012	10	9	11	6	4	3	4	5	8
1923–1924	92,758	10	9	3	6	12	5	3	16	9
1924–1925	95,486	10	15	4	6	13	7	4	1	1
1925–1926	100,642	11	6	6	6	19	11	4	6	7
1926–1927	104,173	11	17	3	7	10	5	4	6	10
1927–1928	99,107	11	7	10	6	19	2	4	8	8
1928–1929	104,133	12	11	8	6	17	6	5	1	2

RATES LEVIED FOR POOR RELIEF IN BRYNMAWR URBAN DISTRICT

Year to 31st of March	Rate in Pound s. d.
1914 . . .	2 11¾
1920 . . .	4 11¼
1921 . . .	6 11½
1922 . . .	11 11
1923 . . .	13 9
1924 . . .	10 6
1925 . . .	7 10
1926 . . .	6 5
1927 . . .	7 9
1928 . . .	14 7½
1929 . . .	15 0
1930 . . .	10 0
1931 . . .	5 3
1932 . . .	4 9

APPENDIX VI

	Brynmawr Urban District	Crickhowell District	Llanelly Parish
Rateable Value 1931–32	£18,884	£21,321 0 0	£6,554 (after de-rating October, 1929)
Loans outstanding March 31st, 1932	(a) Rate Fund account £24,001 (b) Housing Assisted Scheme £124,750	£5,041 11 1 (Waterworks and Housing Substitute Scheme)	£4,265 19 4 (Waterworks)
Indebtedness to Public Assistance Committee March 31st, 1932	£10,961	—	—
Indebtedness to County Council for general purposes March 31st, 1932	£3,982	£715 19 11	£715 19 11

RATES ON LLANELLY PARISH

Year	Total Rate s. d.	Rate for Relief Purposes s. d.
1913–1914	9 11	2 9
1919–1920	12 8	3 5½
1920–1921	15 8	5 3
1921–1922	21 4	9 0
1922–1923	24 8	10 0
1923–1924	20 6	7 6
1924–1925	18 0	6 0
1925–1926	22 8	7 6
1926–1927	22 10	7 0
1927–1928	24 5[1]	10 0
1928–1929	23 1[1]	10 0
1929–1930	25 1[1]	10 0
1930–1931	20 7	5 3
1931–1932	18 8	4 9

[1] The total Rates for the three years 1928–31 include the sums of 1/3, 2/6 and 1/4 respectively levied for re-payment of debts in respect of Poor Rate.

trade and sometimes difficulty in affording steady employment to the workmen.   The value set upon efficiency and
craftsmanship among the workers and the patriarchal over-
sight over their conduct and affairs by the employers has
already been noted.   Messrs. John and Lancelot Powell,
who succeeded the Freres (a Norfolk family who settled in
Clydach and sub-leased the mining rights in Llanelly Parish
from Edward Kendall of Beaufort), seem to have been liked
as well as respected.   Possibly they owed something to their
Welsh origin, which may have brought them into closer
sympathy with the native workers than were the English
industrial leaders at Nantyglo, and other Iron Centres of
South Wales.   The residence of Mr. Frere and later Mr.
Lancelot Powell in the midst of the workers also did much to
promote personal contact with them.

In spite of this, unrest existed in Clydach as in the surrounding districts.   As early as 1804 the Clydach Colliers "brought
in their tools," without, however, causing much concern to
the officials and owners, who concluded that "they could not
do better elsewhere."   The lonely and wild nature of the surrounding country gave opportunities for deeds of violence and
the 1823 Assize Calendars at Brecon show many prosecutions
of men from the district for assaults and disorder.   In that
year an intimidating notice, written in a mixture of English
and Welsh, was put up at the Clydach Works.   The English
translation is as follows:—

"How many times we gave notice to you about going in to work
before you settle all together to go on better terms than were before
or better than what you ask at present?
"Notice to you, David Thomas John, and David Davies, and
Andrew Cross, that the Bull and his friends are all alive, and the
vale of Llammarch is wide, and woe shall be to you, since death you
shall doubtless all have at once, you may depend upon this. It may
be that the night you don't expect we shall come again. We are not
afraid were you to go all at once to work."[1]

It appears from the use of both languages and the names of
the persons cited that the blacklegs were not all of one nationality, and no doubt by that time the community included many

---

[1] See *Old South Wales Iron Works*, by John Lloyd.

N

English immigrants. Its make-up is now very much like that of Brynmawr as regards race and origins, although its roots go deeper into the past owing to the earlier date of the original settlement.[1]

As in Brynmawr, nonconformity was predominant among the workers, and chapels were built early in the nineteenth century. In the Gilwern district, however, there was a tradition of church membership among the wealthy residents as well as in some of the families of farmers and tradesmen, and at one time a stream of carriages could be seen every Sunday making their way up the hill to Llanelly Parish Church.

From the earliest days of industrial development there has been a social and occupational cleavage between the Gilwern district with its rich beauty of wooded valleys, fertile fields and river and the more rugged mining districts of Clydach and Llanelly Hill. The Gilwern area early became the home of members of landed proprietors and of the great employing families, the Crawshays and Jaynes, and later even of a few of the wealthier Brynmawr tradesmen; the social make-up of the population was thus varied and included a local aristocracy of leisured and well-to-do people, which is conspicuously lacking in mining towns in South Wales. In addition, there were not only farmers and small shop-keepers but rural craftsmen such as farm carpenters, blacksmiths, clog-makers, wood-carvers, and sawyers. Colliers and quarrymen also penetrated the district, but not in sufficient proportions to make the outlook predominantly industrial as in Clydach and Llanelly Hill. The picture drawn by a former Rector of Llanelly Parish of the women bringing their three-legged stools and their knitting on to Gilwern Common on Summer evenings in order to listen to the practices of the bell-ringers at Llanelly Church[2] is suggestive of the more slow-moving life of a rural community outside the main stream of revolt and industrial organisation.

[1] The percentages of non-natives living in Clydach and Llanelly Hill in 1929 were 22·5 males and 25·0 females in Clydach, and 11·81 males and 7·54 females in Llanelly Hill as compared with 13·84 males and 12·17 females in Brynmawr.

[2] See *Annals and Reminiscences of the Parish of Llanelly,* by Arthur Griffiths.

While the wealthy industrialists have used the country around Gilwern as their place of residence, the outskirts of Clydach and Llanelly Hill have received another kind of migrant from Brynmawr. The greater age of the former settlements is reflected in the ages of many of the workmen's cottages, most of which were erected more than a hundred years ago, and are structurally dilapidated, damp and badly ventilated. The Annual Report of the Medical Officer of Health and Sanitary Inspector for the Crickhowell Rural District for 1930 states that "Undoubtedly from the standard laid down by the 'Manual of Unfit Houses' issued by the Ministry of Health very few are fit for human occupation." As in Brynmawr, economic depression has prevented both the building of new houses and the repairing of existing ones.   This housing situation has resulted in the creation of "slum" districts in certain parts of Clydach and Llanelly Hill where tenants of the least desirable type both socially and financially tend to crowd into cheaply rented houses from other parts of the two villages and from Brynmawr. A further problem is caused by the fact that a large proportion of the thriftier old-established residents[1] acquired their own houses in former days; thus, even more than in Brynmawr, workers are tied to the district by the locking up of their inheritance or savings in property which has now little saleable value.

The industrial parts of Llanelly Parish have perhaps suffered even more severely than has Brynmawr from successive failures of industry. After the Clydach Iron Works were closed down in 1861, the distress of the population, congregated in the district almost entirely owing to the local demand for labour, was very great and was reflected in the increase of persons receiving Poor Law Relief between 1861 and 1871, and in the sudden decrease in population due to migration. Efforts were made to revive the trade of the Works on other lines, first by the opening out of a gate and hurdle department and later by the development of entirely different industries on the former site, such as a Flannel Factory and Soap Factory. None of these efforts were for long successful, and the district

[1] See Appendix II.

sank back into the status of a dormitory for workers in distant collieries. Since Clydach was even further from the developing mines of the Western Valley than was Brynmawr, the difficulty in obtaining and retaining employment was accentuated. Many of the workers indeed found the expense and difficulty of travelling so great, especially before motor transport was developed, that they returned to their homes and families only at week-ends.

The opening out of new levels and pits belonging to the Blaenavon Colliery Company has alleviated the position for some of the miners living on Llanelly Hill, who on the whole are now better off as regards employment than the men living in Clydach or Brynmawr. Thus in 1929, over 56 per cent of the families living on Llanelly Hill were in receipt of wages as compared with 42 per cent in Clydach and 45 per cent in Brynmawr. Two thirds of the Llanelly Hill families had an average weekly income of over thirty shillings, while in Brynmawr and Clydach only about one half of the men attached to insurable occupations received more than this sum.

Llanelly Parish differs from Brynmawr in that it has one colliery, in addition to small levels, within its boundaries. This colliery shares in the common mining depression; moreover much of its best coal has already been exhausted, and its capital expenditure in endeavouring to open out new areas has been heavy. Hence the employment which it has afforded in late years has been precarious in the extreme. It now employs only about 250 men, and there is little likelihood of any increase in its employment capacity. The district is thus in the main in a position as regards the mining industry which is almost identical with that of Brynmawr.

On the other hand, while mining constitutes the main occupation of men living in Clydach and Llanelly Hill, the Parish of Llanelly as a whole and still more the Crickhowell Rural District, of which it forms part, offers other openings for employment, and there is some tradition of skilled work of a varied nature which may affect the ease with which crafts or other skilled industries can be reintroduced.

The natural resources of Llanelly Parish include limestone and the map of the district between Brynmawr and Abergavenny shows a large number of quarries.[1] Both at Clydach and Gilwern quarrying has been an important subsidiary industry and in the past has provided occupation for considerable numbers of men. Of recent years its employment capacity has been very small owing to the failure of local markets. The quarries at Gilwern and Clydach were largely dependent on the demand for lime for use as a flux in the furnaces at the Steel Works at Blaenavon[2] and, since these have been closed down, the Gilwern quarries have been completely idle owing to lack of an alternative market. The Clydach quarries, which also supplied the Steel Works, have managed to find some other markets by producing lime for agricultural and horticultural purposes and also supplying a limited amount of road stone. These quarries were opened up as early as 1866 and are now leased from the Duke of Beaufort by a private limited Company. Twenty to twenty-five years ago they employed as many as 80 men and produced 3,000 to 4,000 tons of lime and limestone per month. During the three years 1927–30 their output had decreased to about 7,000 tons *per annum* and they could only employ about thirty men somewhat irregularly. It is possible that certain capital expenditure on up-to-date equipment such as a Tar MacAdam plant might enable them to develop fresh markets by producing additional road-stone at a competitive price, and also gravel and poultry grit. Failing such development it is difficult to see what hope they have of affording steady employment to any considerable number of men.

A further subsidiary industry, which once flourished on the outskirts of Brynmawr is brick-making. Suggestions have been made that this should be revived and developed in the district. Ample supplies of fire-clay of good quality in proximity to coal exist, together with good facilities for transport. On the other hand the brick-making industry already

---

[1] See Appendix III.
[2] 44,000 tons of limestone were used in the production of 40,000 tons of iron.

established at Beaufort, like others established throughout
South Wales experienced great difficulties owing to the present
depressed state of the adjacent thickly populated industrial
areas, where there is a housing shortage and where in normal
times a market would be available close at hand. In Brynmawr itself, for instance, there has been no considerable
increase of houses since the completion of the local Authority's
scheme in 1923. Where bricks have to be transported for
considerable distances the cost of freightage is very high, and
the good quality of the local material carries with it the disadvantage that the bricks made of it are heavier than those
transported from Holland and elsewhere. The footnote
below giving examples of freightage and other charges at
brickworks near Brynmawr illustrates the difficulties[1]. It
seems, therefore, that until a general revival of industry and
trade in the coalfield comes about, there is little scope for
extension of the brick-making industry.

Another industry which was opened out for some years,
at Clydach and at Gilwern, was the manufacture of Welsh
flannels. This industry has declined everywhere in South
Wales of late years owing to changes in fashion and the competition of cheaper substitutes such as mixtures and cotton
flannelette.

Flannel petticoats and the linsey skirtings, woollen dress
materials, and aprons, which formed part of the national
Welsh costume, are no longer worn, and a similar fate has
almost overtaken the characteristic Welsh shawls and "turn-
overs." The old striped flannel shirting for men's wear is
giving place to finer and lighter makes, either wool or cotton
or mixtures, such as are beyond the capacity of the majority
of Welsh factories. Hosiery materials have not, however,
altogether supplanted flannel for miners' wear. The demand
for flannel for this purpose forms the principal trade of the

---

[1] Freightage to London : For a guaranteed quantity of three to four thousand
tons £2 per 1,000 bricks. For a guaranteed quantity of 15,000 tons 9s. 6d.
per ton or £1 13s. 3d. per 1,000 bricks. Prices obtainable £2 12s. 6d. to
£2 18s. 6d. per 1,000. Prices at works 12s. 6d. to 18s. per 1,000. Freightage
to Cardiff : The rate is 18s. 1d. per 1,000, and frequently orders are lost by
half the cost of the freightage. During slack periods the cost of stacking
bricks for storage is 1s. 6d. to 2s. per 1,000.

South Wales factories, in many of which the feeling prevails that a revival of the coal trade would put an end to most of their present difficulties. In Llanelly Parish, the industry has been extinct for so long that few experienced workers remain in the district.

On a very much smaller scale than the flannel-making industry, the making of tweeds has been carried on in the Crickhowell district by cottagers engaged in handloom weaving. One such weaver is still producing and selling tweeds a few miles away from Gilwern. As has been seen, there was a time, even as late as that of Carnhuanawc, when all the processes of spinning, dyeing and weaving were undertaken locally in Breconshire, and the making of textiles was an important factor in the life of rural Wales.

Many of the early wool producing areas of England and Scotland were adjacent to the iron and coal deposits, as for example, in Yorkshire and the South of England. Furthermore, in these areas there had always been a tradition of iron working. With the rapid development of the industrial revolution, therefore, it was only natural that, side by side with the great increase in the production of iron there would be a corresponding development in the working of it— resulting in ever-improving machinery, and in turn a consequent development of trade.

In Wales, however, the position was quite different. The textile industry was mainly concentrated in West and Mid Wales, far removed from the coal and iron producing areas of South Wales. Further, in those mountainous and sparsely populated districts, there had never been any real tradition of iron working in the earlier days. When the rapid development took place, therefore, the iron was sent out of the district in its simplest form to be used in other areas, whilst, in the West, cut off as they were by lack of transport facilities, the life of the people carried on in its primitive way; the farmer taking his own wool to the local weaver, who spun and wove it for him on his old-fashioned machinery, untouched, save by rumour, by the seething, tumultuous development of the industrial valleys.

After the War, however, three new features rapidly decreased the local demand; the high price of wool, the advent of the motor-bus, which enabled people to reach the market towns cheaply and rapidly from the villages and surrounding country-side, and the growth of the ready-made tailor with his multiple shop providing suits far below the price of the handwoven tweed made from local wool. In addition, owing to the rise of better organised factories in England and Scotland, the once considerable export trade also disappeared. To-day down many a leafy lane, and by many a quiet stream, may be seen the idle mills and pandys which once played such an important part in the life of the community.

One of the main difficulties in fostering a trade in Welsh tweed is that the traditional Welsh fabric is a coarse, heavy dark-coloured material with good wearing qualities but not suited to modern ideas of cloth for men's wear. An enquiry into the causes of the decline of the industry and the possi-bility of reviving it was made in 1927 by Mr. W. Crankshank on behalf of the University of Wales. His conclusion was that there was "Undoubtedly a trade to be done in cloth for men's wear, plus-fours and light overcoatings for example", which was quite within the scope of the small Welsh factories. Better selection of wool, good dyeing, blending and carding, as well as good finishing were essential. Given an improve-ment in standards of efficiency in production there seems in fact, to be a reasonable prospect of developing the tweed industry in Wales, provided that traditional designs and methods are no longer rigidly adhered to, and that efforts are made to develop new markets through advertising, industrial exhibitions etc., and attention paid to the develop-ment of technical education and the production of new fabric of a kind suitable to modern requirements. An attempt to revive the industry in the Brynmawr district is described in the following chapter.

Both brickmaking and the making of flannel, as apart from tweeds, depend largely for their success on South Wales markets and the prospects of either industry are bound up to a great extent with the renewed prosperity of the mining districts. Agriculture, however, caters for more universal and basic needs and has persisted as the traditional occupation of the bulk of the population of the Crickhowell Rural District outside Clydach and Llanelly Hill. Even in these districts and in Brynmawr the people are not cut off from agricultural interests; there are a considerable number of collier-farmers on the hillsides around Brynmawr, and the mining depression has accentuated the importance of farming as a subsidiary occupation. On the other hand, apart from those already partially engaged on the land, there are comparatively few miners in Brynmawr or Llanelly Parish who claim to have any skill or experience in agriculture. The highest percentage occurs on Llanelly Hill where 6·4 per cent of the unemployed miners give farming or gardening as their alternative occupation.

The use of the land in the Crickhowell Rural District falls into three main divisions; first the production of garden produce and poultry rearing by allotment holders and cottagers; secondly, the cultivation of highland and hill farms, undertaken to a great extent by collier-farmers as a subsidiary source of income; and thirdly, farming on a large scale as a whole time occupation on land in the lower hill and lowland districts.

Cottagers and allotment holders produce fruit and vegetables mainly for their own use, but also sell a certain amount in Brynmawr and even further afield, especially at the weekly market. Garden produce is a substantial help to unemployed families, but the cost of seeds, lime and in some cases, fencing, is a difficulty which is only partly met by assistance to Allotment Associations from voluntary charitable funds.

The highland farmers in Llanelly Parish are all collier-farmers and work their farms wholly by family labour. The income derived from the farms is very largely a subsistence one, the holding supplying the families with dairy-produce, poultry and eggs, while wool, fat lambs, and fat sheep are sold. Somewhat akin to those farms are a group of lower hill farms, again partly farmed as a subsidiary occupation, but also affording the sole means of livelihood to a number of families.   Here, sheep-farming again predominates, but milk is also produced and sold retail or wholesale, while pigs and poultry are kept as sidelines.   Labour is supplied mainly by the family, except on one or two of the larger farms where about 50 per cent of the labour is hired.

Grazing rights on the mountain-sides are a valuable addition to the actual area of all the highland and hill farms.   Some of them are poorly equipped with implements, and the farmers have little knowledge of methods of cultivation of grassland. Lack of capital as well as conservatism prevents them from spending much on artificial manures, feeding stuffs or fencing of the fields.   In addition to better control of the land, improvements are needed as regards breeding of sheep and management, especially with a view to earlier lambing.   Examples are to be seen in the district at present where highland holdings are managed with modern methods which are successful and these farms might be utilised for demonstration purposes.

On the lowland or lower hill farms of from twenty to fifty acres, where the farmer is engaged full time, the success of the holding depends principally on high output of dairy, pig and poultry products.   The same criticisms relating to the management of land apply here as for the highland group. In both groups of farms improved methods would probably result in greater prosperity, and greater employment capacity. This might take the form of more regular and better-paid employment for members of the family, but even if it did not lead to the employment of many additional paid workers not drawn from the family of the farmer, it would indirectly contribute to the well-being of the district.

The first step in developing the district agriculturally appears, indeed, to be the conversion of the part-time industrial farmers to dependence on agriculture as their main means of livelihood and the consequent re-orientation of their interests and those of their families.   Since they are already in touch with farm conditions, they would be the natural pioneers in the change-over from predominantly mining interests to those of the land, and would be important advocates in the struggle with the prevalent closed attitude of mind due to the long-established general conviction that "coal is king." Assistance both with capital and advice as to scientific management and marketing would probably be needed to bring about this change.

The larger farms in Llanelly Parish are for the most part situated in the lowland area around Gilwern. They also employ a considerable amount of family labour, amounting to an average of 63 per cent, excluding casual hired assistance. Like the hill-farmers they have little arable land; their stock included a larger proportion of cattle as compared with sheep, however, and milk production is an important factor. Most of the milk produced is sold wholesale or retail, and there is little butter making; very few pigs are kept and only one farm specialises in poultry keeping. Both milk production and sheep-farming either for fat or store lamb production have been fairly profitable on these larger farms of late years, and, as rents are comparatively high in the lowland parts of the district, are probably more adapted to the needs of the farmers than would be store cattle raising with butter production, from which the turnover would be less rapid. The production of milk might well be increased to the utmost capacity of the farms in view of the distances from which it is brought into the industrial districts.

While the additional number of workers, who might be absorbed by agriculture given some change of methods on the lines indicated above, is limited, there is obviously scope in the district for the development of pig and poultry production and of market-gardening. Some pigs and poultry are kept by cottagers and by farmers, but up to the present little attention has been paid either to pig-keeping or to scientific poultry-keeping on a large scale. There is no doubt that in suitable cases poultry-keeping could be improved and extended and that there would be a market in Brynmawr and the industrial valleys for a much greater production. At present, the Brynmawr market draws its main supplies from as far afield as Crickhowell, Abergavenny, Hereford and Monmouth. Poultry-keeping on right lines with a grading and marketing scheme both for eggs and surplus stock would seem to be a hopeful means of development.

Market produce also is brought into Brynmawr from long distances. Potatoes, which are imported into South Wales generally in considerable quantities, come to Brynmawr from as far afield as Lincolnshire, and Cambridgeshire, although, given proper seed suitable to local conditions and a good marketing organisation, there seems no reason why the needs of Brynmawr and the industrial areas of Monmouthshire should not be met by local production. Other vegetables, such as cabbages, and fruit are also brought in from as far as Worcester and Evesham.[1] Yet the region below Clydach contains all the necessary conditions for successful fruit growing. The soil is not too impervious and the drift soil contains iron and lime. It will be seen from the diagrams in Appendix I that the temperature is very much higher both in winter and summer than in Brynmawr. The only factor modifying this is that, by a process of inversion, the temperature in the Usk Valley may fall very much lower than at Brynmawr during a long period of cold. Thus Abergavenny in February, 1929, was one of the coldest stations in England and Wales.

In any scheme for the development of intensive cultivation too much stress cannot be laid on the fact that the success of small market gardeners and fruit farmers in the district must depend on their organisation for buying and selling, and on opportunities being provided for expert advice on the cultivation of crops. There is a consensus of opinion that the odds are heavily against the individual small holder with small capital and little previous experience, and that it is only by means of co-operation and expert guidance that he is likely to be able to make a living over any length of time.

The question of development of the land in the Crickhowell Rural District as a whole must be considered in conjunction with the need for further avenues for employment for the present industrial population of Brynmawr and Llanelly Parish, the traditional links of even this industrial area with agriculture, the presence of part-time miner-farmers in the

[1] See Appendix III to Chapter VIII.

community, and the demand of the coal-mining areas of Monmouthshire for farm and market-gardening produce.

Two questions arise : the extent to which productivity can be increased from the available land, and the suitability of the unemployed mining population for employment on the land.

The consensus of opinion of experts is that the employment capacity of the land already farmed is not likely to be increased appreciably, although it might be made capable of wholly supporting the families which at present use it as a subsidiary source of income and of producing a much better livelihood for some of those wholly dependent on it. By the use of intensive methods of market-gardening and fruit-growing, possibly in conjunction with poultry-farming, and of a co-operative buying and selling scheme, a number of new smallholders might be settled on the land in the low-lying and fertile area below Clydach. It is also possible that further land might be made productive, as has been done by the laborious efforts of a few small-holders in Clydach Dingle and on the mountainside. This is borne out by a study of Appendix IV which shows the present limits of cultivated land and woodlands at the various altitudes. Such small-holders would be helped by a measure of afforestation, which would enrich the soil and provide shelter, as well as offer some paid employment, but afforestation on a large scale would only be possible with the consent of the farmers and cottagers who have grazing rights over large areas of mountain land.

By a combination of these various methods of increasing the productivity of the land, it seems that the livelihood of those already employed on it might be improved and that it might be made capable of supporting some additional families, although without the concurrent development of other new means of livelihood it would not be capable of providing the solution of the employment problem in Brynmawr, Llanelly Hill and Clydach.

The attitude of the miners and farmers to each other is not altogether sympathetic. Gilwern, and still more the outlying agricultural districts, are opposed to the industrial

area politically, socially and in their method of looking at the
conditions of their respective occupations. The farmer,
relying largely on family labour and conscious of the inter-
dependence of his own efforts and his reward, has little
patience with Trade Union insistence on the regulation of
hours and wages. The miner, proud of his hardly won Trade
Union organisation, looks with pity and contempt on the
agricultural labourer, who appears to him to be a spiritless
and downtrodden beast of burden with little time or capacity
for the association with his fellows and mutual discussion
and effort which give savour to industrial life. There is thus
considerable prejudice on both sides. On the other hand,
the rural origins of many miners, the success of Allotment
Associations and cottage-gardeners especially in Llanelly
Parish, and above all the existence of the collier-farmer
class, suggest that there is considerable interest in the land
among the mining section. The success of any scheme of
land development would depend on the careful selection of
the men, who were to help in carrying it out and consequently
in bringing about a more co-operative attitude of mind in both
the farming and mining communities.

The development of existing industries, the revival of
former industries and the better use of the land in the rural
district together offer some hope of increased production and
employment for the men who live in Llanelly Parish and
Brynmawr, who can no longer hope to find an opening in
the mining valleys. Brynmawr, as has been seen, requires
for the financial basis of efficient and economical administration an extension of its boundaries. Despite the fact that
there are old-standing differences in its point of view and
that of part of Llanelly Parish and of the Crickhowell Rural
District as a whole, it is to their area that it must look for
an outlet in view of its geographical position at a point from
which the heavy industries are receding. The make-up of
the people, historical attachments and present similarity
of conditions have resulted in a real unity of outlook and
interests between it and the northern parts of Llanelly Parish.
Against these common traditions and similarity of fortune,

must be set the memory of old feuds, such as that over the Brynmawr sewage scheme, the sentiment of parochial independence and the differences between agricultural and industrial interests and points of view.

Not only financially, as already pointed out, but also in view of the inter-relationship between possible developments in the production of food-stuffs in the rural district and in the function of Brynmawr as a distributive centre, the ideal region from the point of view of all concerned would probably be brought about by the amalgamation of Brynmawr and the Crickhowell Rural District. If such an amalgamation is ever to be achieved successfully, it can only be by the re-orientation of the outlook of Brynmawr and the growth of a wider outlook in the rural district, so that both parties realise how much they have in common in attachments to the country-side, to its cultural traditions and religious ideals, and how closely their fortunes as productive areas and market centre may be intertwined.

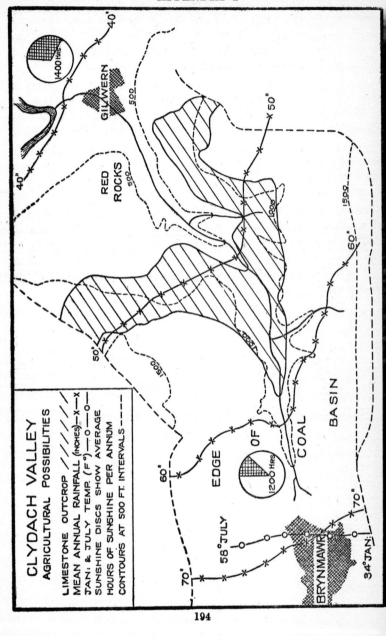

CLYDACH VALLEY
AGRICULTURAL POSSIBILITIES

LIMESTONE OUTCROP ///
MEAN ANNUAL RAINFALL (INCHES)—x—x
JAN. & JULY TEMP. (F°)—O—O—O
SUNSHINE DISCS SHOW AVERAGE
HOURS OF SUNSHINE PER ANNUM
CONTOURS AT 500 FT. INTERVALS———

APPENDIX II

LLANELLY PARISH. HOUSE OWNERSHIP

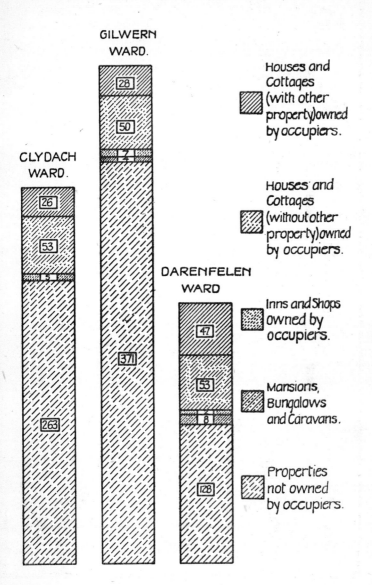

GILWERN WARD.

28

50

7

371

CLYDACH WARD.

26

53

5

263

DARENFELEN WARD

47

53

8

128

Houses and Cottages (with other property) owned by occupiers.

Houses and Cottages (without other property) owned by occupiers.

Inns and Shops owned by occupiers.

Mansions, Bungalows and Caravans.

Properties not owned by occupiers.

195

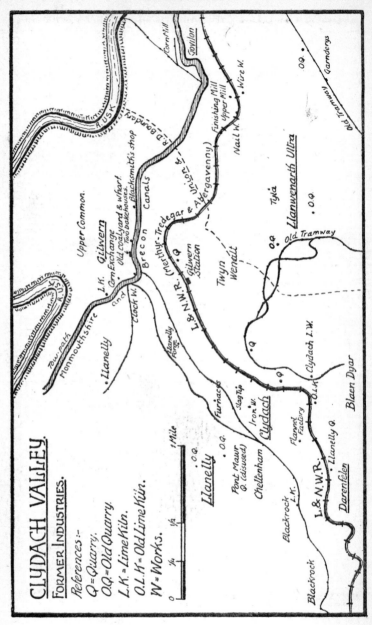

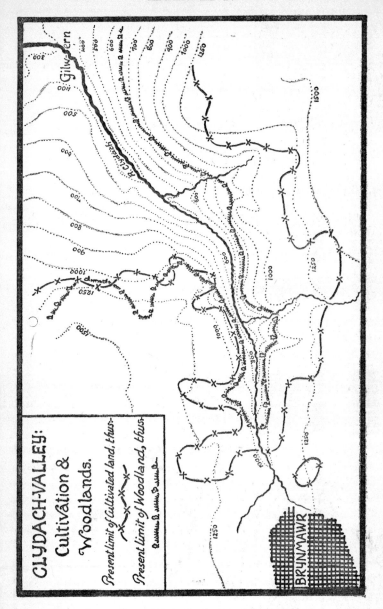

CLYDACH-VALLEY:
Cultivation &
Woodlands.

Present limit of Cultivated land, thus—

Present limit of Woodland, thus—

BRYNMAWR

CHAPTER XIII

AN EXPERIMENT IN RECONSTRUCTION

HISTORICAL events have led Brynmawr, in common with
the other mining areas of South Wales, to look on power
and authority as external. The development of the district
by autocratic English ironmasters and colliery-owners, and
the attempt to impose the Established Church and the English
language on the people caused the twin movements of revolt
in industrial warfare and in nonconformity. Both movements owed their inspiration to belief in individual dignity
and liberty, and both surrendered to the enemy by adopting
methods of coercion. The industrial movement allowed
no freedom of action to "black-legs" and indifferent newcomers, and in its later political development no voice to
persons of a different point of view, no rights to the minority.
It thus denied the claims of the individual as such, which
it had set out to vindicate against the authority of the
"masters." The Nonconformist movement, by its congregational form of government offered liberty to those inside the
fold, but still tried to impose an accepted interpretation of
truth, and thus drove the minority into sectionalism. Hence
within the sphere of the Free Churches there was constant
splitting-off and, without it, an unorganised crowd of individuals whose ideas and desires counted for little in the eyes
of the orthodox. External authority and revolt, compulsion
and ostracism have been constant features in the life of Brynmawr. The result has been the creation of the "closed mind"
and the consequent limitation of the power of co-operative
action in the community by industrial, political and

denominational warfare. Industrial relationships in the South Wales Coalfield provide a striking example of the evil results of this mentality.

A further result has been a jealous guarding of authority and prestige by avowedly democratic organisations which reflected the attitude of mind of the former industrial autocrats rather than that of the believer in the independence and dignity of the individual, whatever his station or influence.

When, in 1928, the resources of the Town Distress Committee were nearly exhausted, and help from outside the distressed areas was brought in by a group of members of the Society of Friends, the administration of the funds thus raised was entrusted to a representative local Committee chosen by the Friends from all sections of the community without respect to political party or denomination. This procedure at once raised a question in the minds of those who by tradition held the view that organised action for the good of the community was the prerogative of the elected Council, and that any departure in the form of action by an independent Committee involved an infringement on their sphere and was derogatory to their authority.

The point of view of the Quaker group was thus early differentiated from that involved by the local conception of democracy. The work of the Distress Committee was thorough and systematic and in its course individuals of very diverse political and religious views were brought together. Relief itself, however, had many disadvantages. Not only was it a palliative, where a cure was demanded, but it proved detrimental to the spirit of self-help and initiative, and, in spite of care and discrimination, caused jealousies, quarrels, and suspicions among those assisted. "I haven't had what I'm entitled to" became only too familiar a phrase, although throughout the period when relief was given, there were many families in dire poverty who refrained from accepting help until they had exhausted all their available resources and endured much suffering. By this time it had become apparent that if Brynmawr was to be self-supporting once more, it was necessary both for it to look for a means of livelihood to supplement and gradually prevent the necessity of dependence on the coal-mining industry, and also to find some unifying factor which would lift the life of the community on to a higher level. The obvious failure of past economic and social methods of living afforded reason for the choice of the district as the place in which an experiment in reconstruction should be made, and the small size of the town made it seem possible to attempt to work out new methods in society and industry at the same time, so that the benefits of the interaction of the two sides of life might be experienced.

It was felt from the first that, while outside help would probably be needed both for financial and psychological reasons, only the community itself could determine its own future.

In order to stimulate a more hopeful and constructive outlook it was decided to ask a local Committee to search out the facts with regard to the history, natural resources and present position of the town, which might provide the necessary basis for an informed plan of reconstruction. Unlike other social surveys, the work was planned as a piece of community self-study, in which educated and uneducated, workers, unemployed, shop-keepers, teachers, transport officials, bank managers, and nurses were all invited to take part on equal terms. As in the formation of the Distress Committee, personal, political, social and denominational differences were ignored, and in the dispassionate search for and study of facts and figures, old-standing feuds were forgotten or deliberately put aside. Advice and guidance on the technical side of survey-making were obtained from Le Play House and other sources, but the final drawing up of questionnaires and the work of enquiry was entrusted to eight local groups of volunteers[1] each of which was made up of persons likely to have some knowledge and interest in their particular subject. For instance, the bank managers, the Postmaster, and various representatives of savings associations were asked to make a study of the financial position of the town, while the Stationmaster and bus company

[1] The eight groups dealt with Population, Transport, Education, Health, Housing, Finance, Commerce, Municipal Services and Industry.

officials, a member of the Main Roads and Bridges Committee, transport workers and others, went into the question of communications and the movement of goods and people into and away from Brynmawr. In the same way, the Head teachers, Attendance Officer, and other persons concerned in education made a special study of educational facilities and after careers of the children who left the Elementary and County Schools. Each of these and the other survey groups made recommendations as to possible developments, always bearing in mind the abnormal situation created by long unemployment both in their own area and in the surrounding districts.

The constitution of the groups ensured the use of expert knowledge and also brought together representatives of the management or employers and the wage-earners.   In order to ensure that the facts obtained were considered, not only from a specialist point of view but from that of the community, the members of all the groups were invited to join a Community Study Council where the results of their enquiries were discussed at regular meetings.   In this way, many questions were considered as factors in the common welfare instead of sectionally.   For example, teachers and parents took part with the shop-keepers and employed and unemployed miners in an attempt to solve the problem created by the excessive and illegal employment of school children out of school hours.   The presentation of exact facts with regard to the extent of this evil by the Education Group led to a real outburst of community feeling and finally to action by the local Education Authority in re-printing and enforcing the bye-laws.

In such ways a community point of view is being slowly evoked, and many small but useful practical pieces of work have been undertaken as a result of the Survey Reports. One of these was an early attempt by the Education Group to provide for classes in such subjects as English Literature and Political Economy, through co-operation with the Workers' Educational Association.   Such classes have now continued for three years, but although the fees for unemployed men are remitted, the response has been very small.   It seems, indeed, that after so prolonged a period of unemployment, organised formal education is too far removed from the difficulties and interests of the unemployed to make any widespread appeal to them.

On the other hand, men who would not join either the County Council Evening Classes or the Workers' Educational Association, were immediately interested in the attempt to get the true facts with regard to the former industries and natural resources of the district, and the reasons why local iron-ore and coal no longer offered hopes of a livelihood, the fate of the boys and girls who left School and other similar points. In researching into these questions something of the habit of scientific enquiry was acquired, and the study of local conditions led on to consideration of problems from a wider point of view. Thus, for instance, it was not possible for a group of people to discuss proposed changes in local boundaries as they affect Brynmawr without learning something of the structure of Local Government and the provisions of recent Local Government Acts. In the same way the study of Transport and Communications induced not only the realisation of the natural advantages and disadvantages of the geographical situation of the town, but also helped to give some idea of the complexity of the economic system by which the population of even a small town has to be fed and provided with the necessities of life. The survey in this way became a vital piece of self-education for all who took part in it.

The Executive Sub-Committee of the Community Study Council spent some months in attempting to define their aims and in doing so were forced to consider the real nature of the community and the conditions of its right functioning. This meant the discussion of abstract ideas from the point of view of everyday life and practical application. The attempt to arrive at common principles by a number of persons of very different views, experience and conditions of life involved also both open-mindedness and a sense of the value of diverse experiences. After long and patient discussion among unemployed, employed wage-earners and comparatively well-to-do salaried representatives of the teaching profession, a statement of aims was evolved which was accepted unanimously not only by the Committee which drew it up but subsequently by the Community Study Council. At the meeting of the latter when the statement was considered and adopted, two remarks were made by representatives of the Trade Union and Labour section and of the staunch adherents of organised religion which, taken together, seemed proofs that a real unity of the historically divorced movements of industrial and political revolt and of nonconformity had been achieved in this matter of a mutual aim for the community as a whole:—"There is nothing in this statement which is not in accordance with pure socialism," and from a life long church member:—"This is pure religion."

How were this unanimity and fusion of ideas reached? The members of the Sub-Committee recognised at their final meetings that out of what had at first been a conscious and difficult exercise of patience, courtesy and open-mindedness there had grown a sense of underlying unity and a mutual conviction of truth which was more than the sum of their individual contributions. Inspiration had visited them and was greeted with fervour.

The statement of aims itself indicates the psychological conditions in which the Sub-Committee believed that such inspiration might guide the discussions and actions of the Community Study Council:—

We have to create that ideal community in which every individual can have the best and fullest life and to which all contribute. As a Community Study Council we can help in this aim of bettering the community in all its activities and aspirations by:—

"Ascertaining all the facts relating to its life for the purpose of promoting the common good; meeting in a spirit which sheds all prejudice and seeks the general well-being rather than sectional interest; laying stress on the similarity of our desires and our common ground as neighbours, while pooling our differences of outlook and experience to enrich the common life and inspire our common action. We feel that our relationships with the Urban District Council and other elected bodies should be one of helpful and cordial co-operation, and that the Community Study Council should serve as an indication to the local legislator and administrator as to what the enlightened citizen wants and feels. We are convinced that by taking counsel together new life is generated and the quality of thought and desire in the community constantly raised. The right functioning of the elected bodies depends on this quality of life and mind."

In this statement is implicit a conception of the neighbour-hood as the basis of the community with the human and social qualities of neighbourliness as the binding link. The inescapable, perhaps half realised, consequences of living together, rather than deliberate organisation for a conscious purpose as in church or Trade Union, give the community its universal appeal to all its members.

Nevertheless conscious association of those who recognise this community bond is believed to be of value, in that it enables the community as such to maintain its life at a higher level. Hence a permanent organisation, through which all shades of opinion can be freely expressed, and action be taken on matters of common concern, is essential. Such an organisa-tion should be complementary to the elected, executive body, and would help to ensure that the varied experience and out-look of individuals and minorities not there represented had their due weight.

The methods of such a Community Study Council would be democratic in that they would be utterly opposed to those of autocracy, majority rule and the suppression or exclusion of dissenting groups, and would be based on the faith that through the unbiased search for truth individual differences would be woven into the finished texture and government by agreement would be reached.

At first sight it appears that no less favourable ground for an attempt to work out this conception of democratic government could be found than Brynmawr. Here the field is divided between warring groups, who have little tradition of courteous recognition that their different points of view may be complementary and necessary ingredients in the whole; here, too, majority rule is enthroned and even within the group there is a tendency to defer to a "King" instead of to seek a leader who will inspire lesser men to the fullest possible self-expression and recognise and carry out the common ideals.

Yet the Society of Friends, in which government by agree-ment based on a common search for truth in matters of principle and of everyday business has for long been accepted, also has its roots in a movement of revolt. It shares too the basic belief which inspired the movement of industrial revolt in South Wales, the faith in individual human values. It seeks, therefore, to discover wherein these values lie and discovers them in the "something of God" which is in every man. It is from this belief in the something greater than the self which is latent in the individual and in the cognate belief that this potential force is released in the right kind of human intercourse that power is derived.

The history of Brynmawr seems to show that such a belief, contrary though it is to the principles underlying the present mode of government of affairs, is yet intimately kin to the basic ideas which have inspired idealistic action in the past. The potential strength of a principle of democracy, founded on a conviction that all men have a natural relationship with goodness and need only a release of the spirit to enable them to play some part in the effort to make its power effective in human life and affairs, is incalculable. In it lies the hope for a common effort to rebuild the community.

In small ways the practical implications of the aim of "creating the ideal community in which every individual can have the best and fullest life and to which all contribute" are already realised. In the winter of 1931–32 after the decrease in the scale of unemployment benefit, it was felt that some voluntary levy on themselves should be made by the more fortunate members, and an appeal for funds for school boots was made by the Community Study Council to its members and to the community as a whole. Weekly collections were made and the response almost everywhere was good; a large number of persons in very poor circumstances made an effort to give a few pence weekly to help the children of the unemployed. The appeal issued shows the intention to relate ideals and practice and reads as follows:—

BRYNMAWR COMMUNITY APPEAL

"On every side the forces of suspicion, mistrust and bitterness based on selfishness are increasing. The release of the spirit of goodwill, trust and neighbourliness based on sympathy and fellowship is desperately needed to-day.

It is realised that there are few in Brynmawr who have not suffered badly in these last few years of depression, but at a special meeting of the Community Study Council held recently it was unanimously agreed that in the present crisis the heaviest burden has been placed on those least able to bear it. The feeling was expressed by those who had not been affected so severely that they would like to make a voluntary levy on themselves, the proceeds to go first to the *replenishing of the School Boot Fund to meet the urgent need of the children during the coming winter*, then to the repairing of the boots when needed, and for the purchase from local traders of materials for the making up of children's garments.

It was felt that others in the town would wish to share in this.

It will be a striking proof of the underlying unity of human sympathy in all who live together as fellow citizens if those who are slightly better off will join in this voluntary levy on themselves to help their neighbours. Such a sacrifice will be both a binding and unifying force in Brynmawr, and a proof of goodwill and self-help which may have great moral and material effects on the outside world.

The feeling was expressed that the levy should be a perfectly voluntary one and that no one should be pressed to take part in it. It is hoped, however, that all who can will range themselves alongside those who believe in the power of goodwill and service instead of suspicion and self interest. The smallest contribution would do this. A collector will call upon you to give you the opportunity of making a small weekly contribution."

An earlier experiment in community service, which preceded the definition of "Aims" was the attempt to clean and beautify the town in order to increase its amenities for the community as a whole and to help to fit it to serve as a residential and holiday centre. Something of the emotional fervour of the Revivals of the past marked the inauguration of this effort. A large town's meeting was held with the local Member of Parliament in the Chair, the whole of the District Council, with ministers, teachers and other leading citizens on the platform, and two thousand people in the Hall. Several hundred people, including not only unemployed men but some shopkeepers, teachers and employed workers, pledged themselves in writing to become members of the "Save Brynmawr Society" and to do all in their power to aid in the work of town development. As in the Revivals, some of these promises were froth and bubble. Yet nearly three years afterwards a few of the original volunteers remain steadfastly faithful to

SITE OF SWIMMING BATHS BEFORE COMMENCEMENT OF WORK.

SWIMMING BATHS AND PADDLING POOL WHEN COMPLETED.

[*To face page* 207

hard manual work in the services of the community, and new volunteers have joined in the movement.

Other forces were at work to deter the enthusiasts. At first the fear of losing their unemployment benefit as a result of giving some of their time to voluntary work deterred many unemployed men from making a start. Two men offered to commence in order to provide the material for a test case. This was decided by the Umpire in favour of the scheme, but in the meantime other objections were raised from the point of Trade Union principle, as it was feared that if the unemployed gave their services to the community the bargaining power of the Union with regard to wages might be affected. Such objections were not shared by national leaders, nor indeed by all the local Trade Unionists. Nevertheless they had their effect on the popular imagination, and, taken together with other forces and prejudices, seriously depleted the number of volunteers. The position was reached later that voluntary work was not considered unsocialistic but was thought to be detrimental to Trade Unionism. At the same time, the weight of the official local Labour Party, which is greatly influenced by its connection with the Miners' Federation, was thrown against the scheme. In spite of this, the work has proceeded and the photographs opposite show the success of one effort to turn a hideous town rubbish tip into beautiful gardens, a children's paddling pool and open-air swimming bath.

The controversy over the scheme of voluntary work for the community had its reactions on the Community Study Council, of which the Town Development Committee was a Sub-Committee. At the moment, the Community Study Council is shunned by many members of the official Labour Party, while the Local Authority, partly by reason of its Labour composition and partly perhaps owing to a lack of understanding of the potential value of machinery by which the community as a whole can express its desires and co-operate actively with the elected body, looks on it with considerable doubt and suspicion. Unfortunate though the effects of such prejudices and suspicions are, they are the natural heritage of generations of industrial strife, in which hard bargaining has been necessary, while suspicions of good faith and disinterestedness have too often been justified. The habit of fighting for one's own hand and of clinging desperately to hard-won gains, whether material or in the form of authority or prestige cannot be overcome except by the contagion of some burning ideal. Such contagion is slower to come when the ideal is brought into the community by persons from outside the district, whose habits of mind and action have not been moulded by the varied forces which have made Brynmawr, and whose temperament lacks some of the qualities which are common among the Welsh. Here too, the memories of previous "foreign" invasions by English industrialists, whose chief concern was the exploitation of natural resources for their personal gain, may subconsciously affect the local attitude of mind.

There is a yet deeper opposition of forces which has become apparent during the progress of the Town Development Scheme. In a community such as Brynmawr industrial and social points of view are closely related. The "mines for the nation" may or may not be practicable, but "the community for a section" is a creed which is utterly opposed to the ideal of community re-building by a common effort. In certain spheres of action where all are affected, class and sectional interests must take the second place. Class warfare can only be a source of weakness in an attempt to build up a new means of livelihood and mode of life for the community as a whole. The clash of loyalties for those who have sacrificed time and personal interests in the industrial and political struggle and who are now asked to put the community first must therefore be severe.

For the fulfilment of human personality and the building up of the good community, which shall provide the right environment for such fulfilment, something more than economic prosperity in industry is required. The study of even the slight sketch of industrial development and Trade Union history contained in the foregoing pages, suggests that all was not well with the men in the mining industry even when profits and wages were comparatively high and employment secure. Not only was there a feeling among many of the employees that their share of the profits was not commensurate with their work, but, as direct contact with the employers became less possible owing to changes in the method of ownership and management, suspicions, bitterness and jealousies became more prevalent. Changes in working conditions have also lessened pride in skill and efficiency, and, as one miner expressed it, even in the prosperous period when wages were high and the miner's money "turned green in his pocket" some men felt that they were missing the best in life in their work underground. Others, of course, still say that they would choose to be occupied as miners, given right working conditions and remuneration, rather than in any other industry or trade.

To the impartial outsider it seems obvious that the spirit of many of those taking part in the industry is destructive both of economic prosperity, and still more of the finest human characteristics. This spirit of course reacts on the community which is so largely made up of workers in the mines, and the art of living together as well as of working together has deteriorated.

The group of workers who had been engaged in relief under the leadership of Peter Scott of the Society of Friends therefore turned their minds to the problem of devising some means of bringing about the permeation of industrial relationships by a new spirit, and at the same time opening out avenues of employment which might gradually obviate the necessity for relief. The Survey had opened the eyes of those who took part in it to the fact that the optimistic outlook with regard to the coal-mining industry was no longer justified as far as Brynmawr was concerned, and had suggested possibilities of developments on other lines. It was felt by the Quaker group and by some of the local Survey workers that something more revolutionary in spirit was required than a mere transplanting of large scale industry with its cleavage between ownership, management and wage-earners, its assumption of an underlying division of interests and its alternate

open warfare and collective bargaining. Was it not possible
to devise a way in industry which would release the constructive forces latent in human relationships and substitute
free co-operation for autocracy or manoeuvring for strategic
position? That such a release of the human spirit from
bitterness, greed and suspicion by the substitution of a mutual
adventure for autocratic domination and unwilling sub-
ordination might have beneficial results even in the economic
sphere was firmly believed, and has been proved in the small
beginnings of the industrial experiment now being undertaken
in Brynmawr.

The first step was the formation of a small *Boot Making
Group* which in August, 1929, commenced to make and supply
boots to the Mansion House Fund and which has since been
registered under the Industrial and Provident Societies Act
with the name of Brynmawr Bootmakers, Ltd. Most of the
members of this little Group had been employees of the Gwalia
Boot Factory, started by Mr. Hicks in 1850, but which since
the mining depression had gradually ceased to be able to
provide regular work for its employees, and which could not
take the Mansion House orders. Starting with a capital of £500
lent by private individuals and with a margin of 10 per cent—
later $7\frac{1}{2}$ per cent—allowed by the Mansion House Committee
in order to help an industry in the Distressed Areas, the Group
successfully competed with larger, old-established firms in the
Midlands and elsewhere. At the end of six months working,
the spirit of co-operation and the general keenness of the Group
resulted in a profit of $12\frac{1}{2}$ per cent.

In the meantime, a larger scheme, of which the Brynmawr
Bootmakers soon became a part, was being thought out and
launched. The plan which was finally adopted was largely
the work of the Horace Plunkett Foundation and the Co-
operative Productive Federation.

The history of Co-operative Productive Societies is mainly
the story of disasters due to the lack of efficient management
in the early stages through the failure of the manual worker
to realise the necessity for efficient organisation.

It seemed probable that owing to past industrial history

many of the workers whom it was hoped to absorb in the Brynmawr scheme would only gradually arrive at an understanding of the practical implications of co-operation and that in the change-over from autocracy to free self-government, the place of the organiser and expert, the right understanding of the function of leadership in industry, might be overlooked. To guard against the natural tendency to swing over to an individualism, which would be the antithesis of co-operative self-government, with its recognition of the need for order and mutual self-discipline, it was sought to set up an organisation which at first would be subject to outside expert control but which would automatically become a co-operatively managed business when the initial difficulties had been overcome.

In March, 1930, the Brynmawr and Clydach Valley Industries Ltd. was registered under the Industrial and Provident Societies Act.

Its object was to encourage and provide work for unemployed miners and others in the neighbourhood of Brynmawr and the Clydach Valley in both industry and agriculture in the following ways:—

1. To enquire into the possibilities of starting new industries.
2. To raise capital for this purpose.
3. To provide an efficient Management Committee of business men of proved ability.

Each industry when started would be a productive unit of the Society. As soon as it passed the experimental stage, it would be registered as a separate company also under the Industrial and Provident Societies Act, the shareholders being the workers with a nominal capital. The actual capital would be in the form of a loan advanced by the parent body, who would thus have control. The Committee of Management would consist of members appointed by both the parent and subsidiary societies. When the business began to show a profit the loan would be repaid, and the outside control automatically disappear. A further advantage would be that services such as accountancy, sales and transport, could be

P

undertaken centrally by the parent body for the various units.

When the loans had been repaid, there would be a group of industries owned and controlled by the workers with a central society carrying out the services and having a certain amount of capital available.

The next stage would start when the separate industries began to invest the surplus by taking up shares in the parent body, until the stage was reached when the latter would itself be controlled by the individual societies jointly and become a co-operative credit bank with funds available for further development.

Perhaps the greatest of initial difficulties was the finding of the right committee of management, and it was only after months of effort that the right people were found who had the necessary experience and ability together with sufficient sympathy and time to give their services voluntarily in this capacity. The application for registration was also signed by the ground landlord of the district, His Grace, the Duke of Beaufort, and Mr. Peter Freeman, the Socialist Member for Parliament.

An appeal was launched for £15,000 either in the form of donations, £1 shares or loan stock. Up to July, 1932, £5,672 2s. 1d. had been given in donations, £3,382 subscribed in shares and £1,525 put into loan stock, making a total of £10,579 2s. 1d.

The former Gwalia Boot Factory was acquired and a considerable sum spent on reconditioning and adapting it. The Brynmawr Bootmakers, Ltd. then transferred there from their temporary premises and were brought into the general scheme by the original loan being invested in the Brynmawr and Clydach Valley Industries Ltd., which re-issued it as a loan.

After the closing of the Mansion House Fund considerable difficulty was found in getting on to the open market, and for a period only part-time was worked. With an increase in the efficiency of the sales organisation, however, this difficulty is being overcome, and the results show a small profit which, considering the serious depression in the Boot Trade, is a hopeful situation which should be steadily improved. The boots being produced are the heavy nailed type suitable for miners and agricultural workers, and children's boots similar to those supplied to the Mansion House Fund.

Among the main objects kept in view in the development of the new industries have been the re-awakening of the spirit of craftsmanship, which was once so strong in rural Wales, and the release of personality in work which is not derogatory to human dignity in the sense that it aims at production of shoddy goods. Thus the bootmakers, for example, have concentrated on the use of good material and the production of a boot of a really good quality for its price.

In the other industries which are in process of development there has been no nucleus of experienced workers to fall back on, and it has been necessary to train boys and youths from the start; in doing so, the place of skill both as a necessary element in the fullest possible human life and as the means by which beauty may be evolved in the production of goods for sale has been kept in the forefront.

The formation of a *Furniture Making Group* was rendered possible by the offer of a skilled craftsman and designer to come to Brynmawr. As a start, youths who were members of the Miners' Training Clubs were given some insight into the elements of the trade even before the Brynmawr and Clydach Valley Industries, Ltd. was registered. The work had to be done under very primitive conditions in the attic of a disused shop, but even so, introduced something of the joy of making to the trainees.

Articles of furniture were designed and made for private orders, and a number of poultry houses, into which an enormous amount of thought and ingenuity were put, were constructed for use under a scheme for starting unemployed men in poultry-keeping.

When the Gwalia Boot Factory was acquired, some up-to-date furniture making machinery was installed and by the use of this for preparation in the early stages, it was possible to train a number of youths to prepare and assemble articles within a comparatively short period. The furniture was all of individual design and followed the trend of modern architecture in its use of flat, unbroken surfaces, relying for its effect on the natural material, proportion and line.

The number of boys and youths who can be instructed at one time, is of course, limited, but already some of the older youths are able to a small extent to supervise the younger boys. The furniture produced is sold out of the distressed areas, and up to the present time there has been no difficulty in marketing it. The problem indeed so far is to bring the output up to the demand.

Perhaps the most important asset of this Group is the fact that the work of a designer craftsman is at its disposal, whose distinctive work places it in a unique position.

The Group is now (1933) making a steady profit out of which the initial loan from the Central Management Committee is gradually being repaid.

A further industry has been opened out by a small *Weaving Group*. For the reasons outlined in the last chapter Welsh tweeds have had only a limited market in other areas, but there seems to be no reason why these defects should not be overcome. It seems also that an attempt to develop spinning and weaving as one of the new industries in Brynmawr might also have a wider influence on the whole industry. Though design and colour were poor, the generations had produced craftsmen of real ability; when once this disappeared, it would be long before it could be regained.

It was necessary to introduce a weaver from outside the locality to take charge of the work of production and the training of youths, as those weavers who lingered in the neighbourhood had no knowledge of up-to-date methods or machinery. The Rural Industries Bureau gave assistance and now tweeds are being produced, which in design and colour can be favourably compared with anything in the same type of cloth. These tweeds are now finding markets both in England and in Wales on ordinary commercial lines.

The generous offer of a Brynmawr resident, who was eager

to do his part in promoting the reconstruction of the community, to transfer the lease of some unworked coal, led to the opening of a small mine, as a slight contribution to the solution of the problem of finding employment for some of the older men who could not be trained for a new skilled trade. After twelve months' working, the management was handed over to a group of workers, although the mine and the capital invested in it still remained the property of the Central Management Committee registered under the Industrial and Provident Societies' Act. The history of the experiment affords a striking example of the clash between the idea of co-operative management and ownership and that of Trade Unionism. At the beginning of 1931 when a reduction of mining wages was enforced by the owners, the Miners' Federation decided on a strike, which lasted nearly a month. The workers in the co-operative level continued to draw the former rate of wages, but in spite of this and of the fact that they were potential owners of the level, they were asked to join in the strike, and, when they refused to do so were reproached as black-legs and traitors to the workers' cause by Federation Officials and fellow-workers. Yet it was obvious that by joining in the strike at a critical time in their own small enterprise, they would have contributed to the failure of the co-operative experiment in which they were engaged and which they hoped might later serve as a model for a more wide-spread revolution in industrial methods and relationships. The strike came to an end before the pressure on the men became too great to be resisted, but the incident showed clearly that the pioneers in co-operative industry might at any moment find themselves required to choose between two loyalties, that of the Co-operative Community based on co-operative industry and that of class and sectional warfare.

Unfortunately, as is so frequently the case in this district where coal has been worked for a long period, it has been found that there are many patches which have already been disturbed, although the existing plans do not indicate this. Owing to this and other reasons, it is doubtful whether the venture will succeed.

As has been seen, the development of agriculture and co-operative market-gardening on an intensive system, might form an important part of a scheme for regional reconstruction. When Brynmawr and Clydach Industries Ltd. first set to work it was hoped that such development might be realised at an early date. A very carefully worked out plan was prepared in conjunction with the Department of Agricultural Economics at Aberystwyth and the Ministry of Agriculture for a scheme of small holdings on co-operative lines designed to fit in with the proposed Land Utilisation Bill. Owing to the failure of the Bill to go through in its original form, these proposals have not so far been put into practice. An experiment with regard to poultry-farming has, however, been made, and a District Association of poultry-farmers was formed for the purpose of obtaining poultry food at wholesale prices for the use of members and arranging lectures and expert guidance on poultry-management. In addition, as already mentioned, a certain number of selected unemployed men were helped to start poultry-keeping and advised as to up-to-date methods. Each man was supplied with thirty day-old chicks, poultry house, hover and credit for foodstuffs for the first six months. When the birds began to lay, the eggs were brought to a central depôt to be sold and from the profits the initial cost was gradually repaid. Through this scheme it was hoped both to stimulate interest in poultry-keeping in the district and to take the first steps towards extending it under expert guidance, so that later a grading and marketing scheme might be instituted and a real contribution be made to the prosperity of the region.

Suggestions that the difficulties of the South Wales Coalfield might be met by the introduction of other industries into the area, so that the whole population shall no longer be directly or indirectly dependent on coal, iron and steel, have been subjected to severe criticism on various grounds. Firstly, even in Brynmawr, in spite of the Survey, there still exists in many minds a tendency to rely on the basic industries. The effects of this tendency and the reasons for endeavouring to overcome it are described in the following passage from the Industrial Survey of South Wales:—

"There exists in South Wales, whose population has for so long been engaged in the extraction of coal and the manufacture of iron and steel, a habit of thinking that the only kind of production which is dignified or worth while is the production of primary commodities. So strong is this habit that some persons may actually be heard deriding the efforts at Brynmawr because they produce 'luxuries' for the well-to-do in Oxford and London. Such persons sometimes argue that the 'new' industries—the manufacture of artificial silk, or gramophones, or radio accessories, for example, cannot 'give employment' as coal-mining or ship-building, or cotton-spinning can do. But a hundred minor industries, each employing a thousand workers, present the same demand for labour as one industry employing a hundred thousand. A community where a number of such industries exists tends, moreover, to be able to employ its population more regularly than one devoted to a single speciality, for when one industry is 'down' another is almost certainly 'up'."

Secondly, it is thought that as long as trade generally remains depressed, if a new factory is opened in the Distressed Areas it will automatically result in unemployment in existing factories elsewhere. Even if this were the case, it may well be better both from an economic and human point of view to spread employment, so that the unemployed shall no longer be concentrated in a few areas where alternative employment is not available and trade tends to be paralysed not only for financial reasons, but owing to the psychological effects of continuous lack of demand. The effects of concentrated unemployment lasting over a period of years throughout an entire region, such as the South Wales Coalfield, are in fact more far-reaching both for the individual and the community than are those of the kind of unemployment experienced in pre-war days and still to be found in such areas as the West Midlands, where the number and variety of productive undertakings afford some scope for initiative both in finding work and in efforts to attract demand from new circles of customers.

Moreover, since demand is not fixed either in quantity or kind even in times of depression, it is fallacious to contend that an additional bootmaker employed in South Wales necessarily means the dismissal of a bootmaker in Bristol or the Midlands. The actual need for boots as opposed to the effective demand for them is far from satisfied, and enterprising manufacturers even to-day are increasing the latter by varying the ranges and prices of their goods so as to attract new custom. The psychological effects of an optimistic and enterprising attitude are perhaps the most potent factors in bringing about a revival of industry and trade. Where distinctive goods, such as the furniture and tweeds now being made in Brynmawr, can be produced, the possibility of creating new markets and actually increasing consumption without necessarily affecting the demand for other classes of goods is most marked. Artistic ability, knowledge of human nature, in fact all the extra values which can be created by the expenditure of personality are commercial assets of equal importance with capital expenditure and technical efficiency.

Rationalisation and other causes have resulted in the assumption that the day of the small productive unit is over. Large scale industry has many advantages in capital resources, range of machinery and goods, in fact on all the material side of production, but the small factory, like the private trader, still seems to have a place in so far as it maintains the qualities of adaptability and distinction of goods and service. In it, both the individual artist, worker and man of inventive genius and the co-operative ideal may have unique opportunities of unhampered expression. It is through this freedom of mind and spirit and through receptiveness to varied and individual demands that small-scale industry persists.

The growth of the co-operative spirit, the belief that agreement can be reached by goodwill and open-minded discussion of difficulties, is no less difficult to attain in the new industries started in Brynmawr than in the community. The working out in practice of the ideals suggested in the articles of association is a long and difficult process, in the course of which the old heritage of suspicions of management, jealousies of foremen, and the temptation to adopt autocratic methods in emergencies have to be overcome. There are many economic difficulties also, which call for a wide industrial and commercial knowledge, and for wisdom and business ability.

Co-operative industries, the inculcation of craftsmanship, voluntary work in producing town amenities and the many-sided work of the Community Study Council in searching out facts and planning a future for the district are all part of one attempt to build up a new and better community in which the human spirit will be released from bitterness and divisions, and find an outlet for its creative energies in craftsmanship and right human relationships. Self-government by agreement, the expression of the higher self by the production of beauty and value, are ideals which are difficult to realise owing both to present social and industrial conditions and to historical forces. Their adoption by even a few persons in Brynmawr is a proof that they are not wholly alien to the spirit of the community. Those concerned in the experiment in reconstruction believe that it is only by the victory of these ideals over sectionalism, exclusiveness and other destructive forces that the community can be rebuilt.

CHAPTER XIV

"HISTORY selects for its study, as really historic, those events of the past which did not exhaust their activity in the moment of their happening but continued to operate and were productive of new events in succeeding ages." Brynmawr and the surrounding areas have fallen upon bad times. What are the historical forces which will determine their future?

Dependence upon one industry, the sharp division between the owners of natural resources and the wage-earners, the consequent movement of revolt, and the permeation of the community by suspicions, jealousies and bitterness, which are part of the "make-up" of the underdog, the conception of leadership as autocracy, on the one hand, and the reaction by which democracy is conceived of as mass control over mandated delegates, the loss of craftsmanship, the racial divisions and the lack of a common culture and idealism, the deterioration of physique and morale due to prolonged unemployment, are not favourable to the reconstruction of the community.

Against these destructive forces must be set the capacity for enthusiasm, idealism and sustained self-sacrificing effort which have been revealed in the history of the churches and of the Trade Union movement. Deep down in the life of Brynmawr, and overlaid by other forces and preoccupations, is a kinship with agricultural workers, craftsmen and the common culture of the Welsh countryside. In the boys who are transferred to an atmosphere of initiative, hope and pride of craftsmanship, these native capacities have once more been

220

awakened. In the mass of the community, love of home and family, a sense of the pre-eminence of human values, belief in the dignity and worth of the individual, the colour of life and the solemnity of death, are joined with a close attachment to place and to the community.

Such positive forces constitute a reservoir of strength. How then can they be evoked and freed from the limitations imposed on them by the other forces which have grown so strong in the last century of strife? In the present crisis, the community will need to call upon all its spiritual and material resources and to use them with wisdom and foresight if it is to make a new future for itself.

To make an effective appeal which will raise its power to the highest possible pitch, unite warring factions and call forth the effort of every member, two things are necessary; the presentation of an ideal which is recognised as related to the nature and intimate desires and aspirations of the people of Brynmawr, and a reasoned and informed plan of action.

Without the native appeal the capacity for enthusiasm, perseverance, unity and self-sacrifice will not be fulfilled; without grounds for the belief in possibility of success, the community will remain paralysed and apathetic in its emergency.

The rebuilding of the community will in itself constitute a sufficiently great ideal and stimulus only if it is consciously recognised as the necessary soil in which other individual and group values are rooted. In that event something of the strength of attachments to such values might be diverted temporarily to the service of the whole. In the present state of disillusionment and apathy, the need of self-preservation will not be a sufficient rallying cry. The community for which men will make sacrifices must be the ideal one, the City of God which men have dreamed of in all times, the setting in which the beauty of all human values and relationships is enhanced.

Looking back on the history of Brynmawr, its needs and desires throughout the past, some characteristics of the Utopia of which its native leaders and prophets have dreamed and for which its people have struggled are apparent. In the ideal

Brynmawr the individual will count, irrespective of wealth or creed; his dignity as a man will be respected and he will receive courtesy as a due from those in authority over him; his right to speak his mind and to associate with his fellows will not be questioned; he will be recognised, too, as a citizen capable of taking his share in government and administration. On the material side, he will be ensured an opportunity to earn sufficient to maintain himself and his family by his labour. He will need also some opening for skill and self-expression in his work and for that spirit of emulation which makes the collier's boy eager to fill his father's tram better than any other boy in the colliery, and which helped to produce the craftsman of rural Wales.

In such a community the deeper human values to be found in attachments to the family and the community will have their proper place. Much of the "colour of life" will continue to be found in family relationships, and there will be scope for ambition for children. The home will be a reason for pride and effort, and the ideal of well-constructed houses, kept in repair, not overcrowded, and provided with a garden, which is expressed now in the saying: "A man should have his own cot and bit of ground" will be realised. To the average dweller in Brynmawr, institutionalism of any kind is alien and distasteful, not only through tradition but by reason of his preoccupation with simple family concerns and human relationships.

Laughter, wit and criticism, the excitement and joviality of social intercourse will find free play, unhampered by any narrow puritanism. Music will broaden its sphere to include ballad and folksong and other secular forms. Welsh history and cultural traditions will be restored to the knowledge of the people, and the keenness of mind and aptitude for debate which are characteristic of all sections find exercise in the discussion of philosophy and history as well as of theology and politics.

Probably the temperament of the people will at all times need to find expression in many and varied social political and religious groupings, each of which may add richness, strength and variety to the common life rather than divide and weaken it. The native temperament demands also the stimulus of a common cause and a great ideal for the realisation of which self-sacrifice, the fighting spirit, and common effort are needed and through which brotherhood and mutual loyalty can be built up. There must be a means of expression also for the new ideas which spring up so easily in fertile minds, scope for experiment, and some accepted moral outlook which will ensure self-control and perseverance.

Brynmawr with its cosmopolitan population, its history of revolt and constructive effort, its versatile and sociable mentality can never be satisfied to stagnate nor to limit or fix its various groupings. To achieve its highest possibilities it will require leaders from among its people, moulded, as they have been, by historical forces, but uniting singlemindedness and vision with that force of character and power to command events which it has admired in the local "Kings" of the past century.

The material basis for such a community can no longer be limited to the exploitation of mineral resources. For the time being coal-mining will probably continue to employ a substantial proportion of the male population, but it is doubtful whether, in view of the distance of the town from the large collieries and the state of the mining industry in South Wales, it will provide them with more than a precarious livelihood. The focus of interest and ambition must move elsewhere if a stable economic foundation is to be laid.

Any plan for the future of Brynmawr must be many-sided, and must take into account the indirect as well as the direct effects of the mining depression upon trade and employment. The reactions of industrial depression are manifold, and the study of the history of Brynmawr reveals the close interrelationships of activities which on the surface are distinct.

Unemployment in collieries and steel works reacts on the trade of Brynmawr; the credit given by the shop-keepers affects their ability to keep up their stocks and so further decreases their trade. Failure on the part of some shop-keepers and property owners to pay their rates involves the imposition of yet heavier rates; heavy rates and arrears of rents prevent repairs to buildings, and depreciation of property, as well as injury to health and family happiness, result; builders and carpenters can employ fewer men; transport workers lose their employment owing to the diminished volume of goods carried and the decrease of passengers due to the stagnation of trade and industry. Public and private debts form a vicious circle.

Against these cumulative and far-reaching effects of the mining depression may be set the fact that any successful effort to improve trade, industry or production also sets in motion ripples which reach far out from the central activity. A number of small experiments in reconstruction made simultaneously would therefore affect the prosperity of the town in indirect as well as direct ways, and, if sufficiently varied, might prevent the recurrence of the widely spread depression which results from the failure of one large-scale industry on which a whole community depends.

The most obvious natural advantage which Brynmawr enjoys apart from its mineral resources is its geographical position, which fits it to serve as a retail and wholesale distributive centre, and as a centre for recreation. At present its traders are suffering from decreased custom and depleted resources. It is for them to take counsel together in order to find means of restoring to the town its former prestige as a shopping centre. Some measure of pooling of resources and co-operation both in buying and in increasing the attractions of the town as a shopping and amusement centre would appear possible if the will to co-operate and, if necessary, to make some temporary sacrifice of individual interests could be evoked.

The project of attracting visitors to the town, which is based on the beauty of its surroundings, would also help trade if it were realised. To make it possible, the Chamber of Trade and other interested bodies might well combine to increase the local amenities and secure lodging accommodation.

In addition to retail trade, the possibilities of the use of Brynmawr as a wholesale distributive centre are great and their exploitation would form part of any comprehensive plan for the future.

In the long run, trade of any kind depends on the volume of production. A distributive centre in the midst of a prosperous industrial or agricultural area may provide a sufficient and stable livelihood for its population. Such a centre, which is mainly dependent for its customers on a declining industry would be in a precarious position, and the consciousness of this might well be a factor in decreasing the initiative and hence the efficiency of its traders.

Brynmawr is thus intimately concerned with the success of the Development Association[1] at work in the mining valleys, along which it must hope to maintain and extend its trade. Since improvement of the position in the valleys must at best be gradual and cannot be assured, it should, if possible, try to foster production in the rural district to the north-east of it and in its own area.

The possible development of agriculture, market-gardening, fruit-farming and poultry-keeping, as well as of forest-holdings, has already been indicated. Such development would form an important part of the Brynmawr plan, and the reclamation of tip and mountain land, the willingness of cottagers and farmers to co-operate, the acquisition of suitable land for intensive cultivation, and the question of grazing rights in connection with afforestation, call for immediate and concentrated study and effort. Many difficulties of a psychological as well as of an economic nature would present themselves, but here again the common will to achieve success would be the determining factor. Even in the depressed state of the mining areas, the problem of finding local markets for market-garden and similar produce would probably not be serious. Co-operative marketing would prevent risk of undercutting by a number of small producers.

The attempt to open out new industries of a skilled type, and on co-operative lines, which is being made by Brynmawr and Clydach Valleys Industries Ltd., as part of the reconstruction

---

[1] An Industrial Development Council for South Wales and Monmouthshire was formed in 1932. Its membership includes representatives of local Authorities, Employers' Associations and Trade Unions and of transport and shipping interests. Its functions include the collecting of information and action calculated to stimulate industry and promote new industrial undertakings.

scheme for Brynmawr, has already been described. Success on these lines would not only make a small section of the population self-supporting, but would also add to the assets of the town by creating a supply of skilled craftsmen, who would form the nucleus around which further development might be built up. Moreover the presence in the community of persons of varied craft and trade interests must be a valuable antidote to the narrowness of outlook born of obsession with one industry only and to the bitterness which springs from the ordinary methods of industrial organisation. The growth and multiplication of such small industries is therefore one valuable means of reconstruction, which would be socially as well as financially beneficial. Even in the event of local failure to extend such skilled work, the men trained in it would have a better chance of maintaining themselves in the outside world than they could have as unskilled labourers.

The popular imagination, influenced by the predominance of large-scale industry in the past, is not at present enamoured of small industries based on skill. Brynmawr hopes against hope that some industrial magnate will build a giant factory within its area which will absorb all the unemployed. Such a magnate would find abundant supplies of unskilled labour in and around the town, and, if he settled in Brynmawr, might well absorb some of the men over forty years of age, who cannot be trained for a skilled trade, and the problem of whose future is the most difficult to solve in any plan so far put forward. Building sites would also be available at reasonable prices, and both road and rail communications are good. Although rates are comparatively high, assessments are low, and in view of this the annual rate charges would probably compare favourably with those in many other areas. Since also, the poor rate makes up the main portion of the present rate, it would probably decrease rapidly if further openings for employment were available.

While, however, a case can be made out for the choice of Brynmawr as a site for a large industrial undertaking and no opportunity of attracting such undertakings to the town should be lost, it would be unwise to make this the main feature of the plan for the future, as it depends to a great extend on factors outside the control of local initiative. It would indeed be fatal if Brynmawr and the other settlements in the distressed areas sat down to wait for good fortune in the shape of a beneficent factory owner from elsewhere or even devoted all their efforts to the attempt to attract such an industrial Father Christmas to their bounds. Moreover in any attempt to create in Brynmawr an ideal community in which the *quality* of human relationships was recognised as of paramount significance, the *motive and methods* of industry are all-important. We are faced indeed in the work of reconstruction with the twofold problem of ensuring a means of livelihood for the population and of releasing the psychological forces in all concerned in industry which would make life qualitatively worth living. Up and down the country there are many businesses which, while not co-operative in name, have achieved a large measure of the spirit of co-operation and good-will. In South Wales the difficulties attending the gradual transformation of capitalistic industry into enterprises which are co-operative in spirit and method are great; it is, however, possible that, *given the right soil and influences in the community in which they are planted*, such a transformation might be brought about. It is essential, therefore, that any attempt to bring new large-scale industry into the district should be regarded as part of the general scheme of reconstruction in which economic and idealistic factors are inextricably interwoven.

In considering the development of production it should be borne in mind that the local South Wales market will probably be very much restricted for some time to come owing to economic depression, and that demand from this quarter would be principally for necessities. The creation of new markets outside South Wales would probably be easiest in the case of specialised products of distinctive kind or value. National or sympathetic interest might help to open out new markets, but could not be relied on for the creation of sufficient demand over a long period.

Development both on agricultural and on industrial lines will involve capital expenditure. In spite of the present

Q

depletion of savings there are indications that, given sufficient incentive, some capital could be raised locally. In any attempt of this kind, small weekly contributions would loom large. The collection of such contributions might serve the two-fold purpose of raising funds and keeping alive the spirit of self-help by enabling the people of the town to take a practical share in the financial side of reconstruction. In addition, it is obvious that additional capital would be needed from out-side the area, and here the experience both of Brynmawr and Clydach Valley Industries Ltd., and of those engaged in the work of town development shows that, given a concrete plan, help for the distressed areas is forthcoming if the appeal is made in the right quarters and in the right way. The main problem of reconstruction is that of finding the right per-sonnel, releasing the spirit of enterprise in the people and making it possible for leaders to emerge from them. If these essentials are ensured, there is little doubt, in view of the response to past appeals, that the material basis could be secured.

Yet another method of creating value is open to Brynmawr in the intermediate stage while the plan is being worked out and the unemployed have not yet been absorbed. This con-sists of the voluntary work of the unemployed for the good of the community. The creation of community values in this way might add greatly to the amenities of the town and its prospects as a trading, amusement and holiday centre. It is even conceivable that a revenue-producing scheme of work undertaken by voluntary labour might help substantially in wiping off the public debt of the town. Local efforts in this direction would do much to bring about a more sympathetic outlook and a willingness to co-operate in reconstruction on the part of the agricultural districts of Brecknockshire. In so far as they reduced the burden of debt they would also of course indirectly conduce to trading prosperity and the introduction of further new industries into Brynmawr.

An improvement in the state of public finance would neces-sarily form one item of any plan for reconstruction. The clear-ing off of debts by community effort would be the ideal; but even if the community were thus enabled to start clear on its new mode of life, it would find it difficult to maintain and improve essential services as long as its boundaries were confined as at present. Especially during the intermediate stage of reconstruction it would be much hampered by the heavy incidence of rates on a comparatively small section of the townspeople and by lack of funds for town development. An agreed plan for the extension of the local government area and for regional development of Brynmawr and the rural district to the north and east would be the ideal solution of present difficulties. With such a plan, the scheme for developing the area as a holiday resort would be much more likely to succeed, as the beautiful valley of the Usk and a number of picturesque little towns and villages would be included in the region to be developed and linked up by transport facilities.

Since the building up of the community on these varied lines must necessarily take some years, the plan for the next few years should include some degree of transfer of unemployed men to other areas. Yet this presents difficulties not only in obtaining openings for such men, but also in the depletion of the human assets of the community by the loss of the men with most initiative and adaptability. Transfer so far has mainly affected the younger men who should be the pioneers in the adventure of re-building. In spite of the drawbacks attached to it, however, the human suffering and deterioration caused by enforced idleness and the strain on public finance involved in it, make it impossible that there should be any hesitation in stimulating transfer to employment by all possible means until the district can provide sufficient local employment for its population. The plan for the future must, in fact, be based on the assumption that for the next few years the population of Brynmawr will continue to decline.

While transfer represents a loss of human material, a policy of training boys and young men, which was related to the plan for the future and the openings for employment which were likely to arise in new industries or on the land, would be an asset to the community. So far, a large proportion of the young men, who have been sent to Government Training Centres,

Q*

have returned to Brynmawr after a short period of employment elsewhere, and have found no means of using such skill as they have acquired. Co-operation between the Government officials or voluntary agencies responsible for training schemes and those engaged locally in working out the Reconstruction plan would undoubtedly have beneficial results.

The Table at the end of the Chapter shows the number of boys who will be free to leave the Brynmawr schools annually during the period ending 1938. It is these boys who constitute the most hopeful material for training as skilled craftsmen. A careful selection of the most suitable for such training, together with close co-operation between the Teachers, Local Education Authority and the Management Committees of the new industries in providing facilities for vocational training and further education would do much to ensure that the best members of the age-group 14–18 would be saved for the town and that their capacities should be developed to the full. For those who could not be absorbed locally during the transitional period, employment or training elsewhere should be systematically sought rather than that the boys should be left to deteriorate in idleness at home.

The closer relationship between education and industry which would result from co-operation with regard to the future of school-leavers might indirectly help to bring the educational system into closer touch with the life of the people. The schools should, in fact, be an important agency in bringing about an understanding of the history and present position of Brynmawr, a sense of communal responsibility and an eagerness for self-sacrificing effort on the part of the younger generation on whose participation the main hope of reconstruction rests.

Brynmawr or the region of which it ultimately forms part can do much to determine its own future, but the social and economic structure of civilisation is to-day so complicated and far-reaching that it is probably impossible for any small region to become self-supporting or self-sufficing. For its members every community appears to be the central point of a series of circles reaching out far beyond their personal knowledge. Not only the state of trade and industry, but ideas current in the wider spheres of South Wales, England and the furthest places of the world react on its life and are to some extent determining causes of its economic success or failure and of its spiritual vitality or disease. It is for this reason that even a small experiment in reconstruction may have such profound and unexpectedly far-reaching effects. One industry or community inspired by the co-operative spirit may provide the spark which will ultimately burn up the dross of selfishness and disharmony in far-off places and times. Even one individual may prove to be the determining factor in battles between good and evil in the hearts of other men, of which he may scarcely be conscious. Throughout the great plane of human life the wind of the spirit blows where it listeth, and the actions of men, their very means and methods of living, are shaped and directed by it.

The plan for the future of Brynmawr will have its reactions in South Wales and elsewhere and must in its turn be affected by the hopes and actions of other communities. A purely local and self-regarding outlook will be fatal to chances of success. Questions such as the mobility of labour within the South Wales Coalfield, the concentration of efforts to transfer men and youths outside the distressed areas in certain areas where there is less hope of their absorption in local industry, plans for the immediate future of localities, and consideration of their ultimate function and place in the life of the wider community, the interdependence and relationships of the "hills," the valleys, and the ports, and the probable reactions of movements of industry upon them severally and as a whole, need common deliberation and an effort to reach agreement. Such common planning for the wider area might well be the function of the Industrial Development Council for South Wales which has recently been set up.

Side by side with this wider effort, the attempt to build up individual regions on lines determined by local history, population and natural resources should be undertaken by the communities concerned. In Brynmawr, as has been seen, the attempt will necessitate many-sided effort to which every section of the community and every phase of life will be called upon to contribute. Such efforts can only be mobilised and maintained by the co-operation of every group or organisation within the community. The capacity for idealism and self-discipline shown in the industrial and political movements of the workers, the fervour and constructive effort of the churches, the formative influence of education and the personal sympathy of the teachers, the initiative of traders and transport authorities, and the civic pride of the District Council will all be needed. Many old antipathies and prejudices will have to be deliberately surrendered in order to bring about the necessary co-operation between individuals and groups. Natural resources, beauty of surroundings, personal attachments are not enough. Only the quality of the people, the height of determination, wisdom and devotion to which the common life can be raised, will bring about a re-birth of the community. The City of the Hills may drift downwards year by year in bitterness and helplessness; it may, if it so wills, become endeared to its citizens by the memory of common efforts and hardships voluntarily endured in the common cause, so that to future even more than to past generations it shines out as the "City of the World."

APPENDIX I

Table Showing the Number of Males Passing Out of
and Attaining the Employable Ages from 1930 to 1938
are as follows:—

Year	Going out of Insurable Occupation on Attaining the Age of 65	Attaining School Leaving Age	Nett Increase in Males of Employable Ages
1930	30	72	42
1931	14	89	75
1932	18	79	61
1933	11	87	76
1934	38	92	54
1935	24	104	80
1936	38	88	50
1937	22	75	53
1938	32	70	37
Total	227	756	528

CHAPTER XV

THE IDEAL AS MOTIVE

WHERE shall we find the ideal which will be great enough to inspire in us the vision, self-sacrifice and determination necessary for the task of re-building the community?

The Distressed Areas are an extreme example of the failure of the economic and social system and of the prevalent confusion of standards. No longer self-supporting, they demand for the maintenance of their people an amount of the national income disproportionate to their contribution in goods and services. Yet, even so, the people are so obsessed by the idea of the insecurity of the bare means of existence, that many of them have little room in their lives for the spiritual values which are the specifically human contribution to the growth of the universe. In the family deep-rooted tradition and instinct still bring into play the forces which make for right human relationships, yet even there the economic and to some extent the social bonds are slackening. In industry, in politics and even in organised religion disruptive forces are at work. The sorry spectacle of the idealist who has become a cynic is all too common.

In Brynmawr, we have a little town set high up in the hills, in which we hope to work out the conditions of the good life. We are spurred on to the attempt by the palpable failure of human effort, as we see it at work at present, to provide us with the requisites for our right growth both individually and as a community. Means of livelihood are precarious; many find no opportunity to exercise strength and ability either for their own or the common good.

Politically all are free and equal, but everywhere we hear politics confused with self-seeking; we have powers of self-government in our own town, but we are hampered in our efforts to create the city beautiful, which shall be the home of citizens healthy in body and in spirit, by a burden of debt due to past and present unemployment, and by the absence of a unifying vision. All too frequent are the miseries of illness, houses which scarcely afford shelter from the winds and rains, poverty and dependence, and the more paralysing evils of bitterness, suspicion and despair. Yet deep within our hearts we feel that our common human nature unites us, that we are capable of a fuller life, have severally and together a high destiny to fulfil, and that, since every desire for good is dynamic and cannot be long withstood by the negative hindrances of want and selfishness, humanity will not remain for ever brutishly ignorant and destructive.

Such a state of affairs is not confined to Brynmawr but is characteristic of many communities in South Wales and elsewhere. Many and diverse remedies have been put forward. National and local economy, State Socialism and nationalisation of industry, co-operative self-help in the community, regional planning for industry and trade, repudiation of debts, nationalism and the co-operative state, all have their adherents. For success any one of these expedients must depend on the strength of a unifying ideal. Too often, plans for economy are thwarted by the selfishness or shortsightedness of individuals and localities, as when a national scheme of economy is defeated by the corruption of elected representatives or their extravagance in administration. Even a co-operative or socialistic system of industry is dependent for its success on the evocation of the co-operative spirit in those who are to take part in it. Nationalism remains an empty name unless men are willing to make private and public sacrifices to bring it into being. A common ideal inspired by some basic conviction alone can raise the individual and the community above the level of apathy, opportunism and ignoble greed.

The following passage quoted from Don Quixote suggests

the three motives by which man may be spurred on to undertake difficult enterprises.

"Difficult things are undertaken for the sake of God, of the world, or of both together. The first are enterprised by the saints, who endeavour to live a life of angels in human bodies; the second by those who traverse boundless oceans, visiting various climates and many foreign nations to acquire what are usually called the goods of fortune; and, lastly, those which are undertaken for the sake of God and the world together are the actions of brave soldiers, who, if they espy in the enemy's wall a breach, though no bigger than may be made by a single cannon ball, laying aside all fear, without deliberating or regarding the manifest danger that threatens them, and borne upon the wings of desire to act in defence of their faith, their country and their king, will throw themselves intrepidly into the midst of a thousand opposing deaths that await them. These are the difficulties which are commonly attempted, and it is honour, glory and advantage to attempt them, though full of dangers and inconveniences."

All three motives have operated in South Wales at different times.

Howell Harris, the Breconshire preacher and revivalist, found himself for the sake of God "a pilgrim and stranger here below." "The world," he said, "and all thoughts of worldly praise and honour vanished from my mind—I only knew this, that God loved me and would, for his own name's sake love me freely to the end." Such was the intensity of his conviction of the spiritual life that he was able to change the lives and habits of the people throughout the countryside.

Of the men who conquer the world for its own sake and in the exercise of their native powers, Wales has known many from the days of the early Iron Masters onwards, and the people of the industrial areas have been brought together and the scenery of the country changed as the result of their initiative.

Neither other-worldliness in the sense of disregard of the conditions of human life, nor efficiency which is wholly self-seeking will suffice for the building of the new community in which the social individual can grow to his full stature. What is needed is an ideal, which, while it has its roots deeper than the present, yet recognises that a part of the Kingdom of

God is in every personality and must, in fact, be realised here and now. Such an ideal, although often dimly recognised, is latent in the minds of many who have not yet allowed it to sway their lives. There is a faith abroad that "Some day we shall catch the gleam."

This faith is justified by many lives of steadfast endurance and self-sacrificing devotion. Almost every accident in the mines bring out the heroic courage of which men are capable; the history of Trade Unionism is full of episodes in which loyalty to comrades and to the idea of brotherhood has conquered fears for self and family, and of long-sustained effort in the common cause. Preachers and laymen have rejoiced to suffer hardships in the cause of religion. Neighbourliness and human sympathies have glorified lives lived in poverty and sordid surroundings; the mothers who have forgotten their weariness or illness, the fathers, who have been content to limit their own activities in order to promote the prospects of their sons, are countless.

Now as always the hearts of men are stirred by the glimpse of something greater than the self which they see in the lives of their fellows. There is no limit to the attractive power of the absolute qualities of goodness, truth and beauty. Perhaps the strength of the ideal lies in the inability of man to remain satisfied with anything less than the perfect of its kind. Whether in human beings or in art or in nature, we have a passionate desire that potential beauty shall be realised, unspoilt by the destructive forces of evil. The twisted tree, the crippled human being, the distorted mind, distress us with a sense of waste and wrong. So too the community rent by suspicions and jealousies, in which personalities remain unfulfilled, calls out our pity and sorrow. The sheep which has strayed on the mountain makes its irresistible call to the shepherd who seeks it, and there is still instinctive rejoicing when that which was lost is found.

Often the ideal of goodness has been restricted in its operation by a narrow creed or sectional application, so that part of its force has been wasted in division. The creative energy must always seek a diversity of expression in man as in the flowers and trees, the varied materials and shapes of mountain, cliff and valley, which make the universe a thing of beauty. Yet while it manifests itself in a multiplicity of ways in the lives of individuals, it remains one, the root of unity which cannot be broken or unharmonious. Those who have felt it flowing through them in natural affection or compelling urge to more than selfish effort, recognise with joy and wonder its presence in the hearts of those who lead their different lives around them. There are few parents, who in the midst of unbelief and even of evidence of a wrong course of life, have not a rooted faith that their children remain "good at heart." In this faith in the universal and indestructible nature of goodness lies power.

Just as the elements of fire, water, earth and air are unique and will not mix, and as certain substances have their own essential properties which cannot be sullied or destroyed, so spiritual qualities are incapable of destruction or change. In the identification of the self with these qualities, revolt, which has flowered so often in disharmony, takes on the nature of a positive assertion of good, which has no need of the weapons of intrigue or bitterness and is incapable of using them. Hence comes the habit of generous thinking, the effort to build a city in which human relationships are determined by the mutual belief in goodwill. In whatever terms we state our faith, in whatever medium we strive to express our vision of beauty, we shall find a unifying power in the belief in "The something of God in every man." No ideal which is less universal will release the force which is now restricted and pent up, or prove sufficient for the task of rebuilding the community.

BIBLIOGRAPHY

Industrial Survey of South Wales made for the Board of Trade by the University College of South Wales and Monmouthshire.

Census Volumes for Breconshire from 1811 onwards.

History of the County of Brecknock, by Theophilus Jones (1809) Glanusk Edition.

Historical Tour through Monmouthshire, by Archdeacon Coxe (1802).

Historical Memoranda, by John Lloyd.

History of Rehoboth Congregational Church of Brynmawr, by Rev. Crwys Williams.

Report of Commission of Enquiry into Industrial Unrest. (No. 7 Division.) (1917.)

A Geographical, Historical and Religious Account of the Parish of Aberstruth in the County of Monmouth, by Edmund Jones.

Annual Reports of School Medical Officer and Medical Officer of Health for Breconshire.

Annual Reports of Medical Officer of Health for Brynmawr.

Annual Reports of Medical Officer of Health for Crickhowell Rural District.

Old South Wales Iron Works, by John Lloyd.

Annals and Reminiscences of the Parish of Llanelly, by the Rev. Arthur Griffiths.

Report on a Survey of the Welsh Textile Industry made on behalf of the University College of Wales, by William P. Crankshaw.

INDEX

A

Abergavenny, 16, 27, 28, 98, 100, 102, 103, 117, 183, 189, 190
Aberystruth, Parish of, 44, 80
Abertillery, 68, 101, 105, 106, 107
Agriculture, 22, 27, 28, 41, 42, 54, 110, 118, 183, 187, 188, 189, 190, 191, 194, 211, 216, 220, 225, 228
Agricultural Economics Department of University College, Aberystwyth, vii
Allotment Associations, 187, 192
Alternative Occupations, 147, 151
Anthracite Coal, 4, 34
Approved Societies, 93

B

Bailey, Crawshay, 18, 30, 31, 65, 66, 121
Bailey, Henry, 64
Bailey, Messrs. C. & J., 18, 33
Bands of Hope, 81, 121
Beaufort, 18, 26, 32, 135, 184
Beaufort, Duke of, 73, 76, 91, 183, 212
Beaufort Estate, 80, 91, 96
Blaenavon, 35, 68, 70, 101, 102, 183
Blaenavon Colliery Company, 182
Blaina, 34, 42, 44, 64, 67, 68, 70, 75, 79, 101, 135
Board of Education, 126
Board of Health (Brynmawr), 20, 21, 24, 49, 64, 72, 73, 74, 75, 76, 77, 78, 80, 81, 100, 101
Board School (Brynmawr), 126
Board of Trade, vii
Brecon, 27, 179
Breconshire County Council, 82, 164, 165, 166, 167, 175
Breconshire Education Committee, 126, 154, 201

Brickmaking, 183, 184, 186
British and Foreign School (Brynmawr), 125, 126
Brynmawr Bootmakers, Ltd., 210, 212
Brynmawr and Clydach Valley Industries, Ltd., 211, 212, 213, 216, 225, 228
  (a) Boot Making Group, 210
  (b) Central Management Committee, 214, 215
  (c) Furniture Making Group, 213, 214
  (d) Weaving Group, 214
Brynmawr Community Study Council, 167a, 201, 202, 203, 204, 205, 206, 207, 218
  (a) Commerce Group, vi
  (b) Education Group, vi, 201
  (c) Finance Group, vi, 172
  (d) Health and Housing Group vi, 91, 93
  (e) Industrial Group, vi
  (f) Municipal Services, vi
  (g) Population Group, vi
  (h) Transport Group, vi, 202
Brynmawr Urban District, 34, 39
Brynmawr Urban District Council, 70, 78, 87, 90, 91, 95, 153, 166, 167, 168, 174, 203, 206, 232
Brynmawr Urban Sanitary District, 33
Buffaloes, Order of, 130
Building Societies, 87
Builth, 117
Bus Services, 109

C

Cambridgeshire, 190
Cardiganshire, 44, 46, 98
Carmarthenshire, 44, 46, 98
Chamber of Trade (Brynmawr), 101, 107, 224

Chapels and Denominations (Brynmawr), 18, 20, 23, 45, 46, 47, 49, 65, 81, 87, 100, 121, 122, 123, 125, 126, 132, 142
(a) Apostolics, 124
(b) Baptists, 18, 49
(c) Calvinistic Methodism, 122
(d) Church in Wales, 121, 123, 124, 125, 126, 142, 198
(e) Congregational Churches, 51, 121, 132
(f) English Baptist Churches, 45
(g) English Congregational Church, 48
(h) English Wesleyan Churches, 45, 48, 132
(i) Free Churches, 121, 122, 124, 198
(j) Independents, 18, 44
(k) Penticostals, 124
(l) Primitive Methodism, 49, 123
(m) Rehoboth, 45, 46, 49, 100
(n) Spiritualists, 124
(o) Welsh Baptist Chapels, 46, 47
(p) Welsh Calvinistic Chapels, 46, 47
(q) Welsh Wesleyans, 45, 132
Chartists, 24, 65, 100, 119
Cheshire, 51
Cholera, 20, 49, 64, 72, 77
Christianity, 1
Church School (Brynmawr), 126
Clydach, 16, 18, 26, 27, 28, 35, 45, 71, 72, 73, 103, 125, 135, 170, 177, 180, 181, 182, 183, 184, 187, 190, 191
Clydach Dingle, 84, 90, 178, 191
Coaching Inn (Brynmawr), 87, 98
Coal Exports, 3
Coalfields Distress Committee of the Society of Friends, 153
Coal-mining Industry, 3, 4, 6, 10, 28, 29, 31, 33, 35, 53, 95, 111, 136, 177, 182, 191, 200, 209, 217, 223
Commerce, 4, 5, 7, 102, 103, 104, 105, 106, 107, 108, 110, 111, 113, 114, 190, 214, 225, 227
Commission of Enquiry into Industrial Unrest, 56, 62, 111, 116
Commission of Enquiry into State of Education in Wales, 48, 64
Communal Kitchen, 153
Communism, 25
Company Shops, 18, 20, 21, 32, 64, 98, 99
Co-operation and Co-operative Societies and Stores, 99, 210, 218

Co-operative Productive Federation, 210
Cornwall, 58
Courts of Referees, 141
Coxe, Archdeacon, 42, 94
Crankshaw, W., 186
Crawshay, Richard, 63, 180
Crawshay, William, of Cyfartha, 99
Crickhowell, 28
Crickhowell Board of Guardians, 164, 165, 172
Crickhowell Rural District, 33, 39, 165, 168, 169, 170, 176, 177, 181, 182, 185, 187, 190, 192, 193

D

David ab Gwyllim, 43
De-rating, 174
Derbyshire, 26, 63
Devonshire, 58
Distress Committee (Brynmawr), 153, 200
Distributive Trades, 3, 5, 6, 7, 10
Domestic Economy Centres, 128
Dorsetshire, 58
Dowlais, 32, 35

E

Eastern Valley (Monmouthshire), 11, 79, 102, 159
Ebbw Vale, 5, 10, 11, 33, 34, 35, 68, 69, 76, 105, 106, 107, 112
Education Authority (Breconshire), 126, 154, 201
Electricity, 35, 108
Elementary Schools (Brynmawr), 127, 201
Employment Exchange (Brynmawr), 137, 139, 145, 155, 156
Enquiry into Sewerage, Drainage and Supply of Water (Brynmawr), 72
Evening Classes and Night Schools, 125, 128, 139, 202
Evesham, 190

F

Fabian Society, 81
Farming, 187, 188, 189, 191
Farquharson, Alexander, vii
Flannel Industry, 181, 184, 185
Folk-Song, 43, 44

Food Importation (map), 116, 190
Forest of Dean, 67
Freemason's Chronicle, 110
Frere, Cooke and Company, 26, 29, 30, 31, 179
Friendly Societies, 157
Friendly Society of Coalmining, 63, 71

G

General Board of Health, 74, 75
General Election (1931), 112
Gilwern, 28, 169, 170, 177, 178, 180, 181, 183, 184, 185, 189, 191
Glamorganshire, 50
Gloucestershire, 51, 58
Goschen Loans, 167
Government Instructional Factories, 145
Government Training Centres, 145, 229
Great Western Railway, 109
Griffin Hotel, 87, 102
Griffiths, The Rev. Arthur, 180

H

Hadow Report, 134
Hanbury, 26
Hauliers' Strike, 68
Herefordshire, 51, 54, 58, 104
Horace Plunkett Foundation, 210
House-building, 6, 87, 91, 92, 226
House-ownership (Brynmawr and Llanelly Parish), 157, 158, 195
Housing, 85, 87, 88, 89, 90, 91, 92, 93, 94, 95, 96, 181
Howell Harris, 121, 236

I

Immigrants into Coalfield, 9, 19, 22, 31, 33, 34, 44, 45, 46, 49, 50, 51, 53, 54, 56, 63, 121, 125, 180
Independent Labour Party, 80, 81
Industry, 5, 9, 40, 147, 167, 183, 184, 185, 186, 192, 211, 213, 218, 226, 233
Industrial Development Council of South Wales and Monmouthshire, 225, 231
Industrial and Provident Societies Act, 211, 215
Industrial Revolution, 9, 88

Industrial Survey of South Wales, vii, 3, 4, 5, 7, 8, 9
Infant Welfare Centre (Brynmawr), 157
Irish or Ireland, 51, 52, 58, 125
Ironore, 3, 18, 22, 27, 33, 38, 178, 202
Iron Strike, 68
Iron Works, 86, 177, 178, 179, 181
   (a) Nantyglo, 18, 26, 27, 29, 33, 46, 66, 67, 84, 117
   (b) Clydach, 18, 26, 27, 29, 30, 33, 46, 84, 181
   (c) Blaenavon, 33, 84
   (d) Beaufort, 18, 26, 27, 30, 33, 46, 84

J

Jenkins, David, 122
Jews, 51, 52, 103
Jones, Edmund, 44
Jones, Theophilus, 42, 43, 178

K

Kendall, 26, 179

L

Labour Party, 82, 112, 141, 203, 207
Lancashire, 51
Lead Mining, 51
Le Play House, vii, 200
Lincolnshire, 190
Llanelly Church, 180
Llanelly Hill, 71, 99, 113, 135, 170, 178, 180, 181, 182, 187, 191
Llanelly Parish, 18, 26, 44, 46, 48, 73, 77, 80, 86, 117, 168, 169, 176, 177, 179, 180, 181, 182, 183, 185, 187, 189, 190, 192, 195 (map)
Llanelly Parish and Govilon Survey Committee, vii
Llangattock Parish, 26, 27, 44, 46, 48, 86, 178
Llangynidr, 98
Lloyd, John, 44
Lloyd, Professor, 42
Local Government, 79, 80
Local Government Act, 1929, 80, 168
Local Government Boundaries, 79, 80

London, 51, 58, 217
London, Midland and Scottish Railway, 109

M

Mansion House Fund, 42, 153, 172, 210, 212, 213
Manual Training Centres, 128
Market Company (Brynmawr), 101
Market Gardening, 189, 190, 191, 216, 225
Market Hall (Brynmawr), 87, 101, 104, 123
Means Test, 155, 170
Medical Officer of Health (Brynmawr), 77, 79
Medical Officer of Health (Crickhowell), 181
Merthyr Tydfil, 5, 16, 45, 98, 102, 104
Metal Industries, 4, 5, 6, 10, 35
Mid-Wales, 98, 185
Mid-Wales Road, 99, 113
Migration, 4, 11, 25, 91
Miners' Federation, 67, 68, 69, 70, 139, 140, 207, 215
Miners' Training Clubs, 213
Miners' Welfare Fund, 71
Ministry of Health, 96, 166, 167, 168, 181
Ministry of Labour, 7, 8
Monmouthshire, 16, 39, 41, 44, 46, 50, 58, 62, 79, 80, 110
Monmouthshire Railway and Canal Company, 102
Moose, the Order of, 130
Mutual Improvement Society, 123, 130

N

Nantyglo, 18, 20, 28, 35, 44, 63, 64, 72, 75, 79, 98, 99, 102, 119, 121, 125, 179
National Savings Certificates and Savings Bank, 163
National Society, 125
Neath, 62
New Industries, Introduction of, 8
Newport, 5, 31, 41, 102, 103, 107
Nonconformity, 43, 121, 122, 123, 124, 126, 180, 203
Northamptonshire, 26, 38
North Midlands, 51
North Wales, 51

O

Oddfellows, Ancient Order of, 130
Origins of Population, 9, 11, 16, 33, 41, 42, 43, 44, 46, 49, 52, 53, 54, 57, 58, 59, 60, 61, 106, 180
Oxford, 217
Oxfordshire, 38

P

Parish Church (Nantyglo), 20, 49, 64
Penry, John, 121
Pembrokeshire, 41
Petty Sessional Division (Brynmawr), 80, 86
Pontypool, 26, 62
Poor Law and Poor Law Guardians, 22, 80, 139, 154, 155, 158, 159, 164, 168, 174, 181, 226
Poundage System, 71, 159
Poultry Production, 189, 191, 216, 225
Powell, Messrs. Lancelot and John, 179
Price, The Rev. Thomas, 118, 157, 166
Public Assistance Committee and Officers (Breconshire), 156, 165, 170, 176
Public Contracts in Relief of Unemployment, 7
Public Utility Society, 96

Q

Quarries, 27, 28, 31, 35, 178, 183

R

Radnorshire, 46, 54
Rates, 155, 159, 164, 165, 166, 167, 168, 174, 175, 176
Reading Room and Library Committee (Brynmawr), 123
Recreation, Facilities for, 107, 158, 159
Relief on Loan, 154, 159
Revivals (Religious), 22, 45, 46, 121, 206
Richards, Thomas, 68
Roman Catholics, 51, 125
Rural Industries Bureau, 214

Ruhr, Occupation of, 34, 137
Royal Commission on Local Government, 168

S

School Medical Service, 128
School Meals, 154, 156
Scotch Cattle, 63
Scotch (Scotland), 51, 52, 58, 102, 103, 185, 186
Scott, Peter, 145, 209
Secondary School (Brynmawr), 87, 126, 129
Shropshire, 38, 51, 58
Shropshire, Staffordshire and Worcestershire Electricity Supply Company, 108
Sliding Scale Agreement, 67, 68
Soap Factory, 181
Social Survey (Brynmawr), and Crickhowell Rural District, v, 3, 9, 10, 11, 16, 20, 41, 42, 43, 44, 48, 49, 52, 54, 62, 64, 65, 92, 200, 201
Society of Friends, 153, 172, 199, 204, 209
Somersetshire, 58
South Wales Iron Strike, 67
South Wales and South Wales Coalfield, 1, 2, 3, 9, 10, 11, 26, 41, 44, 56, 57, 62, 98, 110, 111, 137, 180, 185, 188, 199, 216, 217, 227, 231, 235
South Wales Union Lodge of Coalminers, 67
Spanish Ores, 32, 38
Staffordshire, 38, 45, 51, 58, 62, 63
State Schools, 123, 127, 128
Steam and Bituminous Coal, 4, 33
Steel Works, 4, 183
Sunday Schools, 23, 49, 121, 122, 123, 125, 128, 142, 158
Swansea, 9, 41, 62

T

Thomas, John, 81, 126
Tin Plate Industry, 5, 81
Town Development Scheme (Brynmawr), 207, 208, 228, 229
Town Eisteddfod (Brynmawr), 107, 123, 130
Town Relief Committee (Brynmawr), 153, 158, 199

Trades and Labour Council, 71, 82, 139, 141
Trade Union Movement, 2, 6, 9, 23, 121, 143, 192, 203, 204, 207, 208, 215, 220, 237
Tramroads, 16, 31, 84, 98
Transfer from Distressed Areas, 7, 8, 9, 11, 144, 229
Transfer Instructional Centres, 145, 148
Transport, 5, 6, 7, 24, 202
  (a) Railways, 5, 6, 22, 31, 69, 79, 101, 102, 103, 107, 109, 111
  (b) Roads, 5, 7, 17, 22, 103, 104, 105, 109, 110, 111, 115, 182, 186
Tredegar, 5, 11, 35, 137
Truck System, 19, 62, 99
Tuberculosis, 93, 97

U

Unemployed Lodges of Miners' Federation, 139, 140
Unemployment (Brynmawr), 10, 11, 13, 120, 137, 139, 145, 158, 207, 220
Unemployment (South Wales), 2, 3, 4, 5, 6, 7, 8, 9, 10, 11, 13, 217
Union Clubs, 20, 62, 65, 67, 71
University College of South Wales and Monmouthshire, vii, 186
Urban District Council (Brynmawr), 34, 39, 77, 78, 80, 81, 82, 90, 91, 96, 153, 165, 166, 167, 168, 174, 175, 176, 184, 203, 206, 230, 232
Usk Valley, 16, 110, 178, 190

V

Voluntary Work (Brynmawr), 207, 228

W

Waenavon, 26
Waen-y-Helegyn, 16
Wain, Richard, 102
Warwickshire, 51, 58
Welsh Flannel, 184
Welsh Language, 42, 49, 118
Welsh Nationality, 41
Welsh Renaissance, 117
Welsh Town Planning Trust, 92, 96

Welsh Tweed, 186, 214
West Midlands, 51, 58
Western Valley (Monmouthshire) Sewage Board, 79
West Wales, 98, 185
Whitehaven, 38
Williams, Rev. Crwys, 46
Wiltshire, 58
Worcester, 190
Worcestershire, 51, 58

Workers' Educational Association, 129, 201, 202
Works School (Nantyglo and Brynmawr), 64, 125
Worthing, 153

Y

Yarde Shoppe (Brynmawr), 101
Yorkshire, 38, 51, 185